GM 6.2/6.5 LITER DIESEL ENGINES

HOW TO REBUILD

Dr. John F. Kershaw

CarTech®

CarTech®

CarTech®, Inc.
6118 Main Street
North Branch, MN 55056
Phone: 651-277-1200 or 800-551-4754
Fax: 651-277-1203
www.cartechbooks.com

Edit by Bob Wilson
Layout by Connie DeFlorin

ISBN 978-1-61325-560-5
Item No. SA494

Library of Congress Cataloging-in-Publication Data

Names: Kershaw, John F., author.
Title: GM 6.2 & 6.5 liter diesel engines : how to rebuild / John F. Kershaw.
Other titles: GM 6.2 and 6.5 liter diesel engines
Description: Forest Lake, MN : CarTech, Inc., [2020]
Identifiers: LCCN 2020010209 | ISBN 9781613255605 (paperback)
Subjects: LCSH: Motor vehicles–Motors (Diesel)–Maintenance and repair.
Classification: LCC TL230.2 .K465 2020 | DDC 629.25/060288–dc23
LC record available at https://lccn.loc.gov/2020010209

Written, edited, and designed in the U.S.A.
Printed in China
10 9 8 7 6 5 4 3 2

Cover photos:

Two-tone brown 6.2L pickup (Photo Courtesy Heath Krocker)
Custom-built 6.5L turbo diesel by Quadstar Tuning
(Photo Courtesy John Faddis/Quadstar Tuning)

DISTRIBUTION BY:

Europe
PGUK
63 Hatton Garden
London EC1N 8LE, England
Phone: 020 7061 1980 • Fax: 020 7242 3725
www.pguk.co.uk

Australia
Renniks Publications Ltd.
3/37-39 Green Street
Banksmeadow, NSW 2109, Australia
Phone: 2 9695 7055 • Fax: 2 9695 7355
www.renniks.com

Canada
Login Canada
300 Saulteaux Crescent
Winnipeg, MB, R3J 3T2 Canada
Phone: 800 665 1148 • Fax: 800 665 0103
www.lb.ca

CONTENTS

PREFACE

This is a book for do-it-yourselfers (DIYers) to understand the world of the General Motors 6.2L and 6.5L light-duty diesel engines. It covers engine removal, its overhaul (including the Stanadyne DB2 pump), upgrades, and many service issues. It also provides missing and forgotten information about these engines that does not currently exist in the market.

When I worked for General Motors, I was the senior program developer for Diesel Engine service engineering development. I worked on the service procedure development of all of the GM diesel engines. I was also a senior program developer for the original 6.2L team for GM Product Service Training from 1981 to 1986.

These engines were also used by the military in the commercial utility cargo vehicles (CUCV) and high-mobility multipurpose wheeled vehicles (HMMWV or Humvee), and I was also part of that program.

ACKNOWLEDGMENTS

I want to thank my wife, Joan, for her continued support in all of my projects. I also need to acknowledge my good friend, colleague, and noted author Jim Halderman, who has generously provided photographs, information, and support for this project along with many other projects. Thank you to Steve Christopherson, formerly of Snap-on Engineering and inventor of the timing bracket qualifier. I also want to thank all of the members of the 5.7/6.2/6.5 Facebook group for their generous technical information and photo support. The following members provided help: Kyle Hoffmeyer, Quint McLean, Shane Robinson, Heath Kroeker, Nate Gebard, Bruce Lawrence, Tristan Tennent, Foster James, Steve Huyge, Max Harris, Jordan Regan, Tre Able, Davis Colburn, Roger Dixon, Jerome Sommers, Wes Gottfresson, Evans Bruce, Bryant Calcote, and Matthew Randall. I apologize if I forgot anyone who helped me with this project.

ABOUT THE AUTHOR

Dr. Kershaw has more than 50 years of experience in automotive technology. He has provided classroom curriculum and training as an instructor, educating students and developing personal employee fulfillment, utilizing Passion Test and Passion Test for Business. He is an IASSC-certified Lean Six Sigma Black Belt.

Dr. Kershaw applies his expertise to the forensic investigation of claims involving automotive failure. He determines the cause or causes of automotive failures and validates manufacturer defects or validates the normal operation of vehicles involved in such mechanical claims. He also performs desktop reviews of forensic reports provided by other experts.

Dr. Kershaw received an award of merit for the development and writing of the book *The 6.2 Liter Diesel Engine* for GM Product Service Training. He is the author of 15 GM Technical Training publications as well as the published author of 6 automotive textbooks. He has developed instructional materials for GM, Nissan, Fiat, Hyundai, Honda, Mazda, Corinthian Colleges, Ohio Technical College, Intellitec Colleges, General Mills, Erie Institute of Technology, the University of Missouri at Columbia, and PennFoster College.

INTRODUCTION TO DIESEL ENGINES

A diesel engine operates differently than a gasoline-fueled engine because fuel is not mixed with air entering the cylinder during the intake stroke. Instead, air alone is compressed during the compression stroke, and diesel fuel is injected into the combustion chamber or pre-chamber at the end of the compression stroke. The compression ratio is much higher, providing compressed air temperatures as high as 1,000°F. The temperature is high enough to ignite fuel when the injector sprays or injects it into the combustion chamber.

Combustion is controlled by the speed that the diesel fuel is injected into the combustion chamber. In a diesel engine, combustion is not a rapid burning of the fuel already present in the cylinder, as in a gas engine, rather it is a slower burning that produces an even increase in pressure. The diesel engine operates with a layered air/fuel mixture in the cylinder, and combustion occurs as the fuel mixes with the air. Control of load through variation of the air/fuel ratio benefits efficiency and frees the engine from needing a throttle.

As such, diesel engines do not use a throttle valve. Instead, engine

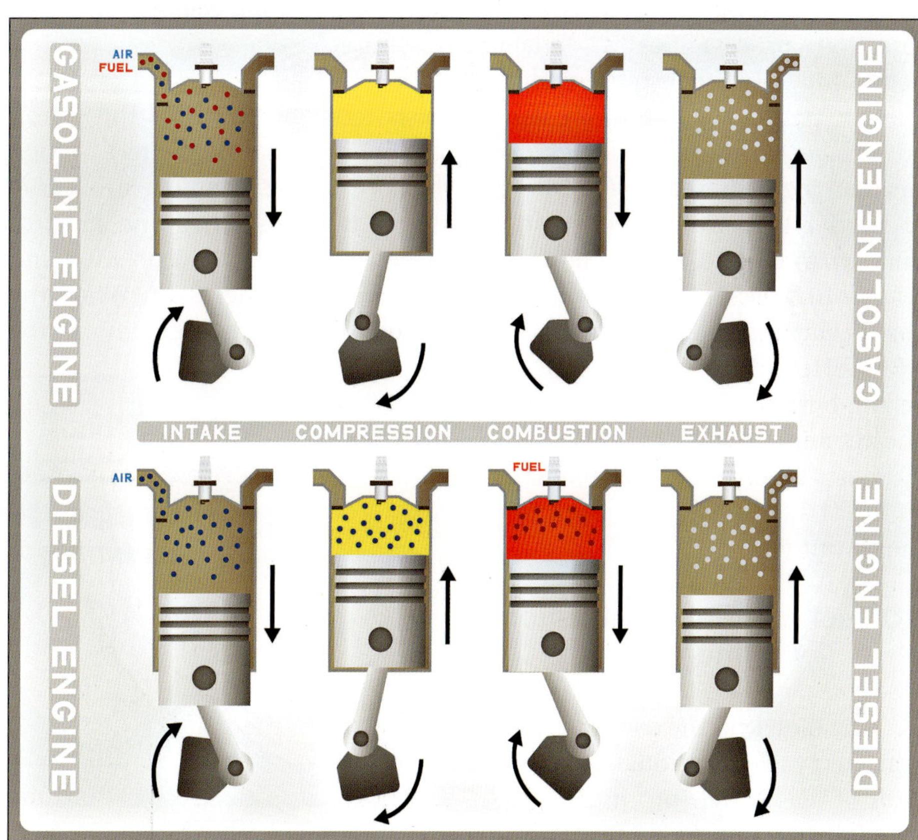

The operation of a gasoline-fueled engine versus a diesel engine is seen here. Note the four-stroke cycles of intake, compression, power/combustion, and exhaust, which are also known as suck, squeeze, bang, and blow.

speed is controlled by the amount of fuel injected and when it is injected. Air intake is constant; fuel injection is the variable. The diesel engine throttle is connected to a fuel-control mechanism to vary the amount of fuel that is injected into the cylinder (with the exception of electronic systems that have a drive-by-wire control).

Diesel engines reduce load at a given speed by injecting less fuel

---

into an essentially constant mass of cylinder air. The air/fuel ratio will be very lean at light loads and idle somewhere around 100:1. This takes place beyond the flammability limit of the fuel. This is possible because a major share of the diesel combustion process takes place in the smaller areas as atomized fuel mixes with high-pressure compressed cylinder air.

The fuel injection pump used with the 6.2-liter and 6.5-liter diesel engines in this text varies engine timing according to speed. The fuel injection process has a variable beginning and constant ending. Diesels provide a thermodynamic advantage. The average specific heat of the cylinder gas is lowered at partial load during combustion and expansion because of both the leaner air/fuel ratio and the resulting lower average temperature. More of the heat value of the fuel in the burning process goes to heat the air, and less is lost to the cooling system and exhaust. This reduction in heat loss increases the work from a unit of fuel.

Diesel Internal Combustion Engine Terms

The diesel engine converts chemical energy released from the combustion of diesel fuel into useful work. The following terms are necessary to know when trying to understand diesel internal combustion engines.

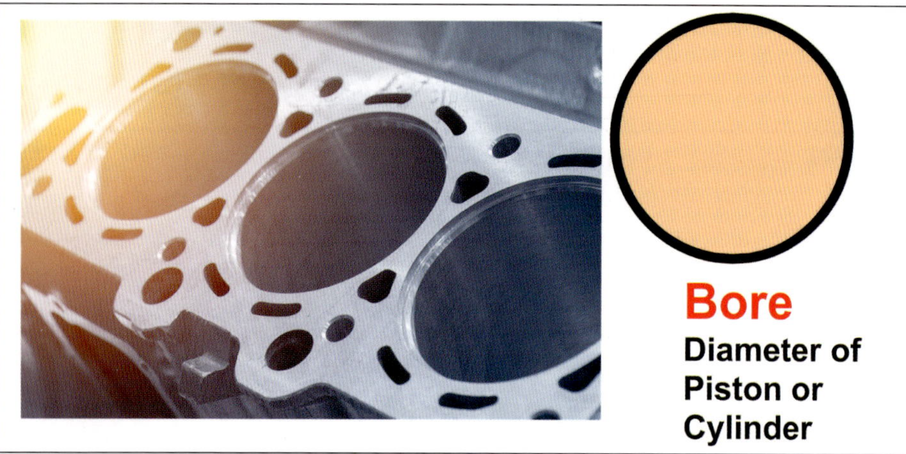

The bore determines the size and power of an engine. Generally, the bigger the bore, the larger the engine and the more torque and power it develops.

Bore

Bore is the width of the piston (or the cylinder diameter). When the bore is larger than the stroke, the engine is over-squared and most of its power is dependent on RPM and generated at higher RPM. When the stroke is larger than the bore, the engine is under-squared with most of its power dependent upon torque development.

Stroke

Stroke is the distance that the piston travels from top dead center (TDC)—when the piston is at the top

Engine stroke is determined by the length of the crankshaft crankpin that is attached to the connecting rod. It is sometimes called the "big end" of the connecting rod, as opposed to the small end that is connected to the piston at the wrist pin.

Rudolph Diesel

The term *diesel* comes from Rudolf Diesel, who is recognized as the inventor of the engine that uses his name. He built the first diesel (compression-ignition) engine in 1893. Other engineers of the time were credited with the diesel invention and became the subjects of controversy.

Rudolf Diesel was the first engineer to understand the full prospective of the compression ignition cycle, which became known as the Diesel Cycle. He published his work in 1892 with the title *The Theory and Construction of an Economical Thermal Motor.* ■

of its stroke—to bottom dead center (BDC)—when the piston is at the bottom of its stroke. At TDC, the crank is at a point nearest the combustion chamber. At BDC, the piston is farthest from the combustion chamber. The space between the piston and the head when the piston is at TDC is the clearance space (or clearance volume). The following terms are also used with respect to piston position:

- Before top dead center (BTDC): The piston position before TDC.
- After top dead center (ATDC): The piston position after TDC.
- Square engine: A term used to define an engine that has a bore diameter that is equal to the piston stroke (or travel).
- Over-square engine: A term used to describe an engine in which the cylinder bore diameter is larger than the stroke dimension.
- Under-square engine: A term used to describe an engine in which the cylinder bore diameter is smaller than the stroke dimension. Most truck and bus diesel engines are under-square.

Piston Displacement

The total engine displacement is the volume in cubic inches or liters (cubic centimeters) of the space swept through by all pistons during two revolutions of the crankshaft (720 degrees). The total piston displacement is easily found using this formula:

$$V = 0.7854 \times D^2 \times S \times \text{number of cylinders}$$

- V = Cylinder volume
- D = Piston diameter (bore)
- S = Stroke

Example: A 6.5L GM diesel engine has a bore of 4.055 inches and a stroke of

Engine displacement is the bore multiplied by the stroke multiplied by the number of engine cylinders.

3.818 inches. What is the total piston displacement?

$$0.7854 \times (4.055 \times 4.055) \times 3.818 \times 8 = 394 \text{ in}^3$$

Compression Ratio

The term *compression ratio* is a volume ratio. In an internal-combustion engine, it is the ratio of the total cylinder volume to the combustion

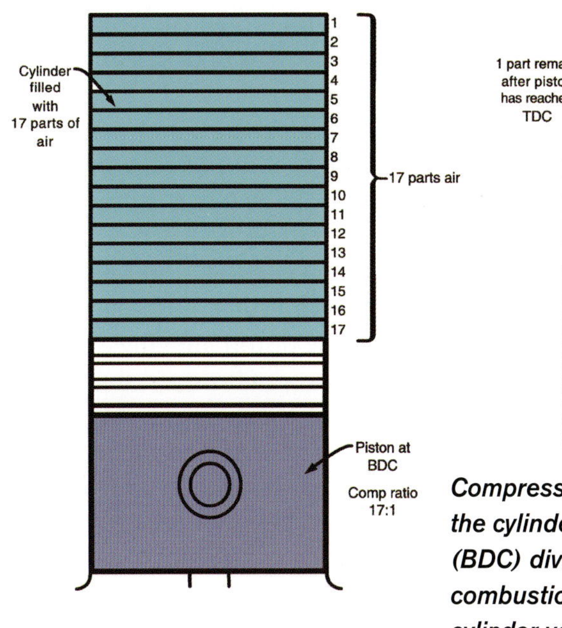

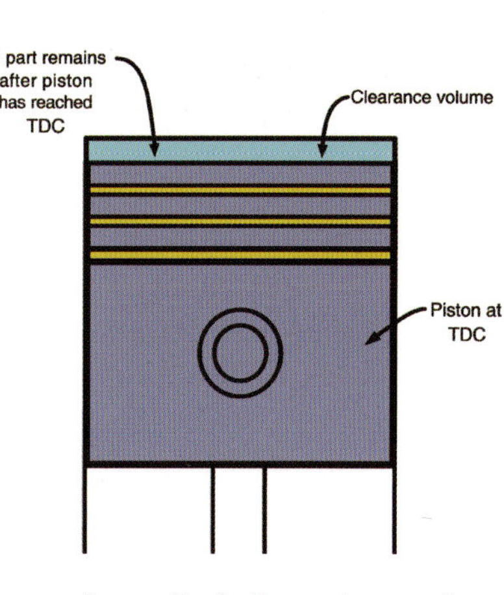

Compression ratio is the volume of the cylinder at bottom dead center (BDC) divided by the volume of the combustion chamber, which is the cylinder volume at top dead center (TDC).

chamber clearance volume. The volume at BDC is added to the volume at TDC, and that is divided by the volume at TDC and calculated in this formula:

$$r = \frac{V_d + V_c}{V_c}$$

- r = Final compression ratio
- V_d = Volume at BDC
- V_c = Volume at TDC

Engine Speed

Engine speed (RPM) is angular velocity, a vector name for the rate of change of position at an angle. It is identified as crankshaft RPM and represented in formulas as the letter N. Typically, speed measurements are performed using a scan tool or a laptop computer on electronically controlled engines. On the 5.7L, 6.2L, and 6.5L, you can use a compression gauge to count the engine puffs to calculate engine speed.

Work

Work is force multiplied by the distance through which the force acts. For an engine and dynamometer, if the engine speed is not known, this formula is used:

$$Wk = 2\varpi FR$$

- Wk: Work (in ft-lbs per revolution)
- ϖ: 3.1416 (a constant)
- F: Force (in pounds or Newtons)
- R: Radius of the shaft (in feet or meters)

The distance through which the restraining force acts in one shaft revolution is 2R, in which R is the radius of the shaft. The constant is ϖ, which is 3.1416. The engine turning the dynamometer and producing

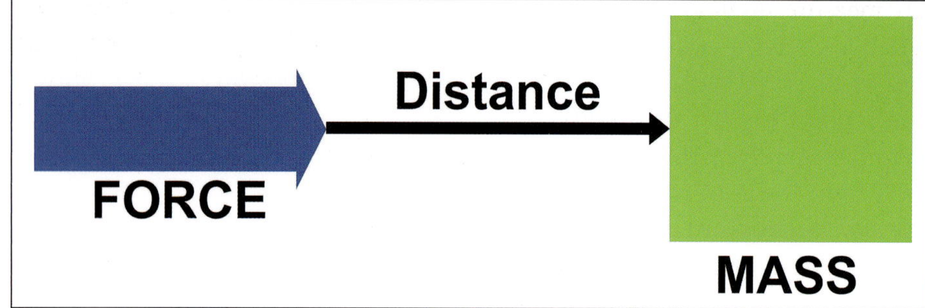

The standard definition for work is force multiplied by distance. Mass (or weight) as pictured is pushed 2 feet by a force of 5 pounds, so 5 pounds times 2 feet equals 10 ft-lbs of work.

a force is comparable to the engine crankshaft standing still and the dynamometer being turned around it with a force (F) acting though a radius arm (R).

Torque

Torque is a force that tries to turn or twist something around another moving object. It is generally defined as the product of a force and the perpendicular distance between the line of action of the force and the axis of rotation.

Torque is force multiplied by length, which is very similar to the formula for work. The length of the lever is the length of the throw of the crankshaft journal. It is a twisting effort expressed as the capacity for the engine to do work, where horsepower is defined as the rate at which the engine can do work.

Diesel engines produce torque by combustion force pushing down on top of the piston, moving a lever that is the throw of the crankshaft. Torque is generally expressed in foot-pounds (ft-lbs) or Newton-meters (Nm), where 1 ft-lb equals 1.355 Nm and 0.737 ft-lb equals 1 Nm.

Torque is expressed mathematically in the following formula:

$$T = FR$$

- T: Torque (in ft-lbs or Nm)
- F: Force (in pounds or Newtons)
- R: Radius or torque-arm distance (in feet or meters)

$$Torque = \frac{hp \times 5{,}252}{RPM}$$

The number 5,252 is a mathematical constant derived from the basic horsepower formula. One

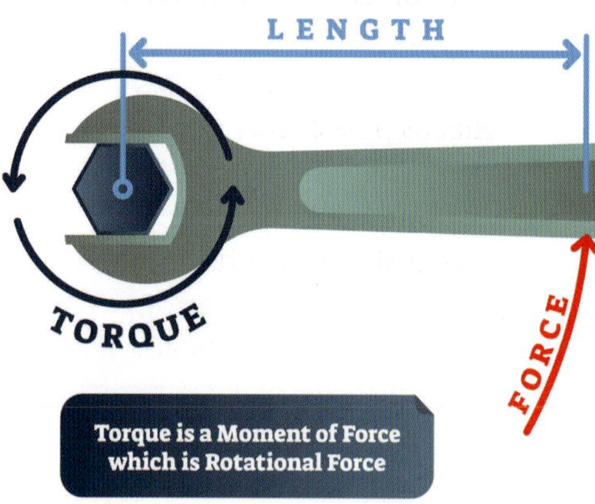

Torque is a form of work, but it is in a circular or turning motion. In this case, the force from the work formula is the force of the engine piston pushing down multiplied by the stroke of the engine, which is the distance the piston travels.

can measure engine torque using a dynamometer.

Combustion Chambers

Diesel engines use two different combustion chamber designs, which are the direct injected (DI) or the indirect injected (IDI) designs. The DI chamber is where the fuel is directly injected into the combustion chamber. The IDI design (as with the 6.2L and 6.5L engines) is where the fuel is indirectly injected by going into a prechamber before going into the main combustion chamber.

A combustion chamber must be designed so that the compressed air will seek out and mix with the diesel fuel. The design must make maximum consumption of the available oxygen and induce total combustion from the autoignition mixture generated from the air-fuel mixture. High oxygen utilization depends at present on the use of high levels of air motion or turbulence. Efficient conversion of combustion energy into work requires:

- Complete combustion of as much fuel as possible by the air in the chamber.
- Combustion completed early in the power stroke and timing the combustion peak to be close to TDC.

The increased heat transfer between the fuel droplet and the air can be compared to that between the car heater with the fan running and a passenger sitting in front of it. Without the fan running, heat transfer between the heater and the passenger is small; with the fan running and creating turbulence, the passenger is subjected to the hot air.

Combustion chamber designs come in two distinct types: open combustion chamber (DI systems) and precombustion chamber (IDI systems). In the DI system, fuel injection and subsequent combustion takes place within the actual working chamber or cylinder of the engine. The IDI system employs a separate combustion chamber that is remote from the working cylinder but connected to it by a channel or passage. It is generally referred to as a prechamber or antechamber and has several different designs.

Open Combustion Chamber Direct Injection

The DI diesel does not use a prechamber because the combustion chamber is open. Fuel is injected directly into the space between the cylinder head and the top of the piston. This is also referred to as an open chamber design. The piston often contains a bowl or has a specially shaped crown to aid in the mixing process for good combustion.

One design called the toroidal piston is used on the 6.2L and 6.5L engines. It has a combustion chamber shaped like half of a four-leaf clover. It is designed to overlay a piston displacement (squish) rotary swirl at right angles to the induction-produced swirl around the piston axis. The resulting dual turbulence spirals around the piston axis and resembles a tornado, hence the term toroidal.

The nozzle is centrally placed in the combustion space and is usually a multi-hole type. The symmetrically placed spray provides even distribution of all available air. Hole dimensions are arranged to give the required penetration and aid in the mixing of air and fuel. The more intense the swirl, the fewer holes are required. DI systems require high pressures in the area of 18,000 to 30,000 psi for this level of fuel penetration. The injector nozzle orifices are located so that the spray pattern fits the combustion chamber without impinging on the cylinder walls or the piston.

The open combustion chamber on the top of a diesel piston actually looks like a small bowl. This is the area in a direct injected (DI) diesel engine where the air meets the fuel and combustion begins. The air spins in this bowl, and the fuel is injected into it.

A properly designed engine uses an opening combustion chamber that is designed for maximum power and good fuel economy. The injection nozzles (or injectors) used should complement the combustion chamber by directing the fuel so that it swirls (or spins) in the mixing bowl.

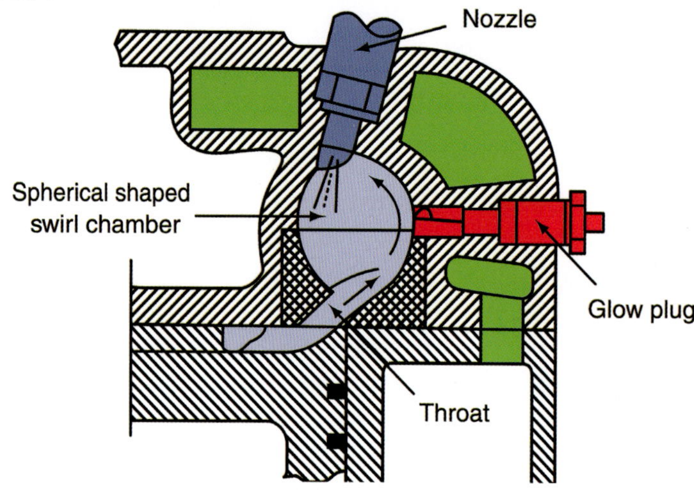

A Ricardo Comet 5 precombustion (prechamber) system has the major chamber in the cylinder head and only a small space between the piston and the cylinder head. The injection nozzle sprays fuel into the prechamber, and virtually all of these designs use a glow plug system for starting.

DI systems have the more desirable torque curve shape for road vehicle applications with a 5- to 10-percent efficiency edge over the IDI chamber design. This fact is mainly due to the lower direct heat losses through lower combustion chamber surface area to volume ratios.

In addition to piston cavities, other chamber designs producing air turbulence include masked intake valves, spiral-shaped intake ports, turbocharging, and aftercooling. A spiral-shaped intake port acts as a forcing cone and twists the incoming air into turbulence. It accelerates the inlet air speed and then transmits a twisting turbulence or swirl that can be further enhanced using a toroidal-shaped piston cavity or bowl. As the piston compresses this air mass, it develops hundreds of miniature tornadoes circling in a forceful vortex. DI engines usually do not use a glow plug system.

Precombustion Chambers and Indirect Injection

The 5.7L, 6.2L, and 6.5L diesel engines use a precombustion chamber and are IDI engines. The IDI diesel uses a prechamber that is joined to the main chamber above the piston by a connecting flow passage. Fuel is injected into the prechamber, which also uses a glow plug to heat the fuel for cold starting. Combustion begins in the prechamber and then spills into the main combustion chamber. As fuel and air are burned, the burning gases emit from the prechamber while the piston descends on the power stroke.

The 6.2L and 6.5L diesel engines use swirl-type (high-turbulence) prechambers. These prechambers have a spherical shape that mixes the air and fuel by air swirl. They assist in promoting high turbulence by creating a swirling mass of air in the prechamber.

The close piston clearance of the 6.2L and 6.5L produces high turbulence in the prechamber because most of the air in the cylinder is forced through a small opening into the prechamber in a very short amount of time. Prechambers promote rapid combustion. The charge is forced out of the thin area, stirring the entire mixture that results in more complete combustion.

This design has an advantage over the open-chamber direct-injection system because it provides a broader operating range for these engines used in light trucks. This results in less diesel noise and more reduced exhaust emissions. It is also less sensitive to fuel characteristics and works well with a less-expensive fuel injection system.

Engine Operation

Diesel engines operate on the principle that high-compression heat is obtained through rapid compression of air in the cylinder, and fuel is injected into this air. After the fuel mixes with the air, it auto-ignites, which is called spontaneous combustion.

The diesel engine is a thermal (or heat) engine that converts heat energy by fuel combustion into mechanical energy through the pistons and crankshaft. They are internal combustion engines, where the fuel and air are burned inside the

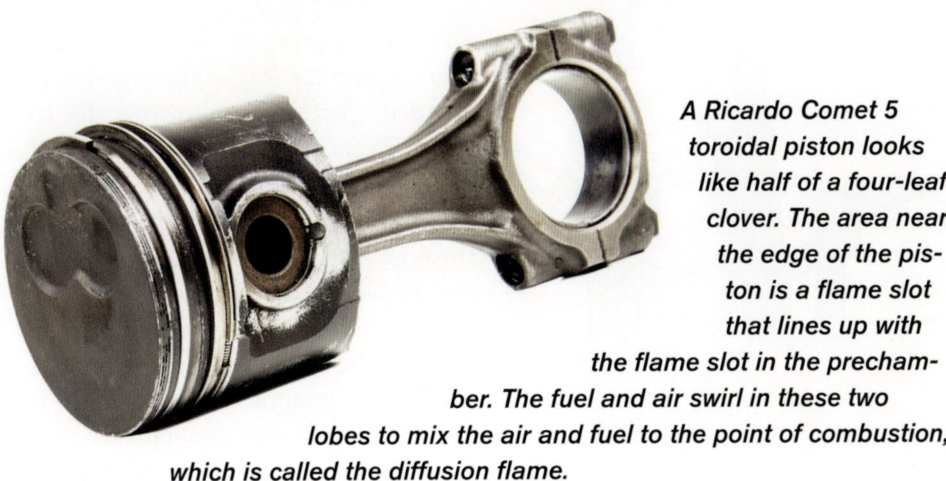

A Ricardo Comet 5 toroidal piston looks like half of a four-leaf clover. The area near the edge of the piston is a flame slot that lines up with the flame slot in the prechamber. The fuel and air swirl in these two lobes to mix the air and fuel to the point of combustion, which is called the diffusion flame.

cylinders and the explosive force of combustion pushes the pistons down and they reciprocate back up. This back-and-forth motion of the pistons is converted into rotary motion by the crankshaft and drives the output.

For an internal combustion engine to operate, it must have these three elements:

- Air: a source of oxygen to burn the fuel
- Fuel: to supply the force, pressure, or energy as it burns and expands
- Ignition: a source of heat to cause a fire

The diesel four-stroke cycle is the same as the Otto cycle (or gasoline four-stroke cycle). However, there are differences in combustion, power control, and compression ratio. The four-stroke cycle consists of intake, compression, power, and exhaust, which is also referred to as suck, squeeze, bang, and blow. When all four are done, the diesel engine has completed the four strokes of one full cycle.

Intake Stroke

The diesel intake stroke starts with the piston at TDC. A lobe on the camshaft opens the intake valve. The piston moves down in the bore due to the rotation of the crankshaft. As the piston moves down, it pulls outside air through the air cleaner, into the air crossover manifold, past the open intake valve, and into the cylinder. The downward movement of the piston creates a low-pressure area above the piston (as the volume increases, the pressure decreases, which is Boyle's law). Air rushes in to fill the space left by the downward movement of the piston because atmospheric pressure is greater than the low pressure in the cylinder. The piston tries to inhale a volume equal to its own displacement.

The air/fuel mixture is not of the same kind or alike. During the intake stroke, only air is inducted. No throttle exists, so the cylinder is completely filled with air at the inlet manifold pressure. The air mixes with any residual gases in the cylinder.

The energy needed to move the piston from TDC downward comes from either the flywheel or is due to overlapping power strokes from a multicylinder engine. As the piston nears BDC, it slows down nearly to a stop. When the piston reaches BDC, the intake valve closes, sealing the cylinder filled with air, and the compression stroke begins.

Compression Stroke

The turning crankshaft forces the piston upward, and since both valves are closed, there is no way for the air to escape (except past the rings). The volume decreases as the piston rises, so air is compressed. The pressure is inversely proportional to the volume, according to Boyle's law.

In the compression of a gas, the volume decreases and the pressure and temperature rise as the gas is

Sir Harry Ricardo

British engineer Sir Harry Ricardo developed the swirl prechamber system in 1931 and called it the Ricardo Comet Head. The newer versions are called the Ricardo Comet 5. His system employed indentation in the piston and a spherical-shaped combustion prechamber in the cylinder head that were designed to promote air swirl when compared with other prechambers of the same type. This design formed a smaller combustion chamber within the main heat-insulated combustion chamber that used a compression-induced swirl to improve the maximum power rating.

This direct combustion type provided a reduced delay period and minimum interference with breathing that preserved high-speed performance. In common with most other indirect systems, a pintle-type injection nozzle is used. The Ricardo Comet 5 prechamber is used in the 6.2L and 6.5L engines but not the 5.7L Oldsmobile diesel. ■

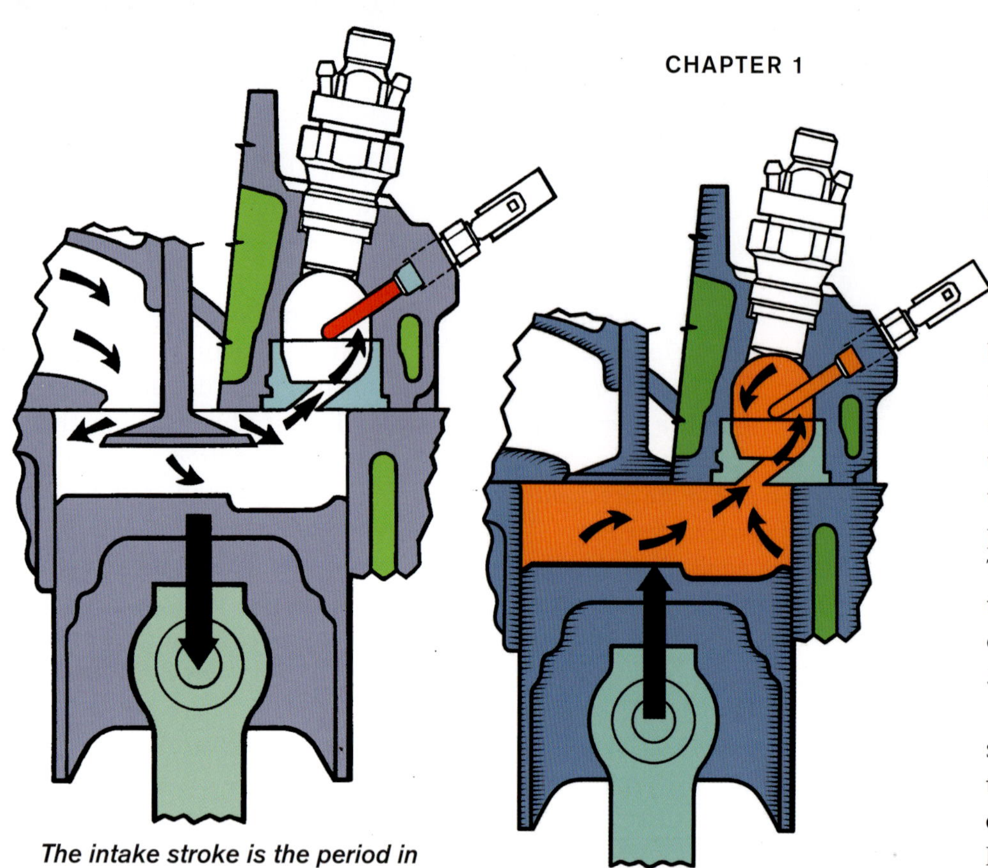

The intake stroke is the period in the Otto four-stroke cycle when air enters the cylinder. This happens due to the pressure being lowered when the piston descends in the cylinder and atmospheric pressure (or turbocharged, induced pressure) pushes the air into the cylinder. This is the sucking in of the air.

The compression stroke is where the air is squeezed (or compressed) by the piston and raises the pressure and temperature of the air to more than 1,000°F. If you cup your hands and bang them together tightly, you will feel the pressure and an increase in temperature.

pressurized. This causes collisions of the air molecules within the cylinder. In the 6.2L and 6.5L IDI prechamber engines, air compression forces air into the swirl prechamber in a tornado fashion, creating a hot swirl of air.

For example, if a volume of air is compressed to 1/22 of its original volume, as it is in a diesel engine, the open space between the molecules is greatly reduced, increasing the number of collisions and the pressure between them. These collisions cause heat due to the kinetic energy of the molecules.

Compression ratio is the ratio of the volume at BDC to the volume at TDC (clearance volume). A higher compression ratio means higher thermal efficiency (or that a portion of the heat supplied to the engine is turned into work). As the compression ratio increases, the expansion ratio also increases, thus thermal efficiency increases. The 6.2L and 6.5L diesel engines have compression ratios in the area of 21.5 to 22.5:1.

The formula is:

$$\text{compression ratio} = \frac{\text{volume BDC}}{\text{volume TDC}}$$

The internal energy of the combustion gas is increased as heat is added. High heat generated by this greater compression will cause the fuel to atomize (break up into finely divided particles), allowing it to mix easily with the air. In the IDI engine, mixing is further enhanced by the addition of more heat through the spinning action of the spherical-shaped prechamber. Ignition will occur as the fuel mixes with the air. The temperature of the compressed air is approximately 1,000°F. The temperature is generally higher than the spontaneous ignition point of the fuel, which is approximately 558°F (292°C).

Near the end of the compression stroke, fuel will be sprayed into either the prechamber in an IDI engine or the combustion chamber in a DI engine. In a DI engine, the compressed air will swirl in a toroidal piston cavity, increasing the friction between air molecules, which will promote mixing with the fuel.

The IDI diesel prechamber is joined to the main combustion chamber above the piston by a connecting flow passage. A swirl precombustion chamber assists in promoting high turbulence by creating a swirling mass of air in the prechamber.

Turbulence is the extreme disturbance of the compressed air in the combustion chamber. It causes the air molecules to move in all directions. They collide with each other and cause friction and heat. This will increase the transfer of heat between the cool, liquid-fuel droplets and this hotter air.

Power Stroke

The power stroke begins after the fuel is sprayed into the prechamber by the fuel injector (or nozzle) mounted in the prechamber. The fuel nozzle sprays and atomizes the fuel into the prechamber in a short burst, forming a fuel-rich core that is surrounded by air zones.

During this period, fuel has entered the main combustion chamber from the prechamber but has not begun to burn. The temperature of the air is much higher than the fuel, so some of it has evaporated, but some has formed into very tiny droplets. It starts to vaporize and mix with the hot compressed air. After about 0.001 seconds, any zones that are hot enough and have the correct air/fuel mixture ratio will auto-ignite.

It is important to note that ignition will take place only where air meets fuel. It is important to note in the 6.2L and 6.5L diesel engines that combustion begins in the prechamber and then moves into the main chamber as fuel, air, and burned and burning gases while the piston descends on the power stroke.

The first fuel burns very rapidly. This rapid burning causes a sudden rise in pressure. This sudden rise causes a highly localized pressure that causes an audible noise known as diesel knock. This diesel knock noise level hinges on pressure rise velocity. The high pressures in the cylinder push down on the piston. This pressure forces the piston down in the bore, which causes the crankshaft to rotate. The pressure falls as the volume increases. The temperature falls as the gas does external work.

The oxygen/fuel burns and the nitrogen expands, pushing the piston down under power. As the piston continues downward, the gases in the cylinder expand and cool as they give up their energy. The power stroke is the only stroke in which energy is used from the fuel, and cylinder pressure is the highest in this stroke. The prechamber on these 6.2L and 6.5L engines use a glow plug to help in cold starting.

The power stroke is the heavy bang of the Otto four-stroke cycle. It is when the fuel ignites (or explodes) and creates the power in a reciprocal internal combustion engine. This explosion is what creates the force along with the flywheel and other cylinders that creates the RPM in an engine.

Exhaust Stroke

As the piston nears the bottom of its travel, the exhaust valve is opened by a lobe on the camshaft. The piston then begins to rise in the cylinder, starting the exhaust stroke. The upward movement of the piston forces the burned gases past the exhaust valve and out of the cylinder. As the piston nears the top of its stroke, the camshaft lobe again opens the intake valve, and the cycle repeats itself. The exhaust valve is allowed to close (by spring pressure) shortly after the piston begins its downward movement. The exhaust stroke produces no work but expends a quantity of energy to push exhaust gases from the cylinder.

The exhaust stroke is the blowing-out portion of the cycle where the engine removes the spent or used gases of combustion. There are several phases in the exhausting of these gases that involve very specific movement of both the exhaust and the intake valves.

Valve Timing

As with all four-stroke diesel engines, intake and exhaust valves are used with 6.2L and 6.5L engines. The intake valve permits the intake of air for combustion during the intake (suction) stroke. The exhaust valve permits removal of the burned gases to the atmosphere during the exhaust stroke. The size and operating mechanisms of the valvetrain are designed so that these operations will occur efficiently at the right time in the four-stroke cycle.

The term *valve timing* is used to

express the time the valve functions in an engine operating cycle. Valve action is stated with degrees of crankshaft rotation from TDC to BDC of the piston in the cylinder. In the four-stroke cycle, the intake stroke occurs only during the piston downstroke and the exhaust stroke only during the piston upstroke. Moving air has inertia (resistance to a change in motion) and requires opening the valves longer than the piston stroke in an operational engine.

The piston moves at varying speeds during its stroke because it must stop at each end of the stroke, gain speed toward mid-stroke, and slow down to a stop at the opposite end. The inertia of the air is used to keep the exhaust gas or intake air moving even though the piston may be stopped. If the valve is held open, the intake stroke now lasts longer than the downstroke of the piston. The exhaust stroke also lasts longer than the upstroke of the piston.

Exhaust Valve Timing

The exhaust valve is timed to open before BDC in the power stroke and to close after TDC in the exhaust stroke. The reason for this timing is to get rid of all of the exhaust gases. The valve is opened before BDC in the power stroke to release the low pressure remaining from combustion and to make sure the exhaust valve is fully open when the exhaust stroke begins. This avoids high back pressure against the piston during the start of the exhaust stroke and reduces withdrawing of the gases through the valve and the seat. There is a small power loss by doing this, but it is canceled out by a gain through the exhaust gases' release. The exhaust valve is open past the end of the exhaust stroke to provide an overlap of exhaust valve and intake valve opening. This permits a thorough clearing of exhaust gases from the clearance space and the creating of a partial vacuum. The inertia of this flow of exhaust gases creates this suction (or partial vacuum) in the clearance volume. All the burned gases are expelled, and the charge of intake air is fresh air.

Intake Valve Timing

In a four-stroke cycle diesel engine, the intake valve is timed to open before TDC and close after BDC of the intake stroke. This is done to achieve the highest volumetric efficiency. The opening of the intake valve close to the end of the exhaust stroke and before the closing of the exhaust valve allows the removal of burned gases before the beginning of the intake stroke.

The intake air partially displaces the small amount of exhaust that remains and reduces the amount of intake air contamination. This is

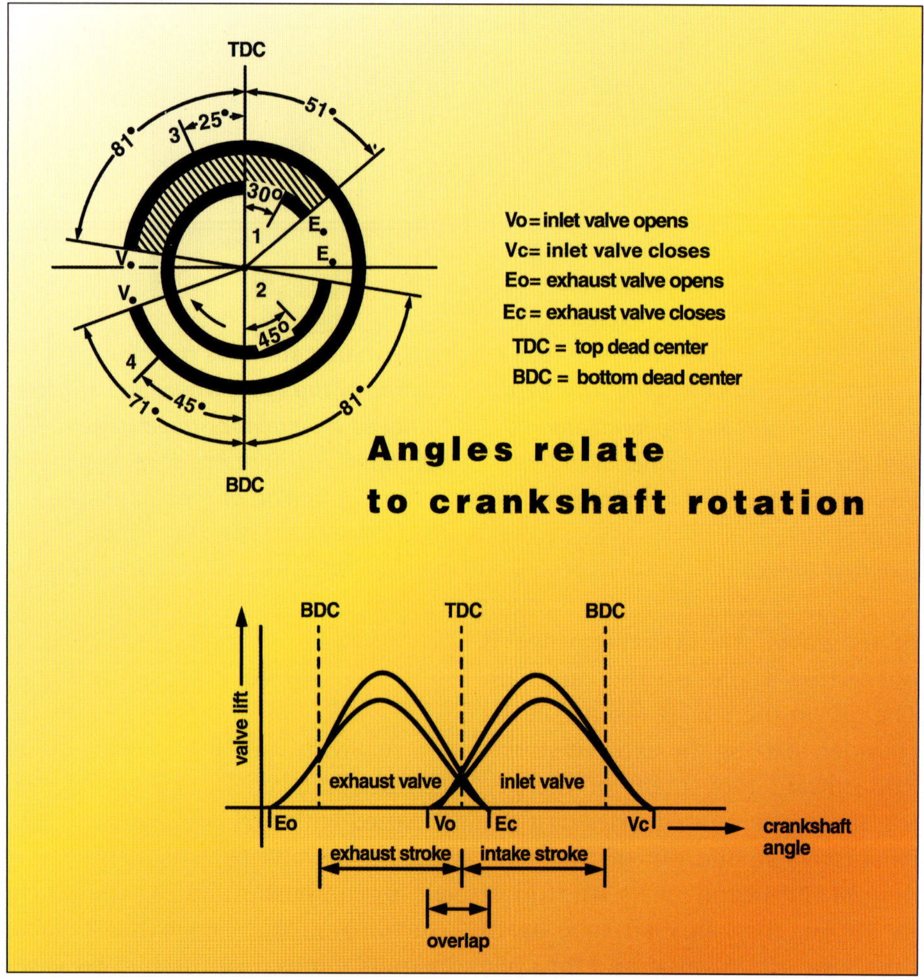

Just like a gasoline-fueled engine, a diesel engine uses intake and exhaust valves that need to be timed to provide the correct operation and exhaust emissions. Valve timing is the time that the valves open and close with respect to crankshaft angle degrees. In this graph, the intake valve opens at 81 degrees before TDC and closes at 71 degrees after BDC. The exhaust valve opens at 90 degrees after TDC and closes at 51 degrees after TDC. So these valves are overlapped.

sometimes referred to as the scavenging period of the four-stroke cycle.

During the period that both valves are open (near the end of the exhaust stroke and the start of the intake stroke) the piston movement is slight. Yet, the volume of exhaust gas that has been forced out into the exhaust path continues outward through the exhaust manifold. The inertia of this flow of exhaust gases creates a suction (or partial vacuum) in the clearance volume. So, all the burned gases are expelled, the charge of intake air is fresh air, and the quantity of oxygen is increased.

The intake valve is held open after the piston has reached the end of the intake stroke. The tendency is for air to continue flowing into the cylinder due to the partial vacuum created by the piston during suction and the inertia imparted to the column of incoming air.

Combustion Process

A substance is said to be combustible if it is composed of elements that will burn when mixed with oxygen and ignited. The elements that will burn are called combustibles. The most common combustible used in a diesel engine is a hydrocarbon, such as diesel fuel. The supply of oxygen comes from the air; thus air is a supporter of combustion.

The compounds created in the process of combustion are gases or vapors. If a hydrocarbon burns in air, the products of combustion are carbon dioxide, water vapor, and nitrogen. The nitrogen is inactive and takes no part in the actual burning, but it pushes the piston down in the power stroke. The water vapor condenses to water when it cools.

As stated, you need three conditions to produce combustion. First, there must be a combustible (e.g., the diesel fuel, which is a hydrocarbon). Second, you need a supporter of combustion, which is the oxygen in the air. Third, you need the mixture of fuel and air at the proper temperature for fuel vaporization so that combustion will start and the fuel will ignite. A source of heat is necessary to cause a fire. In a diesel engine, this ignition source is the heat of compression that causes autoignition, leading to spontaneous combustion. James Ricardo established that the diesel combustion (compression-ignition engine) process takes place in three stages or periods: the delay period (ignition delay), the period of rapid combustion, and the period of controlled combustion.

Delay Period

Ignition delay (ID) is also known as the delay period. It is the time between the start of injection and the start of ignition, which starts the pressure rise due to combustion. It is also called ignition lag.

ID takes place at the end of compression, after the start of injection, because the fuel does not ignite immediately. After the start of injection, the cylinder pressure follows the compression curve. At the end of this curve, the pressure rises at an increasing rate until the maximum pressure slope is reached. ID is much longer than the active combustion period, particularly during the part-load operation.

Fuel injection also continues during the ID period. The longer the ID period, the greater the amount of fuel accumulated in the combustion chamber before the start of combustion. This results in higher rates of pressure rise and maximum gas pressures and temperatures. The length of the delay period depends mainly on the pressures and temperatures in the cylinder gases during ID and the combustion chamber surface temperature against which the fuel hits. The ID in diesel combustion of the 6.2L and 6.5L engines is important because it affects:

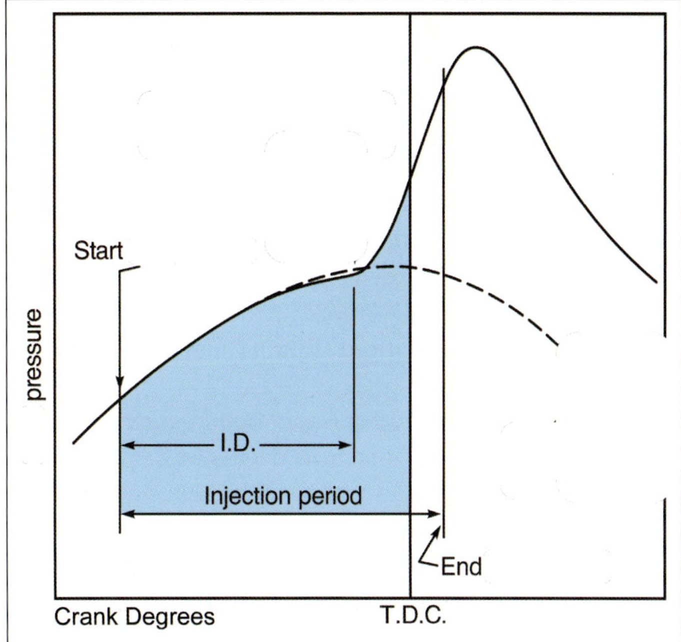

The ignition delay (ID) period begins at the point of fuel injection, which is called the start of injection. It continues until the start of the cylinder pressure rise from combustion. The injection period is generally longer when peak pressure is achieved in the combustion chamber.

- The rate of pressure rise and the maximum gas pressure, causing noise, vibrations, and stress.
- Maximum gas temperature, which affects the nitrogen oxide (NOx) emission, fuel consumption, power, cooling system thermal loads, and the temperature and thermal stressing of the combustion chamber walls.
- Time for evaporation and mixing before ignition depends only on the duration of the delay period.

The ID period contains a series of preliminary reactions that occur before the appearance of a flame. These reactions start in the vapor that surrounds the fuel-drop surfaces as each drop enters into the cylinder. Ignition starts in this vapor layer surrounding the drop, and the combustion rate of fuel drops is limited by their evaporation rate. This burning rate decreases as the fraction of oxygen in the surrounding air decreases. The single biggest factor that changes ID is the average temperature of the cylinder contents during the delay period.

Diesel injection occurs in stratified layers, much like the atmospheric stratosphere. In premixed charges, the air/fuel ratio can change the time between when the flame appears and the completion of the compression process. With diesel fuel injection, as long as the fuel is not completely evaporated, the complete range of air/fuel ratios from 0 (no fuel) to infinite (no air within the fuel droplets) must be present. Ignition will occur where the local air/fuel ratio is most ignitable.

The delay time is independent of speed (RPM) and varies according to the four areas affected by ignition delay. ID does not vary in direct relation to engine speed. In a spark-ignited gasoline-fueled engine,

you have flame speed, which is nearly proportional or increases when engine speed increases. Therefore, the number of crank angles occupied by the combustion process is almost independent of RPM.

However, in a diesel engine, flame speed does not exist. Instead, the combustion rate is determined by how rapidly the fuel and air are mixed. As engine speed increases, mixing increases, but not enough to compensate for the reduced amount of time available for combustion. Thus, the upper speed of the engine is limited. The combination of the Ricardo Comet 5 prechamber and toroidal piston in the 6.2L and 6.5L engines aids greatly in the mixing process because the air swirls in the indentations in the piston during the compression stroke.

Fuel injection timing advance results in longer IDs because the fuel is injected into the air at a lower temperature and pressure. If the increase in ID in crank degrees is less than the injection advance, autoignition occurs earlier in the cycle. Longer ID causes more fuel evaporation and mixing in the lean fuel region of the combustion chamber along with higher NOx. Retarding injection timing is one of the effective ways of reducing NOx emissions. Yet, this results in a loss in brake mean effective pressure (BMEP) and fuel economy. Typically, retarded timing can cause white or black smoke in a diesel engine, and advanced timing causes black smoke.

Period of Rapid Combustion

Injection occurs at or just before TDC to take advantage of the highest compression temperature. The ID is always long enough (about 0.001 to 0.003 seconds) that there is a substantial amount of fuel well mixed

There are four areas affected by ignition delay:
- Nozzle droplet size diameter formation and fuel spray disintegration.
- Air temperature and combustion chamber pressure prior to fuel injection leading to liquid fuel heating and evaporation. Pressure and temperature being high can shorten the delay period.
- Turbulence of combustion chamber air and diffusion of fuel vapor into the air to form a combustible mixture.
- Chemical reason/fuel composition that include the cetane number and the decomposition of heavy hydrocarbons into lighter fuel components.

with air when ignition happens. Ignition delay lasts about 7 crank angle degrees (as shown in Area B).

Once ignited, this fuel tends to burn very quickly due to the collection of ignition points and the high temperature in the combustion chamber. After about 0.001 seconds, any zones that are hot enough and have the correct air/fuel mixture ratio will autoignite.

Flame does not propagate through the combustion chamber as in a gasoline engine. This is because the fuel produced by the injector is too rich to burn and only air exists in other parts of the chamber. Thus, combustion occurs only at the interface where fuel and air come together, which is called the diffusion flame.

The period of rapid combustion takes place when the first fuel is burned. This rapid burning causes a sudden rise in pressure, which creates a highly localized pressure that pro-

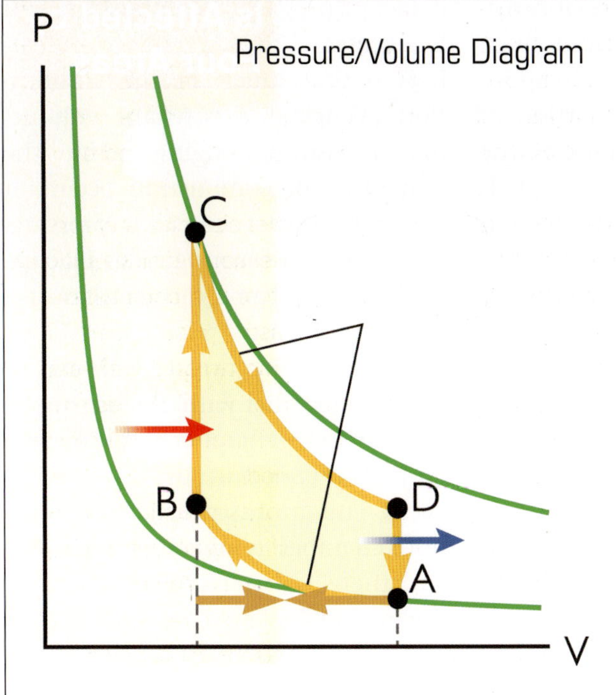

Area A of piston position is the beginning of fuel delivery when the pump or injection pressurizes the fuel. Area B represents the actual beginning of fuel injection into the combustion or precombustion chamber. Area C is the point of ignition until the cylinder reaches peak pressure. Area D represents the end of combustion, when the flame is quenched or goes out.

duces a noise known as diesel knock. This knock happens at the beginning of the combustion cycle, as opposed to a gasoline engine spark-knock (detonation) that occurs at the end of the combustion cycle.

The amplitude of the knock depends on the speed of the pressure rise. Both the rate and the extent of pressure during this period increases as the delay period increases since both mixing time and the fraction of fuel taking part in rapid combustion increase. When the ID is longer than the injection time, the amount of fuel involved is unaffected by ID length.

The rate of combustion is controlled by how rapidly the fuel is mixed with the air. Once the first fuel is burned, a rich core of fuel remains along with zones of air. The remaining fuel is burned as it mixes with the air. The mixing time is the reason some diesel engines have limited speeds and long combustion periods.

A fast rise in pressure can be caused by an extended ignition delay period. During this delay period, most of the fuel is injected, and a large amount of fuel causes a fast pressure rise. Also during a long delay period, more time is available for mixing air and fuel. The sudden rise in pressure can be enhanced by good air-to-fuel mixing. High speeds and good nozzle atomization can increase mixing.

If the fuel and air mixes well, the burning takes place very quickly and a loud knock occurs. If the air and fuel mix poorly, the time required for the air zones to connect with the fuel core increases, the burning takes place more slowly, and the knock is less severe.

This period of rapid combustion or diesel knock can be increased from long delay periods, which will result in more increased mixing. The fuel should ignite quickly and burn quickly to keep the period of rapid combustion to a minimum.

The fuel additive cetane is used to reduce this delay period. The ignition quality of diesel fuels is expressed in terms of a cetane number or rating. A high cetane number indicates a short delay period, and a low cetane number indicates a long delay period. The 6.2L and 6.5L engines use glow plugs as a cold starting aid, so they are not very sensitive to cetane ratings.

Period of Controlled Combustion

The period of controlled combustion is the time period from maximum combustion pressure to the point when combustion is significantly complete. The first fuel is injected, vaporizes, and mixes with the hot compressed air. While it is burning, fuel injection continues, so a rich core of fuel remains along with zones of air. This remaining fuel is burned as it mixes with the air. During this period, when the ID is longer than the injection time, the amount of fuel involved is affected only if it has not mixed with the oxygen during the period of rapid combustion.

Fuel injection continues throughout the delay period and the period of rapid combustion. Fuel injected after the period of rapid combustion, called the first fuel, is burned as it is mixed with the air. The fuel only burns as it is injected into the cylinder so that the rate of pressure rise is moderate. This is called the period of controlled combustion.

Flame speed does not exist in diesel engines. Instead, the combustion rate is determined by how rapidly the fuel and the air mix together. As engine speed increases, mixing increases, but it is not enough to compensate for the reduced amount of time available for combustion and can cause the upper speed of the engine to be limited.

The engine design can go too far with mixing. If all of the fuel was instantaneously mixed with the air, then the mixture would all burn immediately upon ignition and result in an extremely loud knock along with engine damage. The engineers needed to create a design that gets the fuel mixed with the air in a manner that provides quiet, fast combustion.

A diesel engine has a high compression ratio and, therefore, a high expansion ratio. This high expansion can make the diesel engine more efficient than a gasoline engine. Diesel-engine efficiency is also demonstrated by cooler exhaust. Due to the long combustion period, the fuel is more completely consumed. The diesel engine converts more of the fuel's energy into useful work than any other internal combustion engine. Diesel combustion also results in much lower carbon monoxide and carbon dioxide emissions.

Combustion Summary

Optimum efficiency requires that the fuel injected be evenly distributed in the compressed air so that it forms a consistent charge when the burning occurs. To make sure that the combustion occurs quickly, the fuel must be broken up into finely divided particles (atomized) in order to present the largest possible surface area to the surrounding air for mixing. This atomization ensures a rapid transfer of heat from the compressed air to the fuel particles and minimizes the delay period before spontaneous combustion begins. Once started, atomization will accelerate the vapor burning of the fuel surface and bring about early combustion completion.

All compression-ignition engines have a delay period between the first fuel injection and the start of burning, which is then followed by a rapid pressure rise due to the spontaneous ignition of a proportion of the total injected fuel. This is the period of rapid combustion. It is followed by controlled combustion with the introduction of the remainder of the fuel during the period of the controlled-combustion burning phase. Some delay period is essential to make sure that the outer zones of the combustion chamber receive fuel and that distribution is not hampered by premature combustion.

The fuel injection rate for optimum distribution is dependent upon the air turbulence or the speed of the air spiral flowing past the nozzle. Decent air turbulence or swirl maintains the best balance required between uncontrolled and controlled burning phases.

Burning must be complete before the end of the power stroke, and that complete combustion pressure distribution should be at a satisfactory crank angle. In general, the higher the working speed range for a given combustion chamber design, the higher the rate of injection.

Air temperature in the combustion chamber during the compression stroke generally averages between 900 and 1,200 psi on IDI engines. On DI diesel engines, this pressure can run between 1,800 and 2,300 psi. These high pressures result in peak combustion-chamber temperatures as high as 3,500 to 4,000°F (1,926° to 2,482°C).

Late combustion of previously unburned fuel or intermediary products of combustion happens before the afterburning period is complete. Due to ID and combustion time, high-speed diesel engines (such as the 6.2L and 6.5L) do not achieve constant-pressure combustion. It is necessary to start injection earlier so that much of the combustion occurs at a constant volume, like a gasoline engine, while the remainder of combustion occurs at constant or near-constant pressure. More efficient burning takes place at a constant volume rather than at a constant pressure.

Due to incomplete mixing of the injected fuel with the air in the combustion chamber, some fuel droplets do not burn until late in the cycle. This means that the combustion chamber temperature is lower and there is less oxygen to sustain the remaining mixture burning; as a result, incomplete combustion occurs. This results in black or gray smoke coming out the exhaust.

White smoke results from incomplete combustion in lean combustion chamber areas. It also occurs when fuel spray impinges on metal surfaces and with low temperatures in the cylinder, such as when starting an engine on cold days. Fuel with too high of a cetane rating can also cause white smoke when used in high outside temperature conditions. White smoke occurs more often in an IDI engine from retarded timing, as it does on the 6.2L and 6.5L engines. For this reason, these engines use a light-load cold-advance device on the injection pump. Very late timing on a DI engine causes white smoke.

Gray or black smoke is the result of incomplete combustion in rich combustion chamber areas. This is caused by such conditions as engine overload, inadequate fuel injector spray penetration, late ignition due to retarded injection timing, or poor fuel evaporation and mixing due to advanced timing. Air starvation is the major cause of black smoke. Due to the extremely short time available for mixing, the air/fuel rate increases beyond a certain value, and an appreciable fraction of the fuel fails to find the necessary oxygen for combustion. Instead, it passes through the cylinder unburned or partially burned.

Efficient engine operation requires that the combustion duration be less than about 80 degrees of crankshaft rotation. At 3,000 rpm, the combustion duration can be about 0.0044 seconds. In the 6.2L and 6.5L prechamber engines, diesel fuel is injected into a prechamber where combustion starts. To improve mixing, the reacting mixture expands through an orifice in the prechamber into the air-filled main chamber. Intense mixing occurs in the main chamber that results in fast, complete burning of the remaining fuel. Not only does this increase the speed of the reaction but it also results in greatly reduced hydrocarbon and soot emissions. Engine speeds of 4,000 rpm are common for prechamber engines, such as the 6.2L and 6.5L. At 4,000 rpm with an 80-degree crank angle combustion duration, the combustion time is approximately 0.0026 seconds.

Power and Speed Control

In a diesel engine, there is no air throttle valve and therefore no restriction to the intake air. Power and speed in a diesel engine is controlled by the amount of fuel injected and when you inject it. A throttle valve is used in a spark-ignited gasoline-fueled engine to control the air/fuel mixture mass flow or density to control power and speed. In a diesel engine, the same amount of air enters the cylinder during each cycle whether at idle or at full power.

Some air is lost past the rings at low speed, where leakage has time to occur. Varying the amount of fuel (injection duration) injected into the cylinder controls power. For low power, such as idle, there is only a short injection period, and a small quantity of fuel is used. When high power is required, the injection period is longer, a larger quantity is forced into the cylinder, and most of the air is used in the combustion process.

An advantage of the diesel engine is that it has good efficiency at low power because the air/fuel ratio is so lean at reduced power. The air/fuel ratio in a diesel engine varies from 100:1 at idle to 20:1 at full load. At high power, so much fuel may be injected that some of the fuel does not combine with the air in the cylinder. This results in unburned fuel being exhausted as smoke. The air/fuel ratio at this point is called the smoke limit. The smoke limit is reached whenever maximum power is needed. The formation of black smoke begins when the oxygen percentage entering the engine is equal to the percentage consumed by the combustion process.

Fuel Injection Timing

Diesel engine manufacturers, such as Detroit Diesel, determine the best fuel injection timing point using experimental tests in a test cell with the diesel engine on a dynamometer. Actual fuel injection timing is then determined after consideration of the following factors:
- Federally mandated exhaust emissions to include: NOx (nitrogen oxide), HC (hydrocarbons), CO (carbon monoxide), CO_2 (carbon dioxide), and PM (particulate matter)
- Horsepower output
- Fuel consumption
- Engine noise
- Exhaust gas denseness due to incomplete combustion (black soot)
- Exhaust gas temperatures

The actual start of fuel injection varies among makes and models of engines due to design differences. At an idle speed, the variance can be anywhere between 5 degrees and 15 degrees before TDC. As the engine speed is increased and a greater fuel volume is injected, timing must be advanced to allow the fuel to burn to completion because of the now-higher piston speed, since there will be less time available.

At a 600-rpm engine idle speed, the piston can travel 600 feet per minute. In one hour, the piston travels 36,000 feet (60 x 600). If you divide 36,000 by 5,280 feet, we can determine its speed in miles per hour, which in this case is 6.81 mph (11 km/h). At a maximum engine speed of 2,100 rpm, the piston will travel at 2,100 feet per minute (23.86 mph).

If the start of fuel pressurization began at the same number of degrees before TDC at the high-speed as it did at the low-speed setting, then the piston would be closer to the top of its stroke before fuel injection actually began while running at the higher speed. The start of fuel injection has therefore been retarded, where it begins later in the compression stroke of the upward-moving piston at the higher speed. It becomes necessary to advance the start of fuel injection (inject fuel earlier) in the cylinder with an increase in engine speed.

The beginning of fuel pressurization (beginning of compression) starts within the pumping plunger and barrel bore. In an in-line multiple-plunger injection pump that uses long fuel lines to transfer the fuel from the pump to the injector and nozzle, the line length must also be considered.

A speed timing advance device is used in the 6.2L and 6.5L distributor-type fuel injection pump to get better engine performance through the operating-speed range of the engine.

Timing advance is needed to compensate for the two delay periods:

1. The injection pressure wave traveling the length of the injection line.
2. The ignition delay period.

High-pressure injection lines connect the injection pump to the nozzles. Pump pressure travels to the nozzle as a pressure wave, resulting in a time lag. Compensating for inherent injection lag improves high-speed performance. Starting delivery of fuel to the nozzle earlier, when the engine is operating at higher speeds, ensures that combustion takes place when the piston is in its most effective position to produce optimum power with minimum fuel consumption and minimum smoke.

Oscilloscope Traces

The engine is set at 2,700 rpm at a full fuel load with a residual line pressure of 800 psi. The following oscilloscope traces illustrate why it is necessary to provide sufficient fuel injection advance to compensate for ignition delay and line length:

- Trace 2 (from the top) shows the start of pumping at 16 degrees before TDC. The peak line pressure rises to 4,400 psi.
- Trace 4 (from the top) shows the injector nozzle needle valve lifting at 3 degrees before TDC. The pressure rises to over 4,000 psi with needle lift duration of 29 degrees.
- Fuel ignition occurs at 8 degrees after TDC.
- The ignition delay (ID) or delay period is 11 degrees from the time that the fuel injection begins to ignition, or the 3 degrees before TDC plus the 8 degrees after TDC when ignition occurs. ■

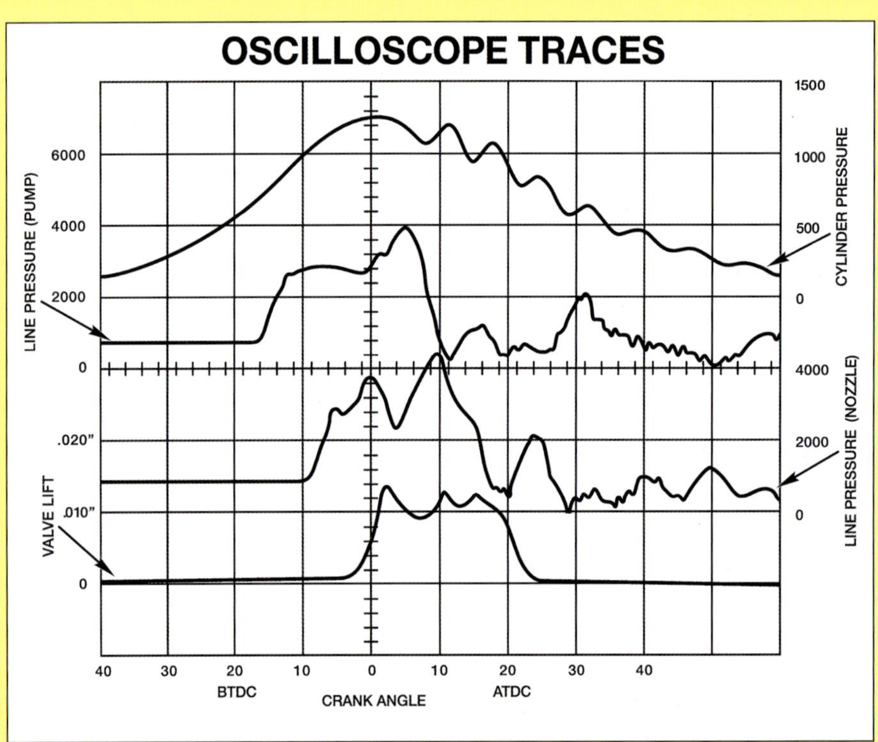

A four-trace oscilloscope pattern was taken under load at 2,700 rpm from an actual engine on a dynamometer at Stanadyne Diesel Systems lab in Hartford, Connecticut. The bottom waveform shows the valve lift of the injection nozzle caused by a distributor-type injection pump. The second waveform shows the injection line pressure to the injection nozzle. The third waveform shows the line pressure in the injection pump, and fourth waveform demonstrates the cylinder pressure. (Graph Courtesy Stanadyne Diesel Systems)

TOOLS, HISTORY, AND ENGINE SYSTEMS

The 6.2L and 6.5L engines require special tools to make the service procedure easier and more precise. Some operations can be done without them by using some backyard ingenuity, while other repairs are next to impossible without the special service tool.

In addition to the engine service tools, there are a number of fuel injection pump service tools that are required to service the Stanadyne DB2 and DS4 injection pumps. They are covered in chapter 5 of this book.

Special Service Tools

Special engine service tools and shop equipment are fundamental to the repair of any engine. They provide the means for work to be undertaken on vehicles, including lifting, diagnosing, removing, installing, cleaning, and inspecting.

Many engine tasks involve the use of some sort of tool or shop equipment. This makes their purchase, use, and maintenance important to the overall success of a rebuild. If buying a tool for $100 saves two hours of working time every time it is used, it only needs to be used a few times for it to pay for itself.

Always use tools and equipment in the way they were designed to be used. Don't abuse them. Think about the task at hand, identify the tools to do the task, inspect the tool before using it, use it correctly, and clean and inspect it after you use it.

Piston Ring Compressor

Using a fixed piston ring compressor to install new or used pis-

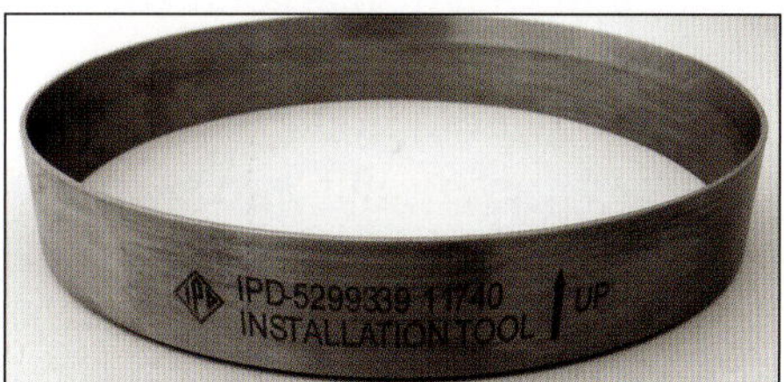

A fixed-dimension piston ring compressor that measures 4 inches in diameter can be used for the 6.2L engine that has a bore that measures 3.98 inches. This tool works well because there is enough tolerance to allow its use. I have used this installation cone for piston installation many times. When the Moraine, Ohio, engine plant was building the 6.2L diesel, the machine shop manufactured this special tool. Chevrolet never provided it to the service field, but the GM special tool for a 350 small-block Chevrolet engine with a 4-inch bore worked fine.

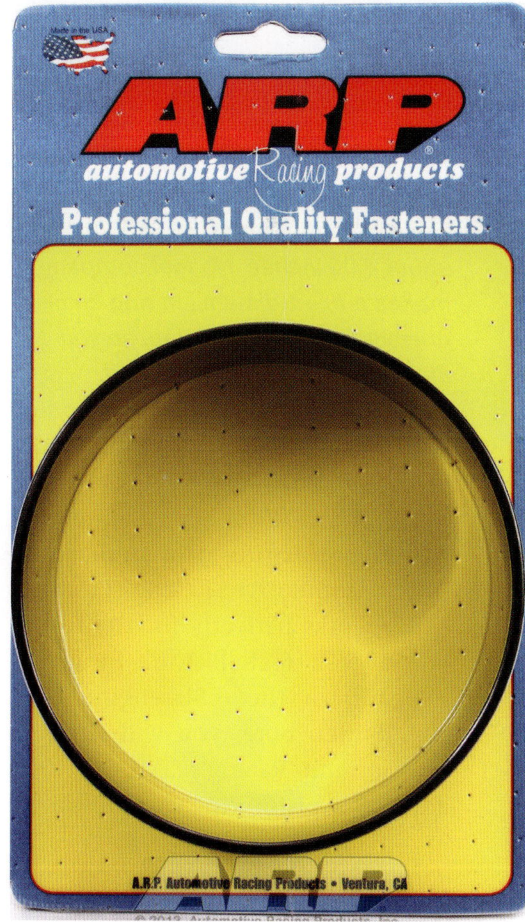

A fixed-dimension piston ring compressor from Summit Racing (SME-904000) non-adjustable 4-inch piston ring or one from Automotive Racing Products (ARP), which is shown, works perfectly for the installation of a 6.2L piston.

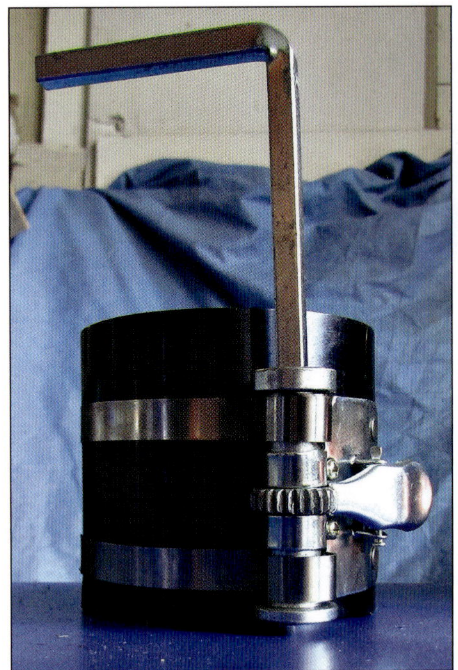

An adjustable piston ring compressor is used with the 6.5L engine. The 6.5L has a bore that measures 103 mm or about 4.05 inches. No tool company makes a fixed-dimension ring compressor for that dimension, so you need to use an adjustable unit.

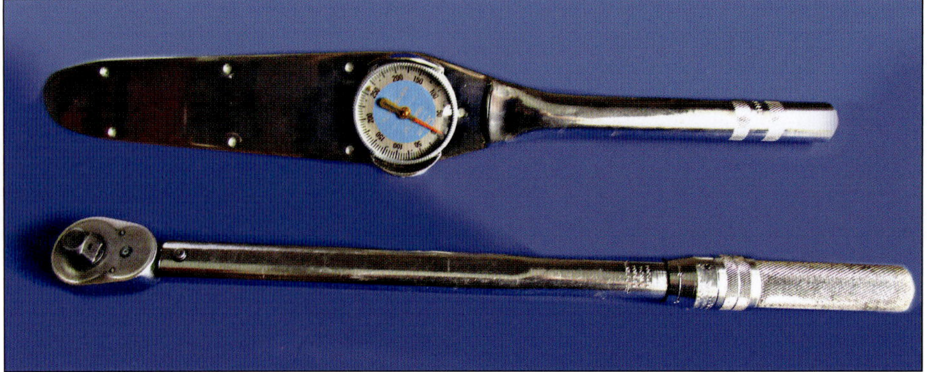

A torque wrench is designed to tighten bolts and nuts using the drive on the end, which fits with any socket and accessory of the same drive size found in an ordinary socket set. Torque all lug fasteners to the proper torque with a properly calibrated torque wrench. Make sure to use the proper sequence.

tons is easier than using the older ratchet-type installer. A Summit Racing (SME-904000) non-adjustable 4-inch piston ring or a similar one from Automotive Racing Products (ARP) works perfectly for the installation of a 6.2L piston. To install a piston in the 6.5L engine with a 4.05-inch bore, you will need to use Summit Racing's SME-90A4000 adjustable piston ring compressor.

Torque Fasteners

Bolt tension is what keeps a bolt from loosening and what causes it to hold parts together with the right clamping force. Torque is needed to create bolt tension. To do this, a torque wrench measures the amount of tightening force required to tighten a bolt or a nut. It also tightens fasteners to a predetermined torque.

The torque value is the amount of twisting force applied to a fastener by the torque wrench. One foot-pound (ft-lb) is described as the amount of twisting force applied to a shaft by a lever that is 1 foot long with a weight of 1 pound placed on the outer end. A torque value of 100 ft-lbs will be the same as a 100-pound weight placed at the end of a 1-foot-long lever.

Chevrolet did not specify torque settings for every nut and bolt, but when it does, it is important to follow the specifications. For example, manufacturers specify a torque for cylinder-head bolts in the first step of the 6.2/6.5 torque turn method. The torque specified makes sure that the bolt provides the proper clamping pressure and will not come loose but will not be so tight as to risk breaking the bolt or stripping the threads.

Straightedge

Cylinder heads and blocks heat up and cool every time the engine starts and stops. Over time, this cycle can warp the head and block mating surfaces, especially if the engine overheats, which is pretty common on the 6.2L engine from a head gasket failure. These parts can also warp if the engine is disassembled while it is still hot and the loosening sequence is not followed.

A straightedge is a precision-ground metal bar used to check the flatness of engine components, such as the cylinder head and block deck in combination with a feeler gauge. Place a straightedge across the length of the cylinder head at each of the combustion chamber fire ring areas and use feeler gauges to check for flatness of the cylinder head and the cylinder block deck to see if they are warped.

Always check head and block gasket surfaces for warping with a straightedge when building an engine. Place this edge on the surface and then try to slip the specified feeler gauge under the straightedge to see if it is flat.

Taps and Dies

A tap and die set consists of a fluted, threaded shank with a drive square at one end and a tap that is used to cut internal threads and clean and restore damaged threads. They are made from hex-shaped or cylindrical sections of hardened steel with threaded holes in the center. Taps come in three different types: tapper, plug, and bottoming. The difference in these types is the length of the chamfer on the cutting end of the tap.

Tapper taps are chamfered or beveled for the first six or eight threads, which makes them easy to start but prevents them from cutting threads close to the bottom of the hole. Plug taps are chamfered up about three to five threads, which makes them a good all-around tap because they are relatively easy to start and will cut to nearly the bottom of the hole. Bottoming taps have a short chamfer of one-and-a-half to three threads and will cut as close to the bottom of a blind hole as is practical.

During use, dies are held firm in a diestock or T-handled holder. Hex-shaped dies are particularly useful because they can be turned with a wrench. Cutting edges are formed where the flutes intersect with the threads. For each tap size, there is a corresponding twist drill that is used to make a hole of the correct size.

Precision Measuring Tools

Superior engine rebuilding starts with the precision measuring of gaps, spans, angles, radii, pitches, forces, pressures, and flows. Basically, the precision of a measuring tool tells how many digits of a measurement you can accurately determine using the tool. The precision of any measuring tool is to 1/10 of the smallest calibration of that tool. The most commonly used precision measuring tools are micrometers (conventional and digital); dial indicators; calipers (vernier, dial, and electric); and a dial bore gauge.

Tapping Instructions

1. Use the correct-size tap drill. Secure this information from a tap drill chart, which is generally included in the tap and die kit.
2. Use a sharp tap and apply sufficient cutting fluid. With some cutting fluids, the area is flooded with fluid; with others, a few drops are sufficient. Read the container label.
3. Start the tap square.
4. Do not force the tap to cut. Remove the chips using a piece of cloth or cotton waste (not your fingers).
5. Avoid running a tap to the bottom of a blind hole and continuing to apply pressure. Do not allow the hole to fill with chips and jam the tap. Both conditions can cause the tap to break, especially small taps.
6. Remove burrs on the tapped hole with a smooth file.

Taps are usually wielded by hand with the square drive end of the tap held in a tap wrench. For smaller sizes, a T-handled chuck can be used. The correct tap drill size is normally marked on the tap itself or on its container.

Micrometer

A micrometer is a widely used device for precisely measuring the thickness of blocks, outer and inner diameters of shafts, and the depths of slots, such as the diameter of a wrist pin or the thickness of a valve spring shim. A set of micrometers that range from 0 to 1, 1 to 2, 2 to 3, 3 to 4, and 4 to 5 inches, is ideal. Digital micrometers are easier to read than conventional models and are just as accurate.

The metric micrometer uses a scale that reads 25 mm from a zero measurement. The thimble must be rotated through 50 complete revolutions to produce a reading of 25 mm.

Thus, each complete rotation of the thimble equals 0.5 mm (25.0 mm = 0.5 mm). The thimble is graduated into 50 evenly spaced lines with each line representing 0.01 mm.

Dial Indicator

Dial indicators are used for measuring valve lift, piston deck clearances, and many other precision measuring tasks. The dial indicator should have a probe with at least 1 inch of travel, graduated in 0.001-inch increments, plus a flexible fixture and a magnetic stand. Another variety of dial indicator, which is designed to measure depth,

has a moveable base that straddles the hole to be measured.

Vernier Caliper

A vernier caliper is a short, graduated scale that slides along a longer graduated instrument and is used to indicate fractional parts of divisions, similar to a micrometer. A vernier caliper is used to measure the distance between two symmetrically opposing sides. The tips of the caliper are adjusted to fit across the points to be measured, the caliper is then removed, and the distance is read by measuring between the tips with a measuring tool, such as a ruler.

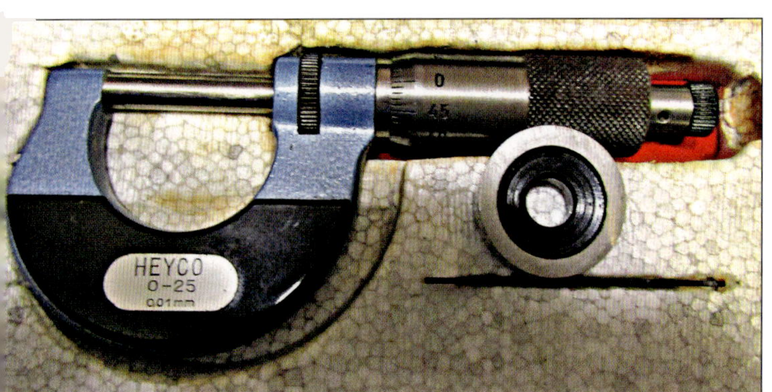

A 25-mm micrometer is the equivalent of a 1-inch English-system micrometer and the smallest micrometer used. The micrometer uses a round or long measuring standard to insert in the micrometer jaws and a special tool to calibrate the mic. Metric micrometers work the same as English micrometers, whether in digital or mechanical configuration.

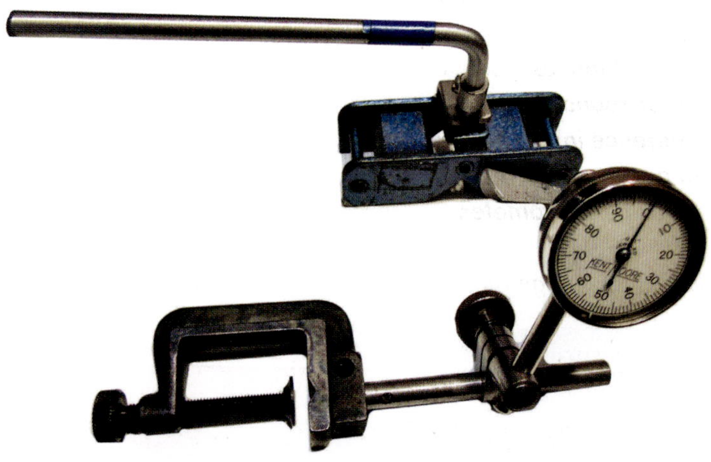

The dial indicator is a precision measuring instrument that indicates movement to a thousandth of an inch or tenths to thousandths of a millimeter with a needle sweeping around a dial face. For example, you can use a dial indicator to measure the flywheel housing bore concentricity or valve guide clearance.

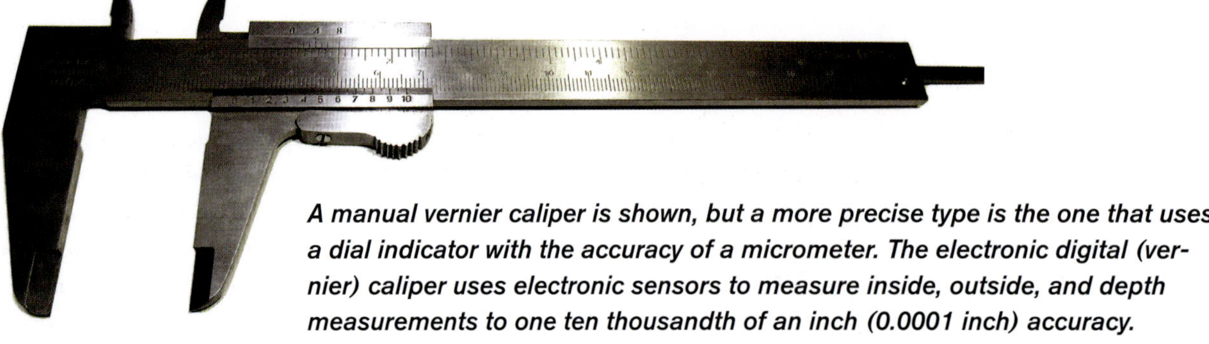

A manual vernier caliper is shown, but a more precise type is the one that uses a dial indicator with the accuracy of a micrometer. The electronic digital (vernier) caliper uses electronic sensors to measure inside, outside, and depth measurements to one ten thousandth of an inch (0.0001 inch) accuracy.

A dial bore gauge has to be adjusted to a dimension, such as the OEM specifications. The reading on the dial bore gauge indicates plus (+) or minus (-) readings from the predetermined dimension. A dial bore is the best tool to measure taper and out-of-round because it shows the difference in cylinder bore rather than an actual measurement provided by an inside micrometer.

Dial Bore Gauge

A dial bore gauge is a very precise measuring device for measuring cylinder taper, inner diameter, and out-of-round along with main bearing (block housing) bores for taper and out-of-round. It is more accurate and easier to use than an inside micrometer. Using various extensions, most dial bore gauges have a range of just over 1 inch in diameter to 6 inches or more. Most are graduated in 0.0005-inch increments.

Valve Spring Compressor

The valve springs, keepers, and retainer should be removed with a valve spring compressor. Many types of compressors can be used, but the most common is the C-clamp type. The 6.2L and 6.5L engines use a simple pushrod-type overhead valvetrain with poppet-style intake and exhaust valves, so a C-clamp type of valve spring is used for head disassembly.

Some OEMs have a special tool for compressing the valve springs on their engine. Both the 6.2L and 6.5L use the C-clamp style of valve spring compressor. The new rocker assembly is completely interchangeable with all previous-model-year engines. The assembly includes rocker arm part number 23500074 (16), shaft part number 23500075 (4), and button retainers part number 23500076 (16).

Engine History

In 1983, the US Army Tank-Automotive & Armaments Command (TACOM) out of Warren, Michigan, contracted with General Motors and specifically Chevrolet Motor Division to build a light utility vehicle to replace the Dodge M880 vehicle that the army was using worldwide. The army called this vehicle the Commercial Utility Cargo Vehicle (CUCV), and it included the 6.2L diesel engine and later the 6.5L engine. There were 11 models of the CUCV.

The CUCV was GM's first major light-truck military vehicle in production since World War II. They were built mostly from existing Chevrolet and GM light commercial truck parts. The CUCVs came in four basic body styles: pickup, utility, ambulance body, and chassis cab. The M1008 was the basic cargo truck, the M1010 was the ambulance, and the M1009 was a Chevrolet K5 Blazer uprated from a 1/2 ton or class 1 to a class 2 with a 3/4-ton capacity. In today's CUCV world, this truck is typically referred

The Commercial Utility Cargo Vehicle (CUCV) squarebody or Chevy Blazer–style military truck from 1983 was named the M1009. There were 11 models. General Motors and Chevrolet Motor Division built 70,000 CUCVs in model years 1984–1987, although most were a 1984 vintage. This build was authorized by TACOM. General Motors continued to build CUCVs in low numbers from 1986 to 1996, mainly to accommodate military markets that needed replacements for existing CUCVs. They were powered by the 6.2L J-series V-8 diesel engine. They used the Turbo-Hydramatic transmission (THM) 400 automatic transmission, and most used an NP208 chain-drive transfer case.

---

to as a squarebody. The rest of the CUCVs were all rated as 1¼ ton or five-quarter truck.

The drivetrain was the 6.2L non-emissions diesel engine using a mechanical injection system and Turbo-Hydramatic transmission (THM400). The THM400 for this application used a third clutch sprag instead of the roller clutch used in the civilian version. The engine regular production option (RPO) code was LL4, which was identified in the vehicle identification number's (VIN) eighth character as a *J*. This engine was rated at 155 hp and 240 ft-lbs of torque. Most of them used the NP-208 chain-drive transfer case. The cab chassis truck had a slip-yoke rear output version of the NP-205, which was mainly for its power take-off (PTO) capacity.

The CUCV's electrical system was a hybrid 12/24-volt system that used a 24-volt starter complete with dual 100-amp alternators. The rest of the truck used a 12-volt electrical system that was connected to the 24-volt system using a bus bar. The ambulance (or M1010) used dual Leece-Neville alternators capable of delivering 200 amperes and had a silicon controlled rectifier (SCR) solid-state system to control it. It also used the standard NATO slave receptacle for jump-starting any NATO vehicle and the military Simplified Test Approach for Internal Combustion Engines (STAICE) diagnostic system.

Arctic Trucks used three diesel-fuel-fired heaters so the vehicle would be operational in 30 minutes at 50 degrees below zero. General Motors built about 70,000 CUCVs from 1983 to 1986 (model years 1984–1987), though most were model year 1984. Chevrolet continued to build CUCVs in low numbers from 1986 to 1996, mainly to accommodate military markets. Three of the original builds were sealed in Cosmoline to ensure that the first production vehicle matched the rest of the vehicles.

In 1979, the United States Army Tank Command (TACOM) out of Warren, Michigan, drafted specifications for the high-mobility multipurpose wheeled vehicle (HMMWV) that was eventually going to replace all the tactical vehicles in the 1/4- to 1½-ton range like the universal Jeep. The specification called for a high level of on- and off-road performance, the ability to carry a large payload, and improved fire survival. It was a larger vehicle with a wider track.

The HMMWV can climb a 60-percent incline and traverse a 40-percent slope. The air intake is mounted flush on top of the right fender, and electronics were waterproofed to drive through 2½ feet of water. The radiator was mounted high, sloping over the engine on a

A high-mobility multipurpose wheeled vehicle (HMMWV or Humvee), also called a Hummer, is a series of light, four-wheel drive (4WD) military trucks and utility vehicles built by AM General. This vehicle was the replacement for the Jeep and the CUCV. After going through a replacement process, the Joint Light Tactical Vehicle (JLTV) was selected as its replacement.

A fully equipped HMMWV military unit is complete with a missile launcher, radar unit, and machine gun.

forward-hinged hood. The drivetrain was also the 6.2L non-emissions diesel engine using a mechanical injection system and a Turbo-Hydramatic transmission (THM400) because they were being used in the CUCV.

One of the big differences between the CUCV and HMMWV was the use of a complete 24-volt electrical system, where the CUCV had a combination 12- and 24-volt system. For example, the CUCV used a 24-volt starter motor. It did not use the 1994 electronic fuel injection (EFI) version of the 6.5L (covered later in this book), which started with the 1994 civilian models. The drive axles were mounted above the axle centerline and used a reduction gear to drive the wheels. Some referred to this design as the rim drive.

There were about 61 firms in the process but only 3 submitted prototypes and bids. AM General, a subsidiary of American Motors Corporation, began work on the HMMWV design in late 1979. About a year later, the first prototype was being tested by TACOM. Chrysler Defense and Teledyne Continental also produced a design. TACOM awarded AM General a contract for development of several more prototype vehicles to be delivered to the government for another series of tests in 1981. The original HMMWV A0 series had a curb weight of 5,200 pounds and a payload of 2,500 pounds. In 1983, AM General was awarded an initial contract for 2,334 vehicles.

During the five-year contract, AM General built 55,000 vehicles, which included 39,000 vehicles for the army with the rest for the navy and marines. There were 72,000 vehicles delivered by 1991, and 100,000 were delivered by the 10th anniversary in 1995.

Construction

The 6.2L diesel engine was designed at Chevrolet's engineering center. It was originally a Chevrolet engine, and the chief engineer's name was Don Riley. The camshaft was manufactured by Detroit Diesel, but that's where it ended at the time. From 1983 to 1987, Detroit Diesel

In 1982, when the 6.2L engine was introduced by Chevrolet Motor Division, it was painted red, as that was the traditional Chevrolet engine color. The block is sometimes referred to as a red block. In 1983, General Motors made a decision to paint all engines black. The thinking at the time was that oil leaks were less visible on a black engine.

The 6.2L engine is shown in an engine compartment that contains many modifications from the factory build. This unit shows an aftermarket spin-on fuel filter and a glow plug relay that looks like a Ford starter relay is mounted on the bulkhead. The traditional mounting was on top of the wheelhouse of the left fender. This system uses the popular field fix of operating the glow plug relay with a manual off-and-on switch instead of a thermal or electronic controller.

The 6.5L used a 46-mm-diameter intake valve and a 39-mm-diameter exhaust valve, and both had mechanical injection and electronic fuel injection.

The firing order for both the 6.2L and 6.5L was stamped on the intake manifold. This firing order was a departure from the standard Chevrolet firing order for V-8 gas engines at 1-8-4-3-6-5-4-2. This was done to reduce distressing on the front main bearing, which was an issue with Chevrolet gas engines. The number-one cylinder is on the left bank.

had design responsibility and service for the 6.2L. However, this ended and reverted back to Chevrolet in 1987 when Detroit Diesel was acquired by Roger Penske Enterprises. The 6.5L diesel was never part of Detroit Diesel; instead, it was part of the newly formed GM Powertrain Division, but most of the people who worked on the 6.2L were transferred to the new GM Powertrain Division.

The 6.2L diesel uses overhead valves and the Ricardo Comet 5 stainless steel swirl-type prechamber, which are serviced separately from the cylinder head. It was an over-square engine design, meaning that the bore was larger than the stroke. This design developed its torque and horsepower at high RPM, as opposed to many diesels that are under-square with a larger stroke than bore so that torque is developed at the lower RPM.

In 1982, Chevrolet Motor Division developed two versions of the 6.2L engine. One was RPO LH6, which used the VIN code *C* and was used in trucks in the 6,000- to 8,500-pound gross vehicle weight rating (GVWR).

The first 6.5L turbo engines used the same mechanical fuel injection system as the 6.2L. In 1994, a fully computer-controlled EFI version was introduced and ran until the end of production in 2000. Production 6.5L engines used a turbocharger that produced between 2 and 8 psi of boost at peak torque based on engine load and other conditions. The 6.5L used oil spray nozzles in the cylinder block to provide additional piston cooling. Both engines use hydraulic roller lifters with anti-rotation guides. In some engines, the anti-rotation guides can cause a lifter-type noise if there are burrs on the guides.

The other version was RPO LL4 and used VIN code *J* for use in trucks in the 8,500- to 10,000-pound GVWR.

These RPO codes were used on all 6.2L engines until it was replaced by the 6.5L engine in 1992. The first version of the LL4 used a 50-mm-diameter intake valve and a 42-mm-diameter exhaust valve, whereas the intake valve size on the LH6 was 46 mm but the exhaust valve was the same size at 42 mm. The 1984-and-later LL4 or J engines used a 46-mm-diameter intake valve and a 38-mm-diameter exhaust valve. Chevrolet engineering used to

The cylinder block (case) was made from one-piece cast iron. The cylinder block castings were originally cast by the GM Foundry, but later blocks (including the 6.5L) were cast and machined by Navistar. There have also been different desig-nations, such as red blocks. The legends regarding the 6.2L go on forever. The term red block *means the first year the engine came out (1982), and there are many special items on that engine, including the Chevrolet red paint on the engine block. Because that was only offered for 1982 and sometimes very early 1983, you'll see carryover engines in 1983 trucks where the engine was painted black. (Photo Courtesy Jim Halderman)*

refer to this as small valves. (For all 6.2L and 6.5L engine specifications, refer to the specifications appendix in the back of this book).

The firing order for both the 6.2L and 6.5L was 1-8-7-2-6-5-4-3. The left-bank cylinders are numbered 1-3-5-7, and right-bank cylinders are numbered 2-4-6-8. The main bearing caps were a 4-bolt design, and the cylinder head used a 17-bolt head design, so you would have 5 bolts around each cylinder to provide the best clamping action.

Both engines use glow plugs to assist starting a cold engine, which will be covered later in this chapter. They also use injection nozzles that are threaded into the cylinder head and a high-pressure distributor-type fuel injection pump to send pressure to these nozzles, opening them in injecting fuel into the prechamber. The 1994 6.5L used electronic fuel injection with a pulse width modu-lated (PWM) solenoid pump.

The 6.2L engine has a 101-mm (3.98-inch) bore and a 97-mm (3.8-inch) stroke. This gives you 6,217 cm³ or 379.4 in³. The 6.5L engine had a bore measurement of 103 mm (4.055 inches) with a piston stroke of 97 mm (3.8 inches), which was the same as the 6.2L, so the difference between the engines is the bore.

The compression ratio on all 6.2L engines was 21.5:1. In 1985, a cylinder head with a 22.5:1 compression ratio was used on the military applications under service part number 14079304. The compression ratio on the 6.5L was 19.5:1 to 21.5:1 based on the applica-tion. (Refer to the specification section in the appendix for the specific com-pression ratio for your engine.) The crankshaft is made from nodular cast iron and cannot be machined, but the camshaft is forged steel and manufac-tured by Detroit Diesel, which is now part of Daimler-Benz.

Block cracks are rare in this engine, but an area that needs to be looked at during a rebuild is the crankshaft webs. These have been known to crack, so during a rebuild, use either dye penetrant or the Mag-naflux process to look for cracks. The main bearing caps are also made from nodular cast iron and then worked in place on the machine line before bor-ing. The center or number-3 bearing is the thrust bearing.

Main Bearings

Main bearings are select fitted to each of the five main bearing bores. The proper size code is also stamped on the pan rail at the correspond-ing main bearing location. The total diameter size range of the main bear-ing bores (number-1 to -5) is 78.826 to 79.850 mm on both engines.

The spread of 0.024 mm is divided into three sizes. These are

Both the 6.2L and 6.5L use a four-bolt main bearing retention design on a nodular cast-iron crankshaft that cannot be machined. There are sev-eral urban legends about a Detroit Diesel forged crankshaft, but other than in a prototype, it never made it into production. The thrust bearing is the center bearing, and this book will cover the unique bearing shell place-ment in the main bearings.

stamped as 1, 2, or 3 on the pan rail. Each of these sizes is matched to the corresponding size of the split bearing insert in the case only. The split bearing insert for the main is match fitted to the crankshaft main journal.

Three bearings will be used for service or rebuild to get the proper clearance. When performing bearing service for rebuilds, Plastigauge is used to obtain the proper clearance. Please note that the values for this engine tend to be in the metric system. The clearance for bearings number-1 through number-4 is 0.045 to 0.83 mm (0.0018 to 0.0032 inch). The clearance on number-5 is 0.055 to 0.093 mm (0.002 to 0.0036 inch). The standard bearing is 0.26 mm (0.001 inch) undersize (US). See the Main Bearing Sizes table.

Cylinder Head

The 6.2L heads for both the LH6 and the LL4 engines are different because of different prechambers and, in some cases, compression ratios and valve sizes.

However, if you have two heads that are identical, they will fit on any of these engines. So, you can use 6.2L heads on the 6.5L and 6.5L heads on a 6.2L. The key is that both heads must be identical on the same engine.

See the Cylinder Head Components table for the different components in the cylinder heads on both engines. Note that 1-2-3 stands for class 1-2-3. The R and V trucks were the older squarebody trucks that were formerly the C-K, now replaced the rounder new C-K. The 6.5L heads have much larger coolant passages and are the best ones to use for a rebuild. Valve sizes are 46 mm (intake) and 39 mm (exhaust).

Main Bearing Sizes			
Main Journal Diameter	**Cylinder and Case Main Brg Bore Diameter**		
Crankshaft Front Center, Intermediate	(3) 79.842–79.850 mm	(2) 79.834–79.842 mm	(1) 79.826–79.834 mm
74.917–74.925 mm, blue	1 0.026 US in case; 1 0.026 US in cap	1 0.013 US in case; 1 0.026 US in cap	1 STD in case; 1 0.026 US in cap
74.925–74.933 mm, orange	1 0.026 US in case; 1 0.013 US in cap	1 0.013 US in case; 1 0.013 US in cap	1 STD in case; 1 0.013 US in cap
74.933–74.941 mm, white	1 0.026 US in case; 1 STD in cap	1 0.013 US in case; 1 STD in cap	1 STD in case; 1 STD in cap
Rear main			
74.912–74.920 mm, blue	1 0.026 US in case; 1 0.026 US in cap	1 0.013 US in case; 1 0.026 US in cap	1 STD in case; 1 0.026 US in cap
74.920–74.928 mm, orange	1 0.026 US in case; 1 0.013 US in cap	1 0.013 US in case; 1 0.013 US in cap	1 STD in case; 1 0.013 US in cap
74.928–74.936 mm, white	1 0.026 US in case; 1 STD in cap	1 0.013 US in case; 1 STD in cap	1 STD in case; 1 STD in cap

The cylinder head on both engines is made from cast iron and is a 17-bolt design that has 5 bolts positioned around each cylinder to provide better clamping action to improve the head gasket retention.

Cylinder Head Components					
Year	**Truck Model**	**Engine Code**	**Nozzle Thread**	**Intake Valve**	**Exhaust Valve**
1982	C-K, 1-2-3	C (LH6)	24 mm x 2 mm	46 mm	42 mm
1982	C-K-P, 2-3	J (LL4)	24 mm x 2 mm	50 mm	42 mm
1983–1984	C-K-G, 1-2-3	J (LL4)	24 mm x 1.5 mm	46 mm	42 mm
1983	C-K-G-P	J (LL4)	24 mm x 1.5 mm	50 mm	42 mm
1984	C-K-G-P	J (LL4)	24 mm x 1.5 mm	46 mm	38 mm
1985	C-K-G-P	J (LL4)	24 mm x 1.5 mm	46 mm	38 mm
1985	C-K-G-P	C (LH6) Fed	24 mm x 1.5 mm	46 mm	42 mm
1985	C-K-G-P	C (LH6) Cal	24 mm x 1.5 mm	46 mm	42 mm
1984–1985	D (CUCV)	J (LL4)	24 mm x 1.5 mm	46 mm	38 mm
1986–1993	C-K-G-P-RV	J (LL4)	24 mm x 1.5 mm	46 mm	38 mm
1986–1993	C-K-G-P-RV	C (LH6)	24 mm x 1.5 mm	46 mm	42 mm

When the head bolts are tightened, there will be line contact around the bore between the cylinder head and the block. When a line-contact design is used, the pressure exerted by the ring to the head and the block is very high. Clamping load is used to compress the metal ring. (Photo Courtesy Jim Halderman)

The prechamber is a press fit into the cylinder head flush to + 0.50 mm (0.002 inch) and marked with an M-N-P and/or a series of dots. The latest replacement design used a diamond stamp. The 1985 LL4 or J engine was a reversed-throat prechamber. The 6.5L is marked with two dots and a T for turbocharged. It is very common for the prechamber to have cracks around the throat, and as long as they do not travel into the fire ring sealing area, they are okay. A crack longer than 5 mm is cause for replacement of the prechamber.

1982–1983 Cylinder Head and Gasket Issues

There are many reasons why a cylinder head may not seal and should be checked before the head gasket is replaced. The pressure within a diesel cylinder head is higher than a gasoline-fueled engine, so it would be 1,000 psi versus 600 psi. The thinking is to use most of the clamping load about 75 percent to seal the cylinder. This is done by placing a round wire ring inside of a thin metal shield that surrounds the cylinder bore, which is called a fire ring.

The body of the gasket is a few thousandths of an inch thinner than the fire ring after it is crushed, so none of the clamping load is used to crush the body. The colored rings around the various holes in the head gasket are cured RTV sealer about 0.005 inch thick on each side. It is

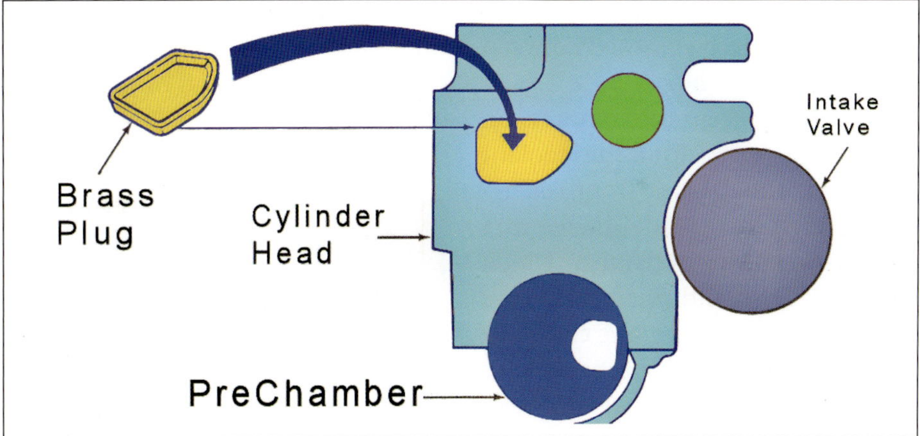

There was a GM Technical Service Bulletin (TSB) on 1983–1984 6.2L cylinder head gaskets that leaked. This bulletin called for the replacement of all 17 head bolts with a newer-design bolt (part number 14077193). Whenever a head is removed from a 1982–1983 engine, replace the head bolts with this newer design. The new bolt provides an increased and more-even clamp load. Coat the thread with Teflon sealer about 3/4 inch from the bottom. The new bolts have about 1¾ inches of thread. You also install a contour-shaped brass plug in a core cleanout hole, but this was discontinued in 2001. I recommend Fel-Pro's 9701PT 6.5 gaskets for those 6.2L engines that do not contain this specific passage in the head. Mahle also makes a head gasket for the 6.2L

TECH TIP

The Brass Plug

Chevrolet Motor Division produced a contour-shaped brass plug (GM part number 14079353) to seal a core cleanout hole. In the middle of 1983, this core cleanout hole was machined out in production. The 1985-and-later engines, including the 6.5L, have this hole eliminated.

When installing this plug, clean any excessive roughness and any casting irregularities with a file. Clean the plug with a wire brush and wash it out with brake cleaner. Coat the sides of the brass plug and hole with Loctite 620 or 271.

Sadly, this brass plug was discontinued in 2001, so if you have one of these early heads, you will need to have the passage welded shut or, better yet, replace the head.

thick enough to be crushed between the head and the block.

The sealer keeps the compression gases from going into the coolant and keeps the coolant from leaking out through the gasket. The fire ring crosses over the prechamber, which should be flush with the head. If the prechamber is recessed, the clamping load in that area will not be enough to seal the cylinder. If it is exposed, the clamping load beside the prechamber will not be as great, and the gasket will fail. Also, any cracks in the prechamber should not extend into the ceiling area around the fire ring.

The prechambers must not be recessed in the head by more than 0.002 inch. The prechamber seats on the cylinder head heat shield and sealing ring. This measurement should be made at two or more points on the prechamber. Use a straightedge and feeler gauge or dial indicator to measure the difference between the flat of the prechamber and the flat surface of the head. A slight variance from one side of the prechamber to the other will result in a good seal, provided that both sides are within the tolerance.

Leaking Cylinder Head Gasket Bulletin

A technical service bulletin issued in mid-1983 referred to a core cleanout hole in the cylinder head that caused a leak. In 1982 and 1983, you could experience coolant loss from the rear lower corner on the left-hand cylinder head and the front lower corner on the right-hand cylinder head. This coolant loss was the result of inadequate sealing around this core cleanout hole in the cylinder head.

Checking the Head for Warpage

With the heads off of the engine, check them for a number of possible conditions.

First, check for warpage using a precision straightedge and the proper-size feeler gauges. Both engines should be checked for 0.006 longitudinally at multiple points and 0.003 transversely in at least four spots. GM does not recommend resurfacing the cylinder heads, but I can tell you that it's done in the field.

Check for surface cracks or cracks in the valve port area of the cylinder head, especially between the intake and exhaust valve ports with the valves removed. Minor surface cracks in these areas is generally normal. (Later in this book, I will show you the process using a die penetrant to check for cracks.) These are cast-iron blocks and heads, so you can use Magnaflux equipment to check for cracks.

There is an indentation in the cylinder block and head surface area where the fire ring contacts both components. The actual measurement of this indentation is 0.001 to 0.002 inch deep and does not affect sealing. Some manufacturers make a head gasket for a 0.030-inch-oversize

Place a precision straightedge on the surface of a clean head. Measure 0.006 inch lengthwise at each fire ring and then across each fire ring with a 0.003-inch feeler gauge. The specified size of feeler gauge should not fit under the straightedge. Cylinder heads should be checked in four planes lengthwise for warpage, distortion, bend, and twist.

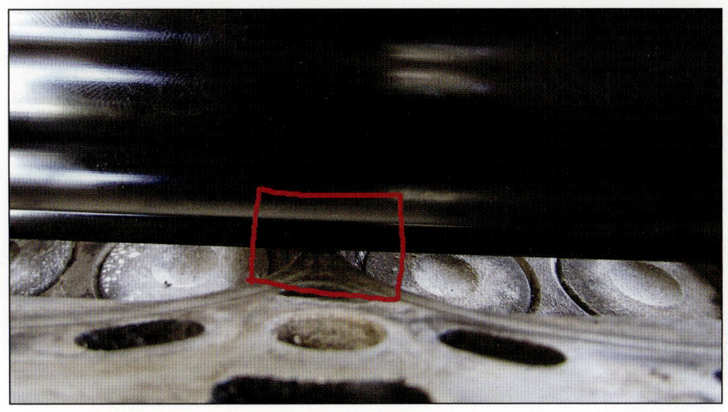

This cylinder head is so badly warped that you can almost see the clearance between the cylinder head and the precision straightedge with the naked eye.

piston head gasket, but toward the end of production, General Motors only used a 0.030-inch-oversize piston head gasket in production and service. The Mahle head gasket has a wider fire ring.

There is another condition to check for by looking at the head gasket when it is located on the dowel pins in the block. Make sure the fire ring is only slightly larger in diameter than the bore. The fire ring may extend into the chamfer at the top of the cylinder, which will result in uneven crush of the fire ring, and it can fail.

To check the fire ring when rebuilding this engine or replacing head gaskets, take the new head gasket and lay it on the block. Look at each cylinder and check that the fire ring is concentric with the bore. Make sure that the bolt holes in the cylinder block are drilled and tapped deep enough. Place the cylinder head on the block without the head gasket and run a 0.005-inch feeler gauge around the edge of the head. There should be no clearance, which will indicate that the dowel pins are not holding the head off the block.

If using head bolts, hand screw each of them in. The head bolts should screw in far enough to contact the head, indicating that the holes are drilled deep enough. Head bolts and studs must have clean threads coated with white Teflon sealant lubricant (GM part number 1052080) only at the bottom for about 3/4 inch. The reason for this is that these bolts go into coolant passages. This lubricant also reduces bolt friction during installation and is included in the tightening calculation. Never put oil in the bolt holes, otherwise you will hydraulically lock the bolt and prevent it from tightening.

In the beginning of production, two different head gaskets were used: The Fel-Pro Print-O-Seal with sealant already applied and the Victor (green) composite gasket. Do not paint the Fel-Pro head gasket with Permatex head gasket sealant because it may attack the RTV in the gasket.

Rocker Train

The 1982–1984 rocker arm and shaft assembly used nodular cast-iron rocker arms and a steel shaft with steel-backed bronze alloy bushings. However, there were problems with this design, so in 1985, they switched to a steel stamped rocker arm and a steel shaft that used individual plastic locator buttons for each of the rocker arms. The 6.5L uses the 1985 design.

To remove the rocker arms on the 1985 design, first remove the rocker arm assembly from the head. Next, insert a screwdriver into the bore of the rocker shaft, breaking off the ends of the nylon rocker arm buttons. Then, remove the rocker arms.

To install the rocker arms, set them on the rocker shaft, lubricating them with engine oil. Line up the rocker arm with the 1/4-inch hole in the shaft. Then, use a drift to install a new nylon rocker arm retainer or button (part number 23500076) in each of the 1/4-inch holes. I use a 3/8-drive extension, which works very well.

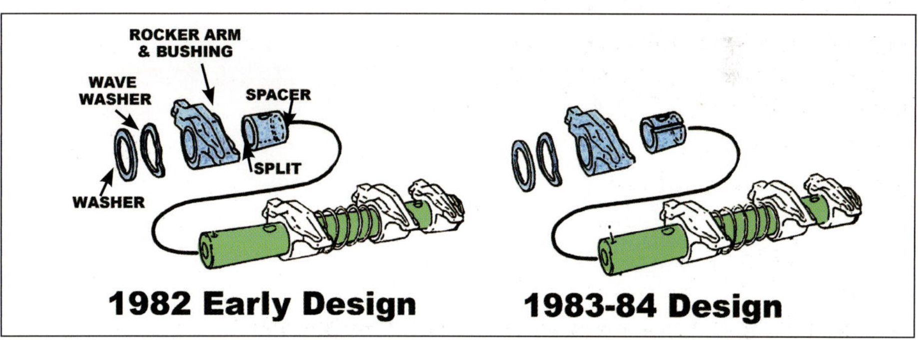

In 1982, when the 6.2L engine first appeared, it used a very traditional rocker arm and shaft design with steel-backed bronze-alloy bushings that rode on a steel shaft with a wave washer and hardened spacer or washer. It was a rigid valvetrain to ensure precise valvetrain motion. The rocker units used four rockers per shaft with two shafts per head. They used a spacer with a lubrication split 180 degrees to the bolt hole. In 1983–1984, the design was changed to an unhardened washer and a steel cleat instead of a spacer. The cleat had a large gap 90 degrees to the bolt to prevent any closure, and the cleat spreads the load.

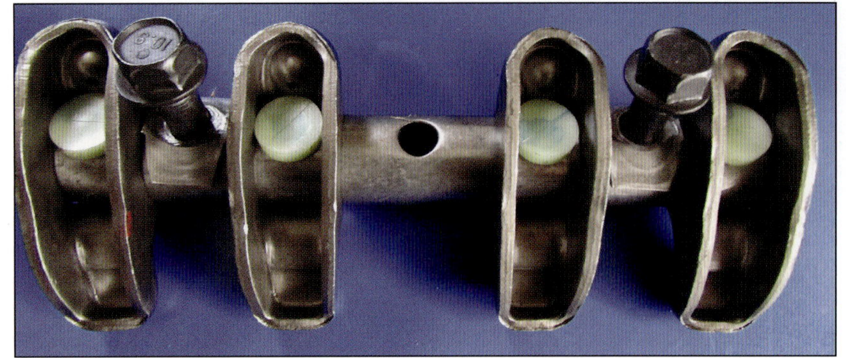

In 1985, the rocker arm design changed to a large-diameter steel shaft bolted directly to the cylinder head pedestals. The stamped-steel rocker arms were held in place with plastic buttons. This design was used on all 6.2L and the later 6.5L engine until the end of production of the 6.5L in 2000.

Connecting the Rod and Piston

The connecting rods are made of forged steel and use a precision-machined bronze bushing in the piston pin bore. The crank pin bore of each connecting rod is split and holds a two-piece bearing insert where studs and nuts retain the cap. Clearance between the piston pin and the bushing must not exceed 0.30 mm (0.0012 inch). The connecting rod bearing clearance should be 0.45 to 0.100 mm (0.0018 to 0.0039 inch). Two sizes of rod bearing inserts are available for service: the standard yellow and a 0.001-inch undersized, measuring 0.026 mm (0.001 inch).

Both engines use pistons that are cast aluminum and use Ni-Resist in the top ring groove. Ni-Resist is a nickel-based compound that resists adhesion to cast iron. Early engines used a three-piece oil control ring, whereas later engines and all 6.5L used a two-piece oil control ring. The 6.5L piston was cooled by an oil jet aimed at the bottom of the piston.

All pistons used a full-floating piston pin. This full-floating piston design was used to eliminate piston scuffing and promote uniform pin loading. The top piston ring is a Keystone design with a tapered shape that promotes a good seal against the cylinder wall. This piston ring is also barrel shaped and does not have a specific top installation position, so it can be installed in either position. The second compression ring is cast iron, has a chrome face, and has a very specific installation position with a mark on the top of the ring that must face up.

The pistons in both engines are match fitted to each cylinder bore of the engine. This is done by measuring the internal diameter of the cylinder bore and stamping the corresponding size code on the panel rail of the block. The piston's outside diameter is measured, and the size code is stamped on the piston face. When the piston is assembled to the block, the sizes are matched to them to make sure that the proper fit and clearance between the cylinder and piston is maintained.

In the 6.2L, there were six matching cylinder bore sizes. Size codes A, B, C, D, E, and G are used to match the piston and cylinder bore. An A-size piston is assembled to an A-size cylinder bore, etc. The size codes are stamped on the case. Pistons are available in standard, high-limit standard, and 0.030-inch oversize.

General Motors balances each of the connecting rods during assembly and does not recommend straightening, bushing replacement, or crank pin enlargement. So, I will not cover any of those procedures in this book.

The 6.2L/6.5L piston has a clover-shaped indentation on the top, which provides an outlet to the prechamber for the swirling and burning combustion mixture when at TDC. As the piston rises during compression, the air's swirl begins in these two indentations. When the piston reaches the prechamber opening, this swirling mixture increases in the prechamber. This piston complements the Ricardo Comet 5 prechamber.

In the 6.5L engine, there are different diameter sizes with number-7 and -8 being slightly larger than cylinders-1 through -6. This difference in bore sizes allows for more piston expansion in the rear two cylinders (numbers-7 and -8). During manufacture of the 6.5L, three piston sizes were used in each of the eight cylinders and were based on the bore size and recommended clearance. Each piston has a size identification mark on its face and the piston boss surface.

The cylinder block will have the piston size identification marking for each bore, just like the 6.2L next to the bore. The piston grades for the 6.5L are different than the 6.2L. There will be five different size codes: production standard (marked J or JT), production standard (marked S or ST), service standard (marked JT), service high limit (marked GT), and service 0.50 mm (marked OS).

Lubrication System Concerns

Watch for these items with the lubrication system:
- Oil filler tube: Use the vented oil filler tube (part number 14071059 or 23500345) on all 6.2L engines up to 1988. After 1988, it was dropped on all applications except the G Van.
- Some 1993 and 1994 G Vans, CUCVs (D Trucks), and P chassis may have problems with the crankcase depression regulator (CDR) valve being restricted or plugged. To fix this, General Motors installed a new oil filler cap. All later-model trucks and engines use the new cap.
- The 6.2L and 6.5L use a traditional oil pump, which is driven by a gear off the camshaft like a Chevy small-block. The vacuum pump is also driven by this gear and shaft. The engine with a belt-driven vacuum pump used a stalk fixture to drive the oil pump.

The Fuel System

The 6.2L and 6.5L low-pressure fuel systems consist of the following components: the tank filter sock, mechanical fuel pump, electric lift pump, fuel filter, and fuel filler cap.

Tank Filter Sock

Inside the tank is the tank filter sock, which strains out large solids. The Saran material is like duck feathers, and it resists water. It acts as a wick to suck fuel out of the bottom of the tank. However, if totally immersed in water, it will suck the water into the fuel system.

The tank filter sock should be checked any time the truck feels like it's running out of fuel. This is done by checking fuel volume and pressure at the lift pump.

Mechanical Fuel Pump

Early 6.2L engines used a mechanical fuel pump mounted at the front of the engine and driven by a camshaft using a pushrod. The early lift pumps were vented pumps, which allowed the fuel to drain back to the fuel tank, so even small leaks would cause air in the system. Air in

Using RTV Sealer

1. The surface must be clean and dry.
2. Remove all traces of oil and old gasket material and clean it with solvent (such as break cleaner). Do not use mineral spirits.
3. Cut the tube extension to 1/8 inch and apply RTV to one of the clean surfaces, circling all of the bolt holes.
4. Assemble the components while the RTV is still wet. Within 3 minutes, it will skin over and then it will not leak. Keep in mind that using RTV is like gluing something together.
5. Torque the bolts to the specifications; do not over-torque. The RTV will be dry enough in 15 minutes to operate the engine. ■

Bohn and Zollner Pistons

In the beginning of the 6.2L's production, Chevrolet used two different piston suppliers: Bohn and Zollner. They differ in exterior finish, so there are two different piston clearance values.

However, you may never see one because, according to my sources, Chevrolet only built 200 engines using Zollner pistons during the 1982 production run. There were no Zollner pistons in production after 1983. Chevrolet issued an engineering change release (ECR) on May 15, 1982, that removed the Zollner piston. Zollner pistons are identified by the letter *Z* with a circle around it near the pin boss. The Bohn piston is identified by the words *Bohnna Lite*, which are also near the pin boss. ■

the fuel system will cause hard starting, white smoke, and poor idle. To fix this, Chevrolet released a pump that had no vents (AC Delco part number 4325 and GM part number 25116503). This pump greatly reduced starting problems.

Electric Lift Pump

Later 6.2L and all 6.5L engines used a solenoid electric lift pump. The 12-volt electric lift pump is a solenoid design that uses oscillating plungers with dual check valves to pump diesel fuel. The pump is 100-percent solid state with no switches. The primary winding is energized when a transistor turns on and the pumping plunger is pulled into the winding. Then, the inlet valve opens and fuel is sucked in by the low pressure created by the plunger. Fuel fills the plunger space and the pressure spring is compressed.

The plunger in the primary winding induces voltage in the secondary winding, which causes the transistor to turn off, de-energizing the primary winding. The compressed force of the pressure spring pushes the plunger and the inlet valve closes, creating the fuel pump pressure.

Fuel Filter

The 1982 and 1983 6.2L engines used a canister spin-on primary fuel filter mounted on the frame, which was eliminated in 1984. These same engines also had a canister-type spin-on secondary filter that was mounted behind the intake manifold, which was also eliminated in 1984.

In 1984, the 6.2L engine used a Stanadyne square filter (model 80) with a water and fuel sensor and a fuel heater as part of the unit. This design was used until the end of production for the 6.2L in 1991. The best modification for the 6.2L engine fuel filter is to the late model GM Duramax 6.6L fuel filter assembly. (This modification will be covered in chapter 8.)

From 1992 to 2002, all 6.5L engines used a spin-on fuel manager filter system that included a water-in-fuel sensor, a fuel heater, a drain valve, and an air-bleed valve. You can use the electric lift pump to push the air out after a filter drain.

Fuel Filler Cap

The fuel filler cap contains a two-way check valve that allows air to escape when the tank heats up and prevents spillage if there is a rollover. No more than 2 psi will exist under pressure. The valve must also allow air to enter the tank to replace the fuel used by the engine. There should be a vacuum of no more than 1 inch of Mercury, and there should be a slight hissing sound when the cap is removed. If you install a cap meant for a gasoline-fueled engine, rough idle and poor performance will result due to the higher pressures caused by the gasoline-type cap.

Evaluating and Diagnosing the Fuel System

Always use #2 diesel fuel with a cetane number of at least 45. If you get air, debris, or water in the fuel system, it is considered contaminated and can cause problems in the injection pump and the nozzles. Fuel contamination should be suspected when the truck stalls, has poor performance, or makes a knocking sound.

To check for contamination, remove the fuel filter and inspect the contents for the presence of dirt, gasoline, or water. If gasoline is suspected, remove the fuel filler cap and check for fumes. Gasoline will not harm the fuel injection system, but it must be flushed out of the system.

Do not remove any of the injection components unless engine operation is considered to be unsatisfactory. The following procedures will eliminate pump and nozzle replacement due to fuel contamination.

Water in Diesel Fuel System

The 1982 and 1983 6.2L used a water drain siphon valve located on the truck frame. Flush the water using the following steps:

1. Drain the fuel tank and remove the fuel gauge unit.
2. Thoroughly clean the fuel tank. If the fuel tank is rusted internally, it should be replaced.
3. Clean and replace the pickup filter and check the valve assembly.
4. Reinstall the fuel tank but leave the lines disconnected at the fuel tank area above the rear axle.
5. Disconnect the main fuel hose at the mechanical or electric lift pump. Use low-pressure air and blow out toward the rear of the vehicle.
6. Disconnect the fuel return line at the injection pump and blow out the line with low pressure toward the rear of the vehicle.
7. Reconnect the main fuel and return line hoses at the tank.
8. Fill the tank to at least 1/4 full with clean diesel fuel.
9. Remove and discard all fuel filters and connect the fuel hose to the fuel lift pump.
10. Purge the mechanical fuel lift pump by cranking the engine until fuel is pumped out. Catch the fuel in a closed metal container. If it is an electric lift

pump, turn the ignition on and operate the electric fuel pump until clean fuel is pumped out into a closed metal container.

11. Install new fuel filters and a clear plastic hose from the fuel return line on an injection pump with a capacity of at least 2 gallons.

12. If the engine temperature is hotter than 125°F, activate the injection pump housing pressure cold advantage (HPCA) solenoid by disconnecting the two lead connectors at the engine temperature switch. They are located at the rear of the right cylinder head. Then, bridge the connector with a jumper wire.

13. On a mechanical pump crank, use the ignition key to turn on the engine of the electric pump and run until clean fuel appears at the return line. Do not crank the engine for more than 30 seconds at a time and repeated the process in 3-minute intervals.

14. Remove the jumper from the engine temperature switch and reconnect the connector to the switch.

15. Crack open each high-pressure fuel line at the nozzle with wrenches to prevent nozzle damage. Disconnect a lead to the HPCA solenoid on the injection pump.

16. Crank the engine or run the electric fuel pump until clean fuel appears at each nozzle. Again, do not crank for more than 30 seconds at a time.

Gasoline in Diesel Fuel System

If gasoline is found in the diesel system, follow these steps to flush the system:

1. Drain the fuel tank and fill it with diesel fuel.

2. Remove the fuel line between the fuel filter and the injection pump.

3. Connect a short pipe and hose to the fuel filter outlet and run it to a closed metal container.

4. Crank the engine on a mechanical pump or turn on the electric fuel pump to purge gasoline out of the fuel pump and fuel filter. Do not crank the engine for more than 30 seconds at a time.

5. Remove the short pipe and hose and install a fuel line between the fuel filter and the injection pump.

6. Try to start the engine. If it does not start, purge the injection pump and lines by cranking the engine with the accelerator held to the floor. Crank until the gasoline is purged and clear diesel fuel leaks out of the fittings. Tighten the fittings, limiting cranking to 30-second intervals. Start the engine and run at idle for 15 minutes.

Air in Fuel Lines

In these engines, air in the fuel is a very big deal. It causes all kinds of running problems, such as rough idle, hard starting, and low performance. First, install a short, clear plastic hose in the return line at the top of the injection pump. Start the engine and see if air bubbles or film is in the line. If bubbles are present, proceed as follows:

1. Raise the vehicle and disconnect both fuel lines at the fuel tank.

2. Plug the smaller line, which is the return line.

3. Attach a low-pressure air pressure source, preferably a hand-operated pump, to the larger 3/8-inch fuel hose and apply 8 to 12 psi.

4. When diagnosing a truck that has dual tanks, this will require a check of the right fuel lines (right tank position) and the left fuel lines (left tank position).

5. Observe the fuel-pump reading of 8 to 10 psi. A decrease in pressure will indicate the presence of a suck leak. The pressure will push the fuel to the leak point, indicating the location of the leak, which is most likely at the lift pump.

Fuel return lines run from the housing pressure regulator on the top of the DB2 fuel injection pump. The lines then run to a metal crossrail front pipe that connects to rubber lines that are in series with all eight fuel injection nozzles. The right bank (or passenger's side) has a cap on the number-8 nozzle where the left bank goes to the crossrail pipe. The crossrail pipe has an outlet that connects via a rubber hose to a pipe on the intake manifold that returns to the fuel tank. Any restriction in the return line will cause severe drivability problems, including rough idle, misfire, and hard starting.

6. Repair the leak as necessary. It's important that the proper-sized clamps are used on all hoses.

7. Fuel pressure is checked at the fuel pump outlet to the fuel injection pump. It should be between 5.5 and 6.5 psi.

8. Always check the owner's manual to see at what interval to drain water out of the filters. Most of the trucks with factory or aftermarket filters will have some kind of water drain that needs to be opened to drain the water when changing the oil.

9. After any filter change, it is absolutely necessary to purge the air from the system, otherwise you will have hard starting and rough idle. Follow whatever procedure is available for the type of filter the truck is using.

Starting After Fixing an Air Leak

1. Install a new spin-on filter with an air bleed valve and a clear plastic line. Place the line in a metal container.

2. Remove the fuel filler cap and disconnect the fuel shutoff pink wire to the injection pump.

3. I recommend installing a solenoid electric lift pump. If a mechanical pump must be used, use the non-vented pump (AC Delco part number 4325 or GM part number 25116503).

4. On electric-lift-pump vehicles, open the air bleed, turn on the ignition, and let the pump run until clean fuel with no air comes out the vent.

5. On mechanical lift pumps, crank the engine for 10 to 15 seconds and wait 1 minute. Repeat until clear fuel with no air comes from the bleed valve. If air continues to come through, the air leak must be found before proceeding.

6. Once clear of air, install the fuel filler cap and connect the fuel shutoff pink wire to the injection pump.

7. Try to start the engine. If it does not start, have someone crank it while you bleed the lines to the injection nozzles. If it starts and has a rough idle, bleed the lines.

Important Tip

While bleeding lines, make sure you wear non-chemical penetrating gloves and safety glasses with side shields.

Lift Pump Checks

To check the lift pump, follow these steps:

1. Check fittings and connections at the lift pump to be sure they are tight.

2. Check the fuel line for bends or kinks in the hoses.

3. With the engine idling, look for leaks at the pressure outlet. A leak on the suction (or inlet) side of the pump will reduce the volume of the fuel on the pressure side of the pump and suck in air.

4. If using a mechanical pump, check for leaks at the diaphragm flange and bleeder holds in the mechanical pump casting.

5. Check the fuel pump cover and its fittings for leaks. Tighten or replace fittings as necessary; if the pump leaks, replace it.

Lift Pump Fuel Flow Test

Follow these steps to test the lift pump fuel flow:

1. Disconnect the fuel line at the filter inlet.

2. Disconnect the pink wire at the fuel injection pump electric shutoff (ESO) solenoid.

3. Place a container at the end of the pipe and crank the engine a few revolutions or turn on the electric fuel pump. If no fuel or a small amount of fuel flows from the open end of the pipe, the pipe is clogged or the pump is inoperable.

4. If fuel flows in a good volume (1 pint in 30 to 45 seconds), then check the fuel delivery pressure.

5. Connect a known good pressure gauge to the outlet of the mechanical or electric fuel pump. It is best to use a T to the pressure gauge. Run the engine or the pump and check for fuel pressure between 5.5 and 6.5 psi.

Vacuum Test the Fuel Pump Inlet or Deadhead

Low vacuum or complete loss of vacuum will provide insufficient fuel to the injection pump throughout the normal operating range. This vacuum test will determine if the pump has the ability to pump fuel. It is one of the best indicators of quality pump performance.

1. Disconnect the hose from the fuel tank to the fuel pump at the fuel pump plug, or position the hose to ensure no fuel leakage.

2. Connect one end of a short hose to the fuel-pump inlet and attach a vacuum gauge to the other end.

3. Start the engine or run the electric pump and check the vacuum gauge. If the vacuum is less than 12 inches of Mercury, replace the fuel pump.

Return Line Restrictions

The fuel injection pump on the system relies on having the right amount of pressure in the housing of the pump. If the return is restricted, it causes the pressure to rise, resulting in poor idle, poor running, and in some cases even a misfire.

To check for this, disconnect the fuel return at the top of the injection pump and install a clear plastic hose with tight connections. Place this hose into a metal container and run the engine. If whatever condition you are experiencing goes away, then there is a return-line restriction to locate.

During the earlier production of 6.2L engines, some of the Bosch injection-nozzle return ports were clocked. If this is the case, it will cause a return-line restriction. The fix is to clean the epoxy out of the return-line ports.

Engine Noise Diagnosis

Diesel engines normally have a noise that occurs because of the sharp rise in pressure at the beginning of the combustion cycle. For this reason, sometimes engine noises are difficult to distinguish from this normal knocking noise. The Diagnosing Engine Noises table outlines some areas that should be checked when encountering noises in 6.2L or 6.5L engines.

An engine with stuck piston rings will have some starting problems due to low compression. If that is suspected, remove all of the glow plugs and use a can of GM top engine cleaner across the eight cylinders.

After soaking for 24 hours, crank the engine with the glow plugs removed to blow out all of the top engine cleaner. Reinstall the glow plugs and start the engine.

If you have hot or cold start problems, it is possible that the cranking speed is too low. This has been a common problem on these engines. When the engine is cold, the minimum cranking speed should be between 100 and 150 rpm. When the engine is hot, the cranking speed should be between 180 and 200 rpm. Use a GM Mag tack or a Snap-on MT480 or MT1480 tool to check the cranking speed. If these tools are not available, there is a procedure using a compression gauge in chapter 8.

Diagnosing Engine Noises		
Concern	**Cause**	**Correction**
Excessive oil loss	External oil leak	Replace gaskets or seals
	Wrong oil viscosity	Use the recommended oil viscosity for the temperature
	Continuous high-speed driving force, such as trailer hauling	This normally happens under these conditions
	Crankcase ventilation	Check the operation of the crankcase depression regulator (CDR) valve
	Valve guides and/or seals that are worn	Ream the guides and install oversize valves and or new seals; some machine shops can knurl the guides, which reduces clearance
	Piston rings not seated, broken, or worn	Could be caused by inadequate time for ring seating, broken rings, or worn rings
	Improperly fitted piston	Replace piston
Low oil pressure (always check with external pressure gauge): Oil pressure 10 psi at idle; max cold start 80 psi; average pressure 40–45 psi at 2,000 rpm	Slow idle speed	Set idle speed to the correct value
	Incorrect or malfunctioning oil pressure switch	Replace the switch
	Defective oil pressure gauge	Replace the gauge
	Defective oil pump or relief valve	Clean pump and replace any worn parts
	Plugged oil filter	Replace filter and oil
	Pick up screen/pipe loose	Repair as necessary
	Hole in oil pickup tube	Replace tube
	Excessive bearing clearance	Replace bearings and/or crankshaft
	Cracked, porous, or plugged oil galleries	Most likely will need a block replacement
	Gallery plugs missing or not installed correctly	Install plugs with the proper procedure
	Excessive valve lifter tube or clearance due to wear	Measure lifter in two spots: parallel with roller and 90 degrees to roller. Wear in area of 0.005 to 0.008 inch will cause low oil pressure. Measure lifter bore in block. Wear greater than 0.003 inch is bad.

Diagnosing Engine Noises		
Concern	**Cause**	**Correction**
Valvetrain noise	Low oil pressure	*See* low oil pressure
	Loose rocker arm shaft attachments	Repair as necessary
	Worn rocker arm and worn pushrod	Repair as necessary
	Broken valve spring	Replace valve spring
	Sticking valves	Use material to free up the valves
	Lifters worn, dirty, or defective; lifter guide plate in the wrong position; or a lifter guide plate with burrs on it	Repair as necessary
	Defective camshaft	Replace camshaft
	Worn valve guides	Repair per GM service information
Engine knocks on initial start-up but only lasts a few seconds	Defective mechanical fuel pump	Replace pump
	Wrong oil viscosity	Change oil and filter with the correct viscosity
	Hydraulic lifter bleed down	Clean, test, and replace lifters as necessary
	Excessive crankshaft thrust bearing clearance	Replace crankshaft thrust bearing
	Excessive main bearing or rod bearing clearance	Repair as necessary
Engine knock continues 2 to 3 minutes and increases with torque	Flywheel or flexplate is contacting splash shield	Reposition splash shield
	Defective flywheel or flexplate	Replace flywheel or flexplate
	Loose or broken harmonic balancer or drive pulley. This is a common problem.	Replace defective parts. Best replacement for the harmonic balancer is the fluid type.
	Over fueling	With the engine off, retard the injection pump by turning it as far in the slot as it will go toward the driver. If the knocking noise is not reduced, then you have a mechanical problem. If it is reduced, then you need to investigate what is causing the over fueling, which is most likely an injection nozzle that is stuck open.
	Improper timing	Adjust the timing based on the information in this book.
	No fuel	Use the no fuel diagnosis process from the service information or information provided in this book.
	Air leak	Air is the biggest enemy of these diesel engines. Install a clear plastic hose in the injection pump return line and look for the leak, which is most likely at the left pump.
	Excessive piston tube or clearance	Refit a new piston using the proper procedure
	Bent connecting rod	Investigate the cause of the bent rod and repair as necessary.
Heavy knock on a hot engine with torque applied	Defective balancer or pulley hub	Replace defective parts. Best replacement for the harmonic balancer is the fluid type.
	Loose torque converter	Tighten
	Accessory belts too tight or nicked	Replace or adjust belt tension to specifications. Check belt tensioner on serpentine belts.
	Exhaust system grounded	Reposition exhaust
	Cracked flywheel or flexplate	Replace defective components
	Excessive main or rod bearing clearance	Resize bearings

Diagnosing Engine Noises		
Light knock during light-load conditions	Air leak	Install a clear plastic hose in the injection pump return line and look for the leak, which is most likely at the left pump.
	Improper timing	Adjust timing
	Loose torque converter bolts	Torque bolts to specifications
	Exhaust leak	Tighten fasteners or replace gaskets
	Excessive rod bearing clearance	Refit rod bearings
Engine knock at hot idle	Loose or worn drive belts	Replace as necessary and check the tensioner on serpentine belt models.
	A/C compressor or generator bearing	Repair as necessary
	Defective mechanical fuel pump	Replace the pump with the same or install an electric solenoid pump.
	Valvetrain	Upgrade to the newer plastic button
	Wrong oil viscosity	Change oil and filter with the correct oil
	Excessive piston pin clearance	Replace piston
	Connecting rod alignment	Most likely major engine rebuild issue
	Insufficient piston tube or clearance	Hone and fit a new piston
	Loose or defective crankshaft balancer	Tighten or replace with fluid type

Glow Plug Systems

Glow plugs are used on all of these engines to aid in cold starting. There were several different glow plug operating systems used:

- 1982–1984: Glow plug thermal controller system
- 1985–1987: Electronic glow plug system that did not use the always-on switch, instead it used a thermal switch that opened when it became hot
- 1988–1993: Electronic glow plug system with an always-on switch, 6.2L engine
- 1992–2002: Electronic glow plug system with an always-on switch, non-EFI 6.5L with a mechanical pump
- 1994–2002: Electronic glow plug system, with EFI and controlled by powertrain control module (PCM)

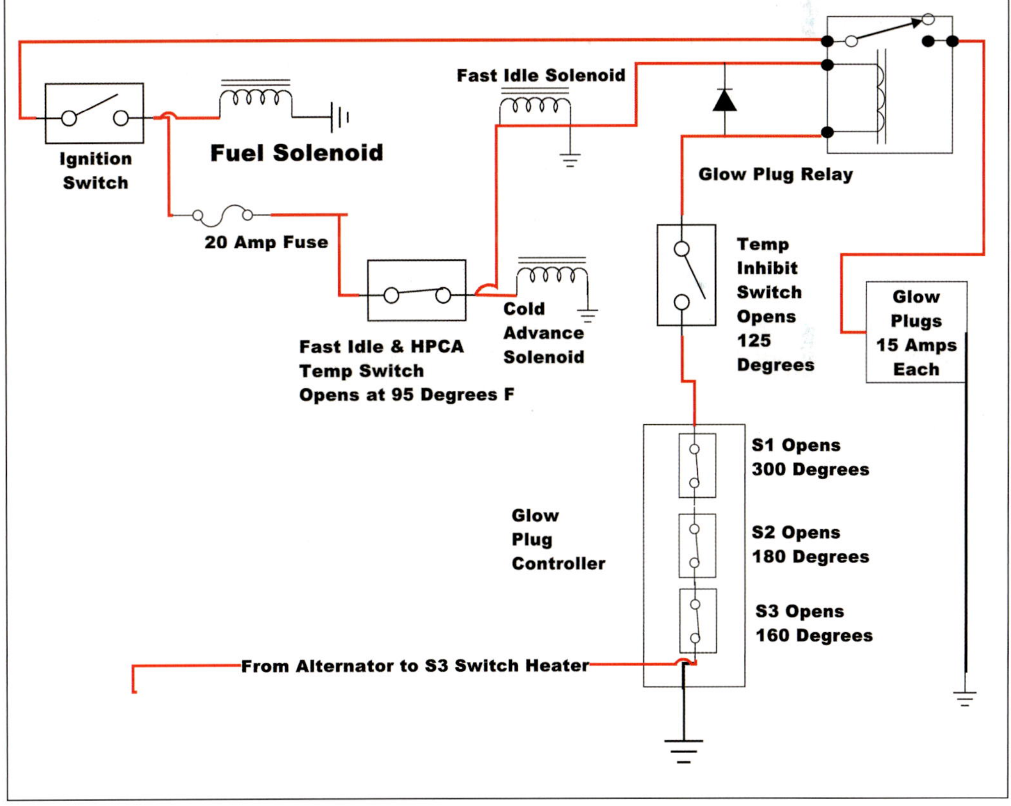

The thermal glow plug controller was used on the 6.2L from 1982 until 1987 with the exception of military applications, such as the CUCV and HMMWV. This thermal controller provides a series circuit ground for the glow plug relay. This series circuit is opened by use of several heaters that either open from engine heat or an electrical heater.

- 1984 all CUCV and all years HMMWV with 6.2L or 6.5L: Military electronic glow plug system that was unique to these applications.

All of these systems used a high-voltage glow plug relay to connect the eight glow plugs directly to the batteries (two parallel 12-volt batteries). There was 12-volt power to this relay whenever the key was on. The control systems grounded this relay to turn on the glow plugs.

The 1982–1985 system used a thermal controller located in a coolant passage in the cylinder head. The yellow wire from this thermal controller activates the glow plug relay by providing a ground to operate the glow plugs. Some systems used a single glow plug light that went on to indicate the glow plugs were on. Other systems used both a wait and a start lamp. When you keyed it on, the wait lamp turned on; when it went off, the start lamp came on and you could start the engine.

Early Thermal Controller System Operation

When the ignition switch is turned on, current flows through the gauge-idle fuse to the positive side of the glow plug relay. When all of the controller switches are closed, the glow plug thermal controller switch terminal "S" to pin 3 of the controller will go to ground.

The controller is the grounding device for the glow plug relay. The different switches inside of the controller open at different temperatures to control glow plug operation. These are thermal switches controlled by engine temperature and alternator output. There is a pre-glow and after-glow period, which is dependent upon engine temperature.

When the glow plug is energized prior to cranking the engine, this is called pre-glow. When the engine reaches 140°F, pre-glow does not take place. When operating the glow plugs, they will remain on for about 60 seconds.

1982–1984 Thermal Glow Plug Controller Wire Color Codes			
Thermal Controller	1982	1983	1984
Pin 6	Black/Ground	Black/Ground	Black/Ground
Pin 5	Black/Ground	Black/Ground	Black/Ground
Pin 4	Pink/Black-Power	Pink/Black-Power	Pink/Black-Power
Pin 3	Light Blue/Glow Plug Relay Control/Ground	Dark Green/Glow Plug Relay Control/Ground	Light Blue/Glow Plug Relay Control/Ground
Pin 2	Empty	Empty	Empty
Pin 1	Brown/Alternator	Brown/Alternator	Brown/Alternator

1982–1984 Thermal Glow Plug Controller Resistance Checks

With the connector removed from the six-pin thermal controller, you can test the bimetal heaters using a digital multimeter (DMM) with high impedance on the 200 ohm scale. The readings should be:

Pins 2 to 3: 0.40 to 0.75 ohms
Pins 4 to 5: 24 to 30 ohms
Pins 1 to 5: 117 to 143 ohms
Pins 2 to 6: Continuity or 0 ohms

Electronic Glow Plug Controller System Operation

When you turn the key on, the glow plugs will come on for 4 to 6 seconds and then go off for about 4.5 seconds. They will cycle on and off for 1.5 seconds and then be on for 4.5 seconds, and they can cycle on and off for a total of 25 seconds. The glow plug electronic controller can be black or gray; early systems were gray, and later systems were black.

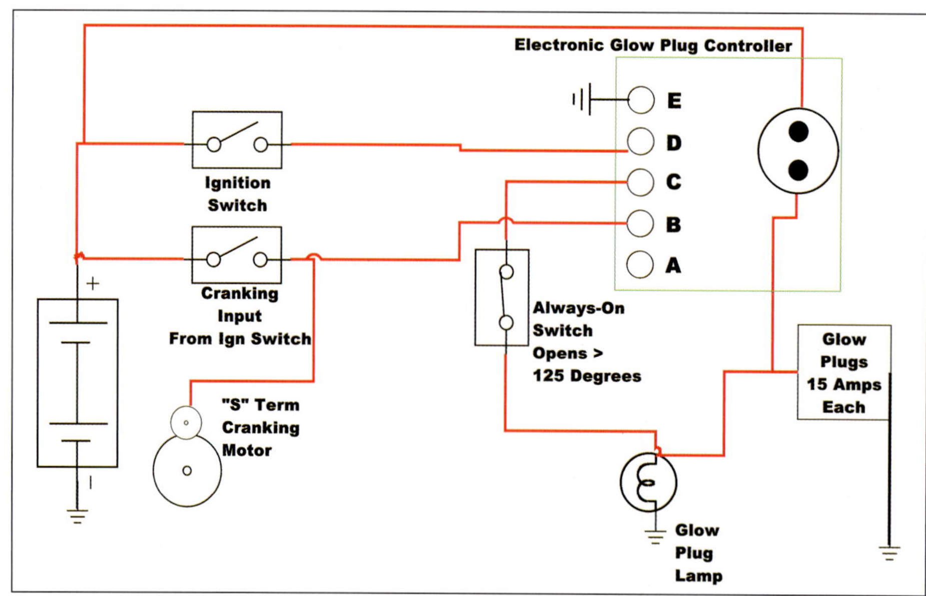

The electronic glow plug controller was used on the 6.2L diesel from 1988 until the end of production in 1991 and on all 6.5L engines from 1992 until 2000. This controller used the always-on or always-closed switch in place of an inhibit switch. This controller can also be retrofitted to replace the thermal controller on the earlier engine.

When you turn the key on, ignition voltage goes to pin D of the controller. Pin B receives engine cranking input. The controller has its own ground at pin E. The always-on switch goes from the positive side of the glow plugs to pin C of the controller and opens above 125°F. Based on all of these inputs, the controller will turn on its relay portion to operate the glow plugs.

Electronic Glow Plug Controller Pin Wire Colors

Pin E: Black ground
Pin B: Purple from starter solenoid
Pin D: Pink B+ power
Pin C: Yellow thermal or always on switch
Pin A: Empty

Glow Plug Types

These engines use three different types of glow plugs. One is the fast glow, which is more common. It is a 6-volt glow plug with a pre-glow of about 8 seconds and identified by a 9G on the plug. The second type is a slow-glow system that used a 12-volt glow plug identified by a 7G on the plug. It was used back in the 5.7L diesel engine days and should never be used in the 6.2L or 6.5L diesels. The third type of glow plug was used in the military application CUCV and Humvee. These were positive temperature coefficient (PTC) glow plugs that used a very specific electronic system to operate them, and they should not be used in the regular 6.2L or 6.5L diesels. They are identified by a 3/16-inch tang (normal tang is 1/4 inch) and the number 13G. The best glow plug to use today is the AC Delco 60G, which is the replacement for all non-military applications.

In 1984, a glow plug temperature inhibit switch was used between the ground side of the glow plug relay and the glow plug controller. It opened at 125°F to terminate all glow plug operation. In 1987, the glow plug switch was dropped from production and replaced by the always on switch.

In 1987–1988 engines, the always-on or always-closed switch was used in place of the inhibit switch. This was done to improve starting a hot engine. This always-on switch can be fitted to all models of the 6.2L with a 1/2-inch thread (part number 2350405) and later models with the 3/8-inch thread (part number 23504006). This switch is located in the water crossover that also contains the thermostat.

In late 1988, an electronic glow plug system was introduced to replace the thermal controller design. Oldsmobile also used a similar system on both its 4.3L V-6 and 5.7L V-8. Yet, the controller is different from these engines and the 6.2L.

The first 6.2L electronic controllers were black in color. The 1983–1991 6.2L trucks had a no-start cold issue caused by bad solder joints on the broad chip components in the black electronic controller. The black controller would chatter, losing about 2 volts to the relay and preventing the relay from engaging. The gray electronic controller (GM TSB number 936519) was released to fix this problem.

The gray controllers must be mounted on the engine because the controller senses engine temperature through the cylinder head. After the release of the 1994 6.5L EFI engine, the controller color was changed back to black when the ECM controlled glow plug operation. The Oldsmobile controller has a black connector and a gold label. Do not use the Oldsmobile 5.7L or 4.3L V-6 controller on a 6.2L because the resistance values are different.

An 11G glow plug is found on a later-model 6.2L diesel. It is a 6-volt glow plug for a fast-glow system using an electronic controller. The most common glow plug for the 6.2L was the 9G. The 13G was the PTC glow plug used in the CUCV that had a thinner tang at 3/16 inch.

The first version of the 6.2L electronic glow plug controller was black (part number 12082153), and the second generation was gray (part number 12088520). They were different internally, hence the color change. The gray controller fixed a cold-start concern for 1983 to 1991 6.2L models.

The 1984 CUCV and HMMWV military system is unlike the other systems. It does not cycle the glow plugs. Instead, they are either on or off because they use a PTC-style glow plug. They also have an electronic control module independent of other systems that operates the glow plugs. If you acquire a CUCV for a civilian application, you should scrap this system in favor of using the 1988 electronic glow plug system and modify the vehicle using the wiring diagram in this chapter.

You can also do what many 6.2L modifiers have done and use the old glow plug relay, which looks like an old Ford starter relay and wire the glow plugs to a dash switch. The driver controls the glow plugs on or off, but be careful to not burn up 6-volt glow plugs by using a timer circuit.

Advanced fuel injection pump timing can cause glow plug failures due to higher-than-normal cylinder temperature. When an advance timing condition exists, several glow plugs may not operate (but usually not all eight). It is also very common for the glow plug tips to expand and break off when they get hot. If this takes place, you can generally remove the injection nozzle, which has a large opening, and fish out the broken tip.

If the glow plug tip just expands, it could be difficult to remove the defective glow plug. Some tool manufacturers make an extraction tool that will assist in removing the glow plug, but Vise-Grips and lots of elbow grease are often used to pull it out. The worst-case scenario would require the removal of the cylinder head.

Injection Pump Timing

In the beginning, all 6.2L engines were timed using a static procedure, meaning you lined up a mark on the pump with the mark on the front cover. If you replaced the timing cover, it didn't come with the mark, so General Motors had a SPX Kent-Moore special tool (J33042) to stamp a mark on the timing cover.

Many do-it-yourselfers (DIYers) out there are people who will tweak the timing a little bit to get better performance or reduce smoke. To advance timing, move the pump and mark toward the driver. To retard timing, move the mark toward the passenger. This pump turns counterclockwise, as viewed from the front of the truck. Make a note to never adjust timing by moving the pump while the engine is running because this can cause a head and rotor seizure and require a new pump.

Static Timing		
Pump Number	**6.2L Engine RPO**	**Timing Mark Offset**
DB2829-4090	LH6 Light Duty	1.5 mm
DB2829-4091	LL4 Heavy Duty	2.5 mm
DB2829-4126	LH6 Light Duty	Aligned
DB2829-4153	LL4 Heavy Duty	Aligned

Timing Meters

There were and still are several different timing meters on the market. Snap-on was the first to come out with the MT480 diesel timing meter, which was a luminosity timing meter. You place a quartz crystal probe in a glow plug hole, usually the number-3 cylinder, and the meter reads the light of combustion as an indication

The DB2 fuel injection pump to front cover static timing marks show two lines: one on the front cover at the bottom and one on the injection pump. They are used to statically time fuel injection. The black dot is a factory timing device used during the manufacturing process. The timing here shows that it is retarded quite a bit, which would result in hard starting. The lines should be aligned or set one line space to the left. This is a counterclockwise-rotation pump, so move the pump toward the passenger's side to advance or toward the driver's side to retard the timing.

The Snap-on MT1480 was a combination luminosity and magnetic timing pickup diesel timing meter. It was the later tool used to time all 6.2L and mechanical-injection-pump 6.5L engines.

The magnetic pickup could be connected to a special fuel injection connector at the number-1 cylinder connection at the injection pump, or the pickup could be wrapped around the injection line. It was a Wheatstone bridge design that worked by changing resistance when the line expanded.

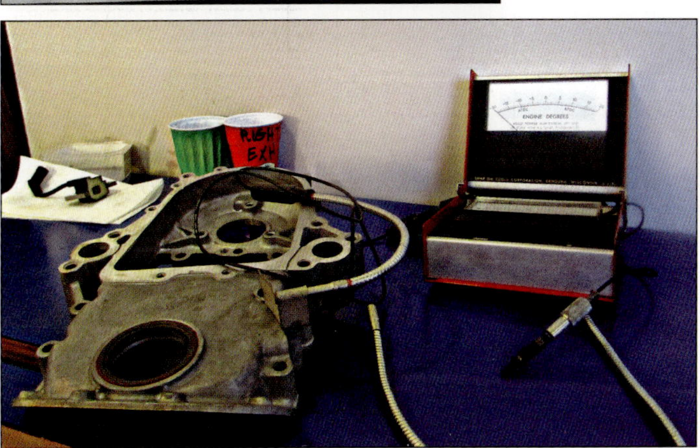

The first version of the MT1480 was the MT480, which operated using only luminosity. The luminosity probe contains a quartz glass center that is screwed into the glow plug hole. The meter reads the light of combustion as the timing event to base pump timing on. Snap-on also provided a light pipe to extend the operation of the quartz luminosity probe for diagnosis of cylinder operation. This occurs after TDC (not before, like typical timing).

of cylinder firing. Readings are at after TDC, and not before TDC as with gas engines.

SPX Kent-Moore offered the TACH-N-TIME, which was a GM essential tool. It used a strain gauge magnetic pickup that was clamped around the injection line to the number-1 cylinder, and a timing light connection was part of the meter. When injection occurred, the line expanded and the pickup read this event, all of which took place before TDC. Later, Snap-on produced the MT1480, which used luminosity timing and also offered a magnetic pickup that wraps around the fuel injection line that worked like the TACH-N-TIME. Stanadyne Diesel Systems makes the injection pumps and also offers a timing meter called TIME TRAC. This meter also uses the magnetic pickup technology as well as a traditional timing light.

1. Place the transmission in park on an automatic transmission and neutral on a manual transmission and apply the parking brake.
2. Block the wheels, start the engine, and let it idle until fully warmed up and then shut it off.
3. Clean any dirt from the engine probe holder and crankshaft balancer rim.
4. No matter what type of timing meter, use the Snap-on MT95

The Snap-on MT95 timing and RPM probe holder timing bracket qualifier is used to align the probe holder to the timing mark on the indicator bracket. It was designed by Steve Christopherson at Snap-on tools, who I worked with during 6.2L diesel service procedures development. If this bracket is not qualified, any electronic timing operation on a 6.2L or 6.5L DB2 pump will be inaccurate.

Place the bracket qualifier magnetic pickup hole and bend the bracket so the arrow on the tool goes in the 0 or TDC position on the timing bracket.

bracket qualifier to qualify the timing indicator. Otherwise, the reading will be inaccurate.

5. Connect the timing meter and follow the manufacturer's instructions for its use.
6. Install the timing probe in the number-1 cylinder and torque it to specifications.
7. Start the engine, adjust the idle to 650 rpm, and set the timing.

Remember that luminosity readings will be ATDC.

1982–1983 Timing Meter Specifications
TACH-N-TIME/TIME-TRAC: All 1982–1983 pumps are timed at 4 degrees before TDC

MT480/1480 Luminosity Meter: All 1982–1983 pumps are timed at 4 degrees after TDC

1984 Timing Meter Specifications

Pump Number	6.2L Engine	Timing
DB2829-4274	LH6 Light Duty	4 degrees BTDC, 4 degrees ATDC
DB2829-4276	LH6 Light Duty	4 degrees BTDC, 4 degrees ATDC
DB2829-4309	LH6 Light Duty	5 degrees BTDC, 3 degrees ATDC
DB2829-4310	LH6 Light Duty	4 degrees BTDC, 4 degrees ATDC
DB2829-4366	LH6 Light Duty	3 degrees BTDC, 5 degrees ATDC
DB2829-4275	LH6 Light Duty	4 degrees BTDC, 4 degrees ATDC
DB2829-4277	LH6 Light Duty	4 degrees BTDC, 4 degrees ATDC
DB2829-4267	LL4 Heavy Duty	6 degrees BTDC, 3 degrees ATDC
DB2829-4268	LL4 Heavy Duty	6 degrees BTDC, 3 degrees ATDC
DB2829-4269	LL4 Heavy Duty	6 degrees BTDC, 3 degrees ATDC
DB2829-4270	LL4 Heavy Duty	6 degrees BTDC, 3 degrees ATDC
DB2829-4355	LL4 Heavy Duty	6 degrees BTDC, 3 degrees ATDC
DB2829-4305	LL4 Heavy Duty	6 degrees BTDC, 3 degrees ATDC
DB2829-4266	LL4 Heavy Duty	6 degrees BTDC, 3 degrees ATDC
DB2829-4266	LL4 Heavy Duty	6 degrees BTDC, 3 degrees ATDC

1985 Timing Meter Specifications

Pump Number	6.2L Engine	Timing
DB2829-4425	LH6 Light Duty	4 degrees BTDC, 4 degrees ATDC
DB2829-4427	LH6 Light Duty	4 degrees BTDC, 4 degrees ATDC
DB2829-4437	LH6 Light Duty	3 degrees BTDC, 2 degrees ATDC
DB2829-4439	LH6 Light Duty	3 degrees BTDC, 2 degrees ATDC
DB2829-4426	LH6 Light Duty	4 degrees BTDC, 4 degrees ATDC
DB2829-4428	LH6 Light Duty	4 degrees BTDC, 4 degrees ATDC
DB2829-4267	LL4 Heavy Duty	6 degrees BTDC
DB2829-4410	LL4 Heavy Duty	4 degrees BTDC, 4 degrees ATDC
DB2829-4411	LL4 Heavy Duty	6 degrees BTDC, 3 degrees ATDC
DB2829-4412	LL4 Heavy Duty	6 degrees BTDC, 3 degrees ATDC
DB2829-4413	LL4 Heavy Duty	6 degrees BTDC, 3 degrees ATDC
DB2829-4471	LL4 Heavy Duty	6 degrees BTDC
DB2829-4386	LL4 Heavy Duty	6 degrees BTDC
DB2829-4440	LL4 Heavy Duty	6 degrees BTDC
DB2829-4441	LL4 Heavy Duty	4 degrees BTDC, 4 degrees ATDC

1986 Timing Meter Specifications

Pump Number	6.2L Engine	Timing
DB2829-4502	LH6 Light Duty	4 degrees BTDC, 4 degrees ATDC
DB2829-4503	LH6 Light Duty	4 degrees BTDC, 4 degrees ATDC
DB2829-4506	LH6 Light Duty	4 degrees BTDC, 4 degrees ATDC
DB2829-4507	LL4 Heavy Duty	3 degrees BTDC, 2 degrees ATDC
DB2829-4544	LL4 Heavy Duty	5 degrees BTDC
DB2829-4509	LH6 Light Duty	4 degrees BTDC, 4 degrees ATDC
DB2829-4510	LL4 Heavy Duty	5 degrees BTDC
DB2829-4511	LL4 Heavy Duty	4 degrees BTDC, 4 degrees ATDC
DB2829-4512	LL4 Heavy Duty	5 degrees BTDC
DB2829-4520	LL4 Heavy Duty	6 degrees BTDC
DB2829-4521	LL4 Heavy Duty	6 degrees BTDC
DB2829-4524	LL4 Heavy Duty	6 degrees BTDC
DB2829-4523	LL4 Heavy Duty	6 degrees BTDC
DB2829-4548	LL4 Heavy Duty	4 degrees BTDC, 4 degrees ATDC

1987–1993 Timing Meter Specifications

Pump Number	6.2L Engine	Timing
DB2829-4554	LH6 Light Duty	3 degrees BTDC
DB2829-4581	LH6 Light Duty	3 degrees BTDC
DB2829-4555	LH6 Light Duty	4 degrees BTDC, 4 degrees ATDC
DB2829-4582	LH6 Light Duty	4 degrees BTDC, 4 degrees ATDC
DB2829-4502	LH6 Light Duty	4 degrees BTDC, 4 degrees ATDC
DB2829-4503	LH6 Light Duty	4 degrees BTDC, 4 degrees ATDC
DB2829-4506	LL4 Heavy Duty	4 degrees BTDC, 4 degrees ATDC
DB2829-4507	LL4 Heavy Duty	4 degrees BTDC, 4 degrees ATDC
DB2829-4544	LL4 Heavy Duty	5 degrees BTDC
DB2829-4509	LL4 Heavy Duty	4 degrees BTDC, 4 degrees ATDC
DB2829-4510	LL4 Heavy Duty	5 degrees BTDC
DB2829-4511	LL4 Heavy Duty	4 degrees BTDC, 4 degrees ATDC
DB2829-4512	LL4 Heavy Duty	5 degrees BTDC
DB2829-4520	LL4 Heavy Duty	6 degrees BTDC
DB2829-4521	LL4 Heavy Duty	6 degrees BTDC
DB2829-4524	LL4 Heavy Duty	6 degrees BTDC
DB2829-4523	LL4 Heavy Duty	6 degrees BTDC
DB2829-4548	LL4 Heavy Duty	4 degrees BTDC, 4 degrees ATDC

For all other later years up to the last year of 6.2L production, use 4 degrees before TDC, 4 degrees after TDC. These later-year specifications are no longer available.

Check for Sticking Advance Piston

To check for a sticking advance piston, go to the passenger's side of the injection pump. Take a 10-inch-long screwdriver and push on the injection pump's rocker lever at the lower end toward the pump. There should be a sharp drop in RPM, indicating that the piston is not stuck. If there is no change in RPM or timing, the advance piston is sticking and will need to be replaced. Normally, engine timing will retard 3 to 5 degrees and the RPM will drop.

Compression Testing

When checking compression, cranking speed must be at least 180 rpm and the engine must be fully warmed up. The lowest reading should not be less than 80 percent of the highest, and no cylinder reading should be less than 380 psi.

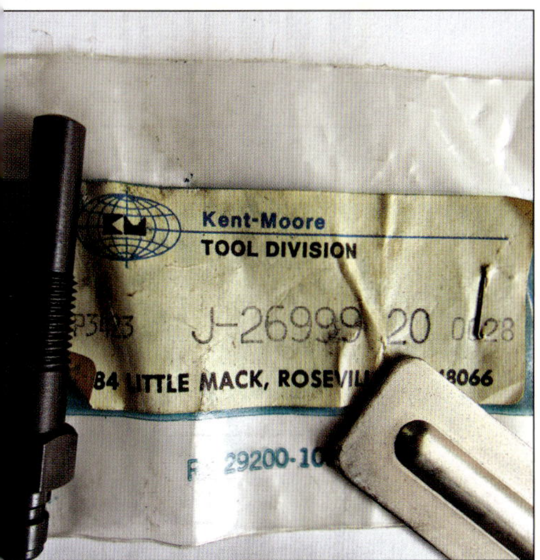

A 6.2L/6.5L compression adapter tool (part number J-26999-20) is for use with the J-26999 compression tester.

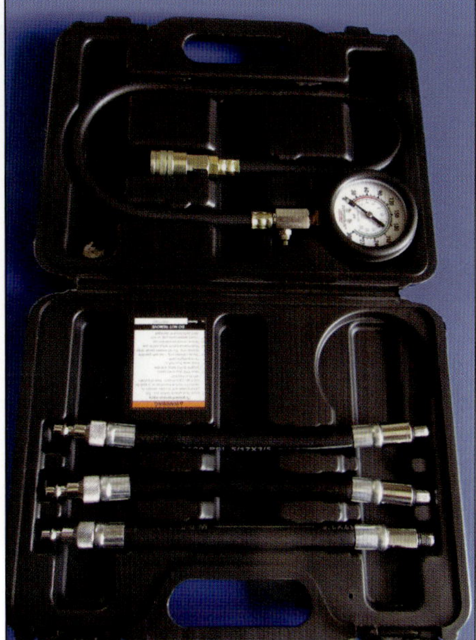

You can also use an aftermarket compression tester like the one from Harbor Freight that is very inexpensive compared to the GM factory tool. You cannot measure engine compression without these special adapters that screw into the glow plug hole.

1. Remove the air cleaner and install the intake manifold cover special tool (J29664-1).
2. Disconnect the wire from the fuel solenoid terminal of the injection pump.
3. Disconnect the wires from all of the glow plugs and remove all of the glow plugs.
4. Screw in the compression gauge adapter special tool (J26999-10) into the glow plug hole of the cylinder that is being tested.
5. Crank the engine and allow six pops per cylinder.

When normal, compression builds up quickly and evenly to the specified compression on each cylinder. Leaking compression reads as low on the first stroke and tends to build up on following strokes but does not reach normal.

Checking Turbo Boost Pressure

In 1994, General Motors added electronic fuel injection to the 6.5L and also used an Ishi-Warner turbocharger to increase the density of the charge and push more air into the engine. Throughout the years of 6.2L production, many people have added a turbocharger to that engine. Many of them used the Banks turbocharger, although there are some other aftermarket turbo manufacturers. A lot of DIYers remove a turbocharger from an old 6.5L and adapt it to the 6.2L. No matter which turbocharger is installed on your engine, there will be times when you need to check its operation to see if it is performing correctly. Here is a suggested checking procedure:

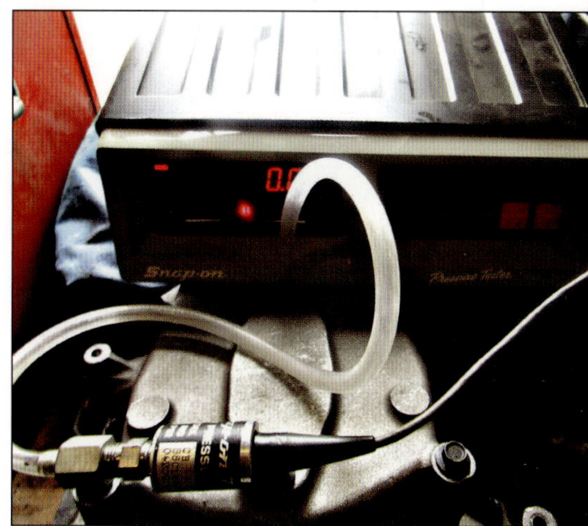

There are several pressure gauges that can be used to check turbocharger boost pressure. A Snap-on digital pressure tester can measure a number of pressure values.

1. Remove the front center mounting bolt for the upper intake manifold and install SPX Kent-Moore special tool J39307.
2. Connect a vacuum hose to this adapter so that a gauge can be

---

connected to it and be seen while inside the truck.

3. Install a pressure vacuum gauge, such as the Snap-on unit shown, on the vacuum hose and route the hose so that the hood can be closed during a road test.

4. Road-test the vehicle with an assistant to observe and record the pressure vacuum gauge readings. Allow the vehicle to coast at idle speed with the transmission in first gear. Press the accelerator to the floor and direct your assistant to observe and record the gauge reading.

5. Compare your gauge reading to the specification, which is 2 psi minimum. If the reading is greater than 2 psi, remove the gauge and adapter and install the upper manifold bolt. If the reading is below the specification, conduct further diagnosis tests to isolate the cause.

Cooling System Issues

The 6.2L and 6.5L engines use a somewhat-traditional cooling system that has gone though some changes from 1982 to 2002. This cooling system is very similar to ones used in Chevrolet gasoline engines of the same time period. The difference is that diesel engines have much larger capacity. Both engines use a viscous clutch fan drive. A truck with air-conditioning is designed to engage at 200°F; on a non-AC truck, it will engage at 180°F.

Water Pump

All 6.2L water pumps flow at 70 gallons per minute (gpm) and have a scroll impeller design using an inverted impeller. The 1992–1996 6.5L water pump flows at 87 gpm. The 1997–2002 water pump flows at 130 gpm. The cooling system capacity is 6.2 gallons with 3.2 gallons in the engine.

Professional Mechanic Tip

Best Clutch Replacement

PRO TIP

The best replacement clutch assembly for all engines is the 6.5L unit or a Hayden Viscous Clutch (part number 2840). ■

Use a hand-operated pressure tester to test the cooling system to simulate the engine operating pressure listed on the radiator pressure cap. Please note that you do not pump up the pressure beyond that specified by the original equipment manufacturer (OEM). The system should not be pressurized beyond what is stamped on the radiator pressure cap. If too much pressure is put in the system it may cause the water pump, radiator, heater core, or hoses to fail.

The 6.5L 1997–2000 water pump (AC Delco part number 252-776) flows at 130 gpm and is my recommended replacement for all of these engines. The GM Parts unit boasts a superior bearing and seals at double the cost. The coolant passages in this pump are deeper, and the impeller is about 1/4-inch larger in diameter. You should also install the 1997 cooling bypass fitting. This is done to get the maximum cooling efficiency and flow through the engine.

Critical Inspection Tip

If you're evaluating the pump, the clearance between the veins and the land of the pump body is 0.005 to 0.042 inch. If it's greater than 0.042 inch, you must replace the pump.

The system uses a very traditional radiator cap, and the radiator uses a low-coolant sensor. There is no expansion tank used, but there is a coolant reservoir. A temperature sensor activates the temperature gauge. The temperature gauge and check gauge light are used to indicate an overheating condition. On the 1988 and 1989 6.2L, the gauge red zone begins at 228°F. The check gauge light is designed to illuminate at 230°F plus or minus 10 degrees.

The 1990-and-later engines use the same gauge as the gasoline

Water Pump Upgrade

When upgrading your 6.2L or early 6.5L water pump, use an OEM 6.5L water pump for model years 1997–2002 (ACDelco part number 252-776) and a nine-blade Duramax cooling fan (part number 15080690). ∎

engines. The red zone begins at 245°F, and the check gauge light will come on at 250°F plus or minus 10 degrees. In 1992, the check gauge light was recalibrated to come on at 245°F plus or minus 3 degrees.

Fan Clutch

Two fan clutches were used on the 6.2L diesel. The air-conditioning application (part number 15548578) was designed to engage at 200°F fan air temperature. Non-AC fan clutches (part number 15548579) were designed to engage at 180°F fan air temperature. The fan air temperature is the temperature the outside air must reach after it has picked up heat by passing through the AC condenser (if equipped) and radiator core.

Fan clutch engagement should take place before the coolant reaches the gauge red zone at 228°F on 1988 and 1989 engines or 245°F on 1990-and-later engines. When clutch engagement takes place above these temperatures, the temperature will still come down. Yet, if the fan clutch disengages before the engine cools down, it is miscalibrated and should be replaced with a Hayden clutch. Fan engagement below 215°F causes noise and is not good because the thermostat will not be open enough

to allow full coolant flow through the radiator.

It is possible to experience higher coolant temperatures on AC-equipped trucks if the ambient temperature is 85 to 96°F and the AC is not on. The air reaching the fan clutch will not be heated up by the AC condenser (about 20°F). This air must be heated up by a higher coolant temperature before the fan clutch will engage. Once the fan clutch engages, the coolant temperature should drop several degrees and then stabilize.

Thermostat

Both engines use a remote-mounted thermostat that is installed in a water crossover. The early design was a wax-element thermostat with a bypass hose that operated in the traditional Chevrolet design like any small-block Chevy engine. The 1982 thermostat had an opening point of 180°F with a temperature range of 175 to 182°F and was fully open at 202°F. The 1983–1987 and later thermostats opened at 190°F with a temperature range of 175 to 182°F. It was fully open at 202°F. Both of these thermostats were of the non-blocking type.

The 1988-and-later 6.2L engine used a unique full-blocking thermostat (part number 23500827). There are no other thermostats that will work in this application. This unit starts to open at 190°F and does not fully open until 215°F. The full-blocking design allows all flow through the water pump bypass hose to be blocked when the thermostat is fully open. All of the coolant then flows through the radiator for better cooling. If using a non-blocking thermostat in this engine, it will fit but may overheat. This design was used from 1988 until 1991, which was the end of production for the 6.2L.

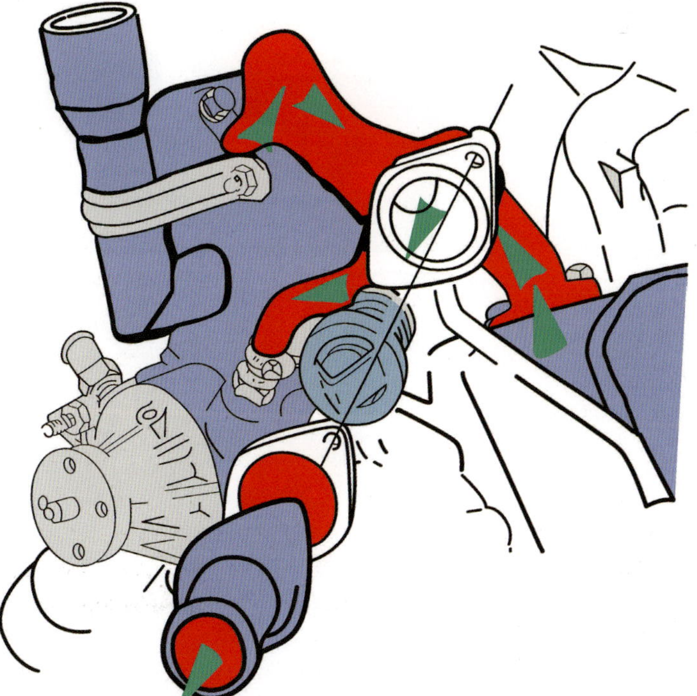

The 1982–1987 thermostat is a key component in the cooling system because it accelerates engine warm-up and improves performance but can be a big flow restriction, even when fully open. All 6.2L and 6.5L engines used a remote-style thermostat for a higher flow rate.

The 1982–1987 wax-pellet type automotive thermostat had a small cylinder that was filled with a wax that began to expand when the calibrated opening temperature was reached. A rod connected to the valve pressed into this wax. When the wax got hot, it expanded and pushed the rod out of the cylinder, compressing the return spring and opening the valve to allow coolant flow into the radiator.

The 6.5L water crossover for 1992–1995 was a different design than the 6.2L. The 6.5L thermostat was a full-blocking thermostat that was mounted vertically, unlike the 6.2L. In 1996, Chevrolet went to a horizontal single thermostat mounting using the same thermostat. From

The 1982–1987 non-blocking thermostat was placed in a water crossover as the remote location.

1998 until the end of 6.5L production in 2002, dual thermostats with the same full-blocking feature were used, which were similar to the Duramax engine in 2001. Note that the 6.5L remained in production for the Hummer for some time after 2002.

The 1988–1991 full-blocking thermostat has a dual-valve bypass that provides a tighter control of temperature and is less sensitive to thermal shock caused by the coolant surge. This design allows for a constant inlet temperature. In this arrangement, the inlet cooling to the engine is controlled by a double-valve thermostat that mixes a recirculating sensing flow with the radiator cooling flow. These employ a single capsule but have two valve discs. Thus a very compact and simple but effective control function is achieved.

Water Crossover and Thermostat

When building a 6.2L diesel, make an effort to locate a 1988–1991 water crossover, a full-blocking thermostat, or a 6.5L 1992–2002 water crossover and thermostat. For better flow, drill four 1/8-inch holes in the thermostat. ■

The water crossover and thermostat housing with internal passages accommodates the full-blocking thermostat.

The early 6.5L water crossover used a full-blocking thermostat that was mounted vertically. This design was used to improve coolant flow through the engine and reduce the possibility of engine overheating. It was a 195°F-opening thermostat.

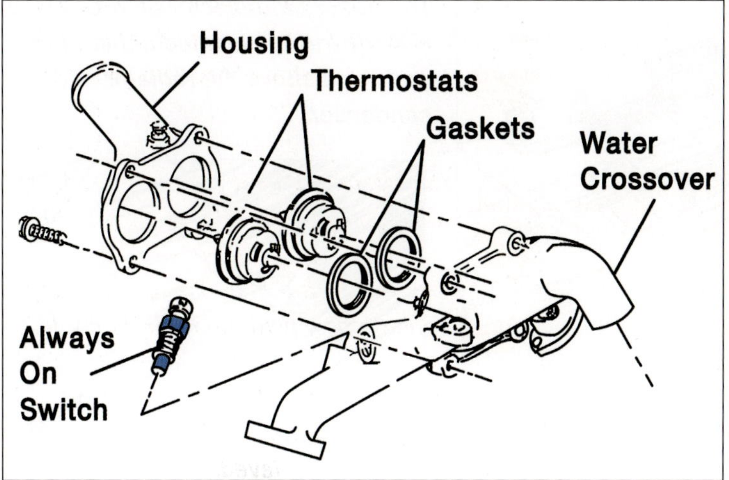

Late 6.5L diesels use two full-blocking thermostats to provide improved temperature control. The rear or primary thermostat is a non-blocking, two-stage design. The first stage of the rear thermostat begins to open at 180°F (82°C). During the first stage, a small passage is open so coolant can flow to the water outlet and begin to circulate to the radiator. The second stage begins to open at 185°F (85°C), and more coolant is allowed to pass through to the radiator. The rear or primary thermostat is fully open at 203°F (95°C).

This is a combustion leak chemical detector using a blue liquid to detect combustion gases in the cooling system on a running engine. Remove the radiator pressure cap on a cold engine and place the tapered end into the radiator or expansion tank. Remove the top cap with the vacuum port on it and pour some of the blue fluid into the tube. Place the top cap back on. Using engine vacuum or a vacuum pump, suck engine coolant into the tube to mix with the blue fluid. If combustion gases are present, the liquid combination will turn yellow.

History of 6.2L and 6.5L Thermostat Usage				
Year	Engine	Thermostats	Position	Opening Temp
1982–1987	6.2L	1 non-blocking	Horizontal	1982 opens at 180°F, fully open at 202°F; 1983–1987 opens at 190°F, fully open at 202°F
1988–1993	6.2L	1 full-blocking	Horizontal	Opens at 190°F, fully open at 215°F
1992–1995	6.5L	1 full-blocking	Vertical	Opens at 190°F, fully open at 215°F
1996–1997	6.5L	1 full-blocking	Horizontal	Opens at 190°F, fully open at 215°F
1998–2002	6.5L	2 staged opening with blocking to by-pass passage	Horizontal	Primary thermostat opens at 180°F, fully open at 203°F; secondary thermostat opens at 185°F, fully open at 212°F; when both are fully open, flow is 80 gpm

6.2L Engine Overheat Condition

The 1988–1989 6.2L diesel cooling system is designed to run at 220°F at 70 mph at wide-open throttle (WOT) on 100°F days with the air-conditioning running and 225°F while towing at maximum gross combination weight rating (GCWR) up a grade. The 1990-and-later engines can run 225 to 236°F at 70 mph up a grade.

If fueling on the injection pump is increased beyond what it is calibrated for, you may experience increasing coolant temperature—so be careful if increasing the fuel rate. This cooling system is very sensitive to airflow on both engines. Any disruption of flow due to anything placed in front of the radiator will most likely result in elevated coolant temperatures and possible overheating.

It is extremely important to keep the radiator full of coolant at all times. When cold, the radiator cap can be removed. If more than 1 gallon of coolant is needed to fill the radiator, severe engine damage may have already occurred, such as a blown head gasket or a warped head.

Never trust the coolant recovery tank to indicate if the cooling system is full on these engines because it is not an expansion tank. The cold level in the recovery tank is only accurate if coolant is being expelled to the bottle during warm-up and drawn back into the radiator after cooling down. Coolant may not be drawn back to the radiator if the radiator cap is not working properly or there is an air leak in the cooling system. Remember that air is the enemy of any cooling system, and all air leaks must be fixed.

If you suspect a head gasket is leaking combustion gases, check this out. A leaky head gasket can push excess coolant into the recovery bottle and result in the radiator running low on coolant, which may appear as coolant boiling in the recovery tank. Running the system low can result in aerated coolant with a reduction in cooling efficiency and a complete loss of coolant flow.

Check this by removing the water outlet, thermostat, and serpentine belt. Fill the thermostat housing full of coolant. Start the engine, let it idle, and look for bubbles rising to the top of the thermostat housing. A leaky gasket will result in a steady stream of bubbles rising from either leg of the thermostat housing to the top. The leaking cylinder bank can be identified using this process.

Do not run the engine more than 1 minute during this process.

Other Coolant Temperature Issues

Many folks modify their 6.2L and 6.5L applications with a DB2 mechanical pump and increase the fueling rate by turning the leaf-spring screw clockwise. This has an effect on coolant temperature because the engine will run hotter when the fuel rate is set above the specified limits without additional cooling capacity, such as a 130-gpm water pump, a nine-blade fan, dual thermostats, or a larger radiator. Exhaust back pressure will also affect coolant temperature due to the use of aftermarket exhaust systems with a higher restriction. So, measure back pressure when installing a different exhaust system.

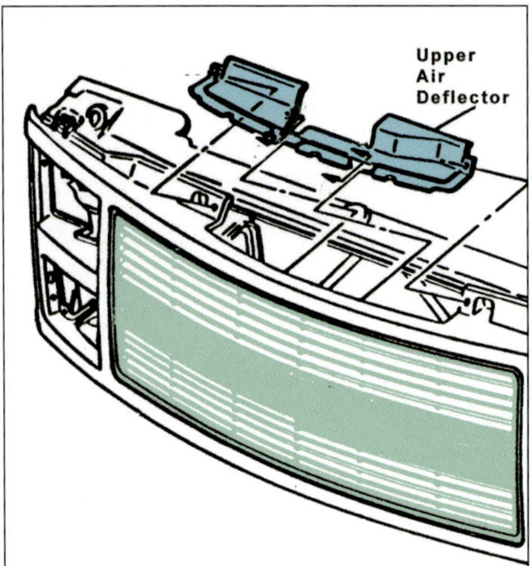

The upper air deflector on a GM C- or K-Body truck is located behind the grille and above the radiator and condenser.

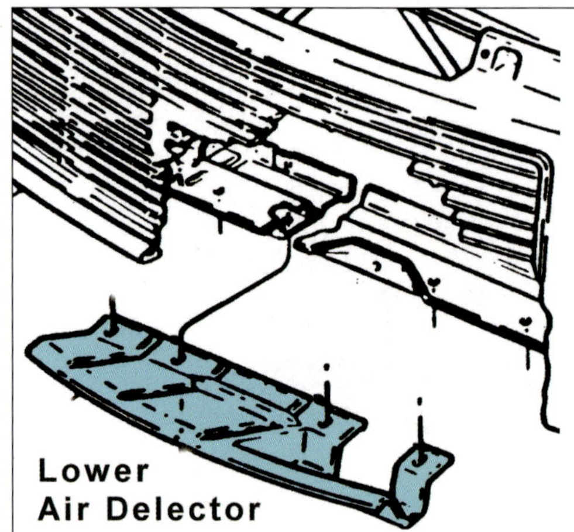

The lower air deflector is under the radiator and behind the front grille. Do not confuse this deflector with the 4WD truck engine pan shield. Make sure that the upper and lower air deflectors are in place because they affect airflow through the radiator and shroud and over the engine.

The 6.2L and 6.5L cooling system is very sensitive to airflow over the engine. Any disruption in the flow of air through the radiator or over the engine due to snowplows, missing baffles or air dams, or a bug screen in front of the radiator will likely result in higher coolant temperatures.

It is extremely important to keep the 6.2L radiator full of coolant at all times. Never use the recovery bottle level as a gauge to determine if the radiator is full. On a cold engine, remove the radiator pressure cap and check the coolant level. It should be full. If you need to add more than 1 gallon of coolant, engine damage may have occurred, so check the compression.

Hose Clamp

A new design of hose clamp was used in production starting with the 1992 model year on C- and K-Body trucks. Usage of this clamp expanded to include other models in the

The Mubea clamp must be installed on a hose that will be put on a clean, dry, paint-free surface. If lubrication is necessary for assembly, use GM part number 1051717. Production of trucks with the clamp began in 1992, starting with the water pump and radiator connections. The heater hoses followed on most applications. If the vehicle was originally built with Mubea clamps, the clamp should be replaced with the same part number Mubea clamp and not a screw-type hose clamp.

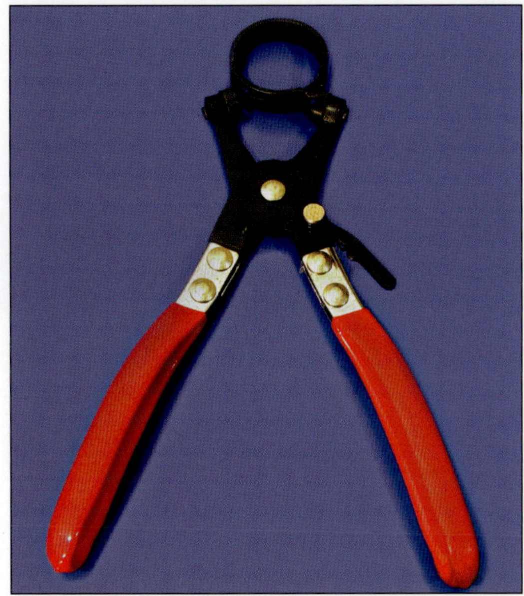

Standard pliers or hose clamp pliers will not work well on the new style of clamp. Various tool companies have developed special pliers to install and remove these hose clamps. Some companies may have a plier available that is effective in removing the larger size of clamps but may not open wide enough to accommodate the clamp once it is off the hose and relaxed. Do not compress the clamp (permanently) to make the tool fit because this will decrease the effectiveness of the clamp.

1993 model year. The Mubea constant-tension hose clamp was designed to reduce the amount of coolant leakage from radiator and heater hoses. With the previous design (screw-type clamps), it is difficult to maintain a constant load on the hose connection. Some of the load is lost under certain temperature changes. The Mubea clamp exerts a relatively even and constant pressure that is maintained under varying temperature conditions.

Cooling System Overheating Diagnoses for 6.2L or 6.5L Engines			
Step	**Action**	**Yes**	**No**
1	Check for a loss of coolant. Is there a loss of coolant?	Go to Step 2	Go to Step 3
2	Fill the system to the specified level. Check the service manual for "Loss of Coolant" and locate the problem and fix it. Does the engine overheat?	Go to Step 3	System okay
3	Check for low-coolant protection; go to "Coolant Concentration Testing" in the service manual. Is the coolant at the correct concentration?	Go to Step 5	Go to Step 4
4	Check for a loss of system pressure. Refer to "Cooling System Leak Testing" in the service manual. Is there a loss of system pressure?	Go to Step 5	Go to Step 6
5	Check for a faulty engine coolant temperature (ECT) sensor. Go to "Cooling System Diagnosis" in the service manual. If the ECT is at fault, a DTC will be set and the malfunction indicator lamp (MIL) will be on. Is the sensor operating properly?	Go to Step 6	Go to Step 7
6	Check for a cracked coolant recovery reservoir or a leaking hose. Go to "Loss of Coolant" in the service manual. Is the reservoir cracked or is a hose leaking?	Go to Step 7	Go to Step 2
7	Repair or install new parts as necessary, then retest. Does the engine overheat?	Go to Step 8	System okay
8	Check for incorrect drive-belt tension. Go to "Drive Belt Tensioner Replacement" in the service manual. Is the belt at the right tension?	Go to Step 9	Go to Step 7
9	Using a scan tool or a timing light, check for incorrect engine ignition timing. Is the ignition timing incorrect?	Go to Step 7	Go to Step 10
10	Check for a damaged water pump. Is the water pump damaged or is the seal leaking?	Go to Step 7	Go to Step 11
11	Check for obstructed radiator airflow or bent radiator fins. Is the radiator airflow obstructed?	Go to Step 7	Go to Step 12
12	Look up the "Engine Coolant Flushing Procedure." Add the recommended coolant to the engine. Are the cooling system passages blocked?	Go to Step 3	Go to Step 13
13	Check for inoperative cooling fans, either viscous clutch or electric cooling fans. Are the cooling fans working?	Go to Step 14	Go to Step 7
14	Check the thermostat by using diagnostic information from the service manual. Is the thermostat stuck in the closed position?	Go to Step 15	Go to Step 16
15	Replace the thermostat. Does the engine overheat?	Go to Step 16	System okay
16	Check for a faulty water pump. Are the impeller blades broken or eroded from cavitation erosion?	Go to Step 7	Go to Step 17
17	Check for a missing or damaged radiator upper air deflector and/or center air deflector or air dams. Are the deflectors or air dams missing or damaged?	Go to Step 7	Go to Step 18
18	Check the radiator cooling capacity. Is the proper size of radiator being used on the vehicle?	Go to Step 2	Go to Step 19
19	Replace the radiator. Is the repair complete?	System okay	

ENGINE REMOVAL

There are a number of shop tools along with some special tools that are needed to remove a heavy engine (the 6.2L and 6.5L diesel engines weigh in excess of 700 pounds). The fasteners on both the 6.2L and 6.5L engines are metric, so you will need both English and metric hand tools. The best engine removal tool is the shop crane, or cherry picker, as it is known in the trade. You will also need an engine stand that is strong enough to hold the engine.

Before beginning, determine what engine is being pulled to ensure that you have what you need for an overhaul. A typical engine number is broadcast code HH0311, which indicates that it is a 1983 6.2L engine built on March 11. See the table for other engine years and numbers:

A shop crane works best for removing the 6.2L or 6.5L diesel engine. Never skimp on the lifting capacity of the shop crane. The 6.2L weighs 701 pounds and the 6.5L weighs 750 pounds without any accessories, and most likely the engine is being pulled with most of its accessories still attached. In some cases, you may remove the air-conditioning compressor to avoid having to recharge the system. You must use a shop crane with a capacity of at least 2,000 pounds. The most common cranes have a capacity of just 1,000 pounds, which is cutting it very close with an assembly that could reach 800 pounds.

Use a robust engine stand to manipulate either the 6.2L or 6.5L engine due to its weight of up to 800 pounds. When connecting the engine to the engine stand, use four Class 8 bolts with 3/16-inch diameter and 18 threads per inch.

Safety is Critical

Safety is the most important consideration when working on a heavy diesel engine. It should always be your first consideration when performing any engine service procedure, including connecting the engine to the shop crane, lifting it out, and connecting it to the engine stand. The moving parts of the engine can be very hazardous.

Also, this engine is very heavy at 701 pounds for the 6.2L and 750 pounds for the 6.5L without accessories, so if the lifting device is not secure, serious injury can occur.

Always have a complete first aid kit and fire extinguisher available for an emergency. It is a good idea to have another person present when you are performing difficult tasks. Diesel engine components, especially the cylinder heads and the crankshaft, are very heavy, so get assistance when lifting these components from the engine. Never lift the engine out of the truck by yourself. ■

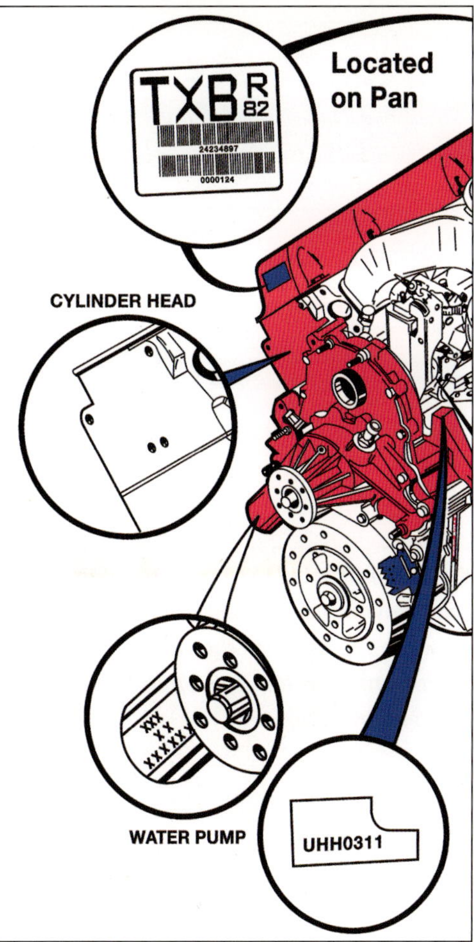

The engine identification number is stamped in the cast-iron block at the number-1 cylinder intake runner. The stamp identifies the broadcast code and defines the engine configuration plus the month and date that the engine was built. My engine has the engine broadcast code 1YJF8 26, which means that it is a 1999 6.5L engine built on August 26.

Engine Codes	
Model Year	**Engine Code**
1982	T
1983	U
1984, CUCV	F
1985–1988	D
1986–1989	H
1987	J
1990–1991	K
1992–1993, 6.5L	L
1994, 6.5L	M
1995, 6.5L	Y
1996, 6.5L	P
1997, 6.5L	R
1998, 6.5L	S
1999, 6.5L	V
2000–2005, 6.5L	W

The traceability label is glued to the engine pan on the passenger's side and the passenger-side valve cover at the front. It contains two barcodes. The first bar code includes the number 10, indicating an engine, plus the broadcast code, which could be one of 37 different codes that are presently released, such as YJF on the 6.5L engine that I am using for this book.

The second barcode contains a computer letter plus the component identification, component manufacturing location, Julian date, and the vehicle identification number (VIN). The first piece of information on the

The traceability label is glued to the engine and contains two barcodes. The first code may include the number 10, indicating an engine, plus the broadcast code, which could be 1 of 37 different codes that are presently released. The broadcast code on this engine is YJF.

barcode is a *1*, which is simply for programming in the computer. The next information is a number *10* to define the component as an engine. The next bit of information in this case is the letter *R* to signify that the engine was built at the Marine, Ohio, engine assembly plant.

The Julian date code and engine identification are found on the driver-side bank of the engine on the block runner at the front to the right of the injection pump.

For the code UHH 0311, *U* is for 1983 and 0311 is March 11. That is the 70th day of the year and would be 070 on the traceability label.

After that date, the VIN appears. The VIN starts new for broadcast codes at the beginning of the model year. For each of the many broadcast codes, it is a separate set of serial numbers starting with the number 1 for whatever model year, and it is continued until the last product of the current model year was manufactured. The end of production for the 6.2L was in 1991. End of production for the 6.5L was around 2005 with some extension of the military applications, but these were built by AM General and not General Motors.

Pulling the Engine

1 Gather Service Information

Go to either the OEM website or one of the online service manual websites and look up the engine removal instructions to make sure that you don't miss any steps on the particular vehicle you are using.

Do this because certain components may not have to be removed while other components may have to be removed to get the engine out.

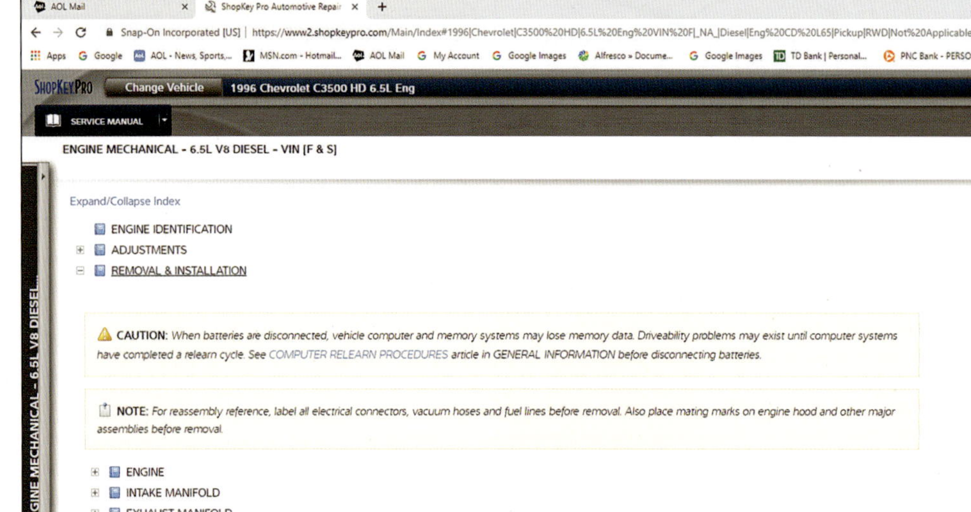

Visit one of the service information websites, such as ALLDATA , shopkeypro, or Mitchell On-Demand, and download the OEM instructions for engine removal. You will have to enter the make, model year, model, and engine information for your build before you can get to the specific instructions.

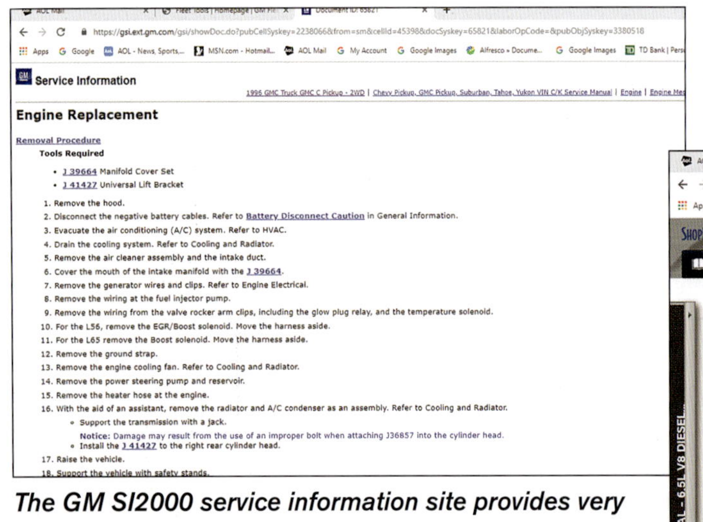

The GM SI2000 service information site provides very detailed instructions on engine removal. However, if your vehicle is more than 10 years old, the GM site will not contain any service information for that engine. You will need to use one of the generic service information websites.

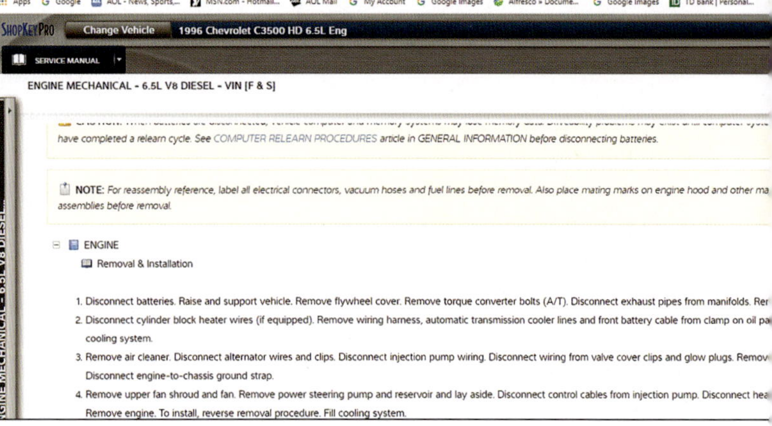

Use a generic service information site to locate engine restoration and replacement instructions for older trucks.

2 Document the Engine

Before beginning engine removal, get a phone camera or a good digital camera and take detailed pictures of the engine. Take photographs of the connections and key components that need to be removed to get the engine out.

Take photographs of the engine to document where the wiring and connectors from the vehicle will reconnect to the engine at reinstallation.

3 Hood Removal

Pulling the engine from the typical pickup truck or Suburban always requires removal of the hood. This provides the additional working area and light that is needed when pulling a big, heavy engine like the 6.2L. It's important to mark the hinges to make reinstalling the hood easy during the reassembly process. The hood is very heavy, so have an assistant help with removal. Store the hood in a safe place with some furniture blankets or other soft materials so that it is not damaged.

Mark the hood hinges with a permanent marker so you will maintain hood alignment when reinstalling the hood.

4 Label Wire Connections

I recommend using tags to label the connectors. These tags mark critical component connections on the vehicle wiring connections to make reinstallation easier.

Use a wire tag connection at the fuel filter fuel heater assembly.

5 Disconnect Battery

Important!

Always disconnect the ground cable on both batteries before doing anything else. This ensures that no short circuits take place, engine wiring is not damaged, and serious injury does not result (in the case of the 24-volt CUCV).

Disconnect the negative cables from both batteries. If this is a CUCV, the system uses two 12-volt batteries in series, which is 24 volts aboveground. Be very careful with that level of voltage.

6 Drain Coolant

Drain the cooling system into a clean and suitable container if you plan on reusing the coolant, which is unlikely on a rebuild. If disposing of the old coolant, follow all local, state, and federal laws regarding the disposal.

7 Drain Motor Oil

Drain the motor oil and dispose of it according to local, state, and federal hazardous waste disposal laws. Wal-Mart will take up to 20 gallons at a time of used engine oil.

8 Remove Accessories

Remove the upper intake manifold cover on engines equipped with factory or aftermarket turbochargers if you want to reduce engine weight by removing the turbo. (The engine I am removing has a factory turbocharger.) Next, remove the air-conditioning compressor from the accessory mounting bracket vehicle and secure it out of the way. This is done to avoid having to recover the refrigerant, which is a process that requires special tools.

9 Remove Alternator

Remove the alternator from the accessory mounting bracket.

Alternators

The new and smaller Delphi CS series alternators (far right) were used from 1986 to 2000 on 6.2L and 6.5L diesel engines. All SI models (far left) have a capacitor installed in the rear housing to protect the diodes from sudden voltage surges and to filter out voltage ripples that could produce electromagnetic interference (EMI). Voltage is adjusted by removing the adjustment cap, rotating it until the desired setting (low, medium, medium-high, or high) is opposite the arrow on the housing, and reinstalling it in the new position. The two alternators in the center are for medium and heavy truck diesel applications.

The GM Delco (now Delphi) 10-DN series alternator used an external electromagnetic voltage regulator. Six individual diodes were mounted in the rear housing with a capacitor for protection. A 14-pole rotor and Y-type stator provide current output. Field current is drawn from rectified output and travels through a B-circuit. The terminals on a 10-DN are labeled BAT, GRD, R, and F. The DN series was used from 1963 to 1973 on all models, with the exception of the 1969–1972 Corvette. It had a Y-stator design with a 60–70 ampere output at full load but not at idle.

The Delphi Systems Integrated (SI) series was the first GM alternator with a Delta wound stator capable of delivering 40 amps at idle or start-up and was first used in the 1969 Corvette. Most SI models have a rectifier bridge that contains all six rectifying diodes. The regulator is a fully enclosed unit attached by screws to the housing. Field current is drawn from unrectified AC Generator (alternator) output and rectified by an additional diode trio.

The SI series was used on the 6.2L diesel engine from 1982 to 1985. The new and smaller GM Delphi CS series alternators were used on the 6.2L and the later 6.5L from 1986 to 2000. The charging system (CS) produced current output similar to larger truck alternators. This series includes models CS-121, CS-130, and CS-I44. ■

10 Remove Radiator and Power Steering

Remove the radiator assembly from the vehicle and the power steering lines from the power steering pump.

11 Disconnect Fuel Lines

Disconnect the fuel lines from the fuel filter, making sure that the lines are securely plugged to prevent any leakage of diesel fuel.

12 Remove Hoses

Disconnect the engine wiring harness assembly at the left rear of the engine block. Then, remove the ground straps from the right-rear cylinder head, remove heater hoses from the heater core, and remove the radiator hoses from the engine assembly.

13 Install Lift Brackets

Install a balance design lifting fixture on the shop crane.

Install an engine lift bracket to the rear of the right cylinder head. Damage may result from the use of improper bolts. Install an engine-lifting device, such as the SPX Kent-Moore Special J 36857, along with GM bolts (part number 94282217) and GM washers (part number 15650963) to the right rear cylinder head. Tighten the lift bracket bolt to 30 ft-lbs.

14 Remove Components

Lift the vehicle and support it with safety stands at the correct support areas of the frame as found in the service information. Remove the following components: front driveshaft (4WD truck), oil filter adapter, starter from the engine block, bolts from the torque converter, and the exhaust pipe from the turbocharger (if equipped).

15 Disconnect Electrical

Disconnect the electrical connector for the block heater. Remove the battery ground in the front of the engine block. Disconnect and remove the oil cooler lines from the engine block and secure them out of the way.

16 Remove Bellhousing Assembly

Remove the transmission oil cooler lines from the radiator and tie these lines out of the way. On automatic transmissions, remove the bellhousing bolts from the transmission to the engine block. On manual transmissions, such as the SM465 or the NV4500, remove the transmission from the bellhousing. Remove the bellhousing, flywheel, and clutch assembly, and then remove the safety stands and lower the vehicle.

The balance design lifting fixture allows you to hold the engine level during removal from the truck in addition to being able to attach the engine to the engine stand.

Oil Cooler Lines

Whenever the oil cooler lines are disconnected from the quick connectors on the radiator or the engine block, the retaining clip must be replaced with a new one. ∎

17 Attach Lifting Hooks

Attach the lifting device hooks to the two engine lifting brackets. Remove the inner splash shield from the wheelhouse and the frame and raise the engine enough to remove the engine-mount through bolt. It may be necessary to remove the engine-mount bracket from the engine block to gain enough clearance to remove the engine assembly.

For better clearance and working area, remove the front grille and sheet metal on the C-K series. The front grille and bumper must be taken off on a G Van to remove the engine.

18 Remove Engine Mounts

Remove the left engine-mount through bolt.

19 Reinstall Engine Mounts

Remove the right engine-mount through bolt. Support the transmission by wiring it to the body, lift the engine slightly, and reinstall both motor-mount bolts back into their sockets.

20 Remove Engine

Remove the engine from the vehicle with the help of an assistant. To prevent injury, never pull a heavy engine alone. When removing a 6.2L diesel from a G Van, it comes out the front or out the bottom, as is the factory process.

21 Document Engine Assembly

Before placing the engine on the engine stand, take another photo of the engine with any remaining accessories or brackets and remove them. Next, place the engine on an engine stand that can handle the weight of a 6.2L or 6.5L engine and remove the lifting device from the engine.

22 Align Engine with Stand

Using the shop crane, lift the engine to the same height as the engine stand. You will need Class 8 3/16–18 bolts.

24 Bolt Engine to Stand

Make sure that the engine is stable on the engine stand and that you can rotate it to ease the process of disassembly and reassembly.

23 Align Engine Stand Arms

Align the top two engine stand arms to the two top engine bolt holes and the bottom two arms to the two bottom engine bolt holes.

ENGINE DISASSEMBLY

To disassemble, overhaul, repair, or assemble the 6.2L or 6.5L diesel engine, use the disassembly, overhaul, and servicing sequences listed in this chapter.

It is helpful to have GM service information available for this process. Most of these engines are too old for General Motors to still have service information on its SI2000 website, so you will need to use one of the aftermarket websites, such as ALLDATA, shopkeypro, or Mitchell On-Demand. Most of the OEMs only keep service information for vehicles that are less than 10 years old.

Disassembly

1 Download Disassembly Information

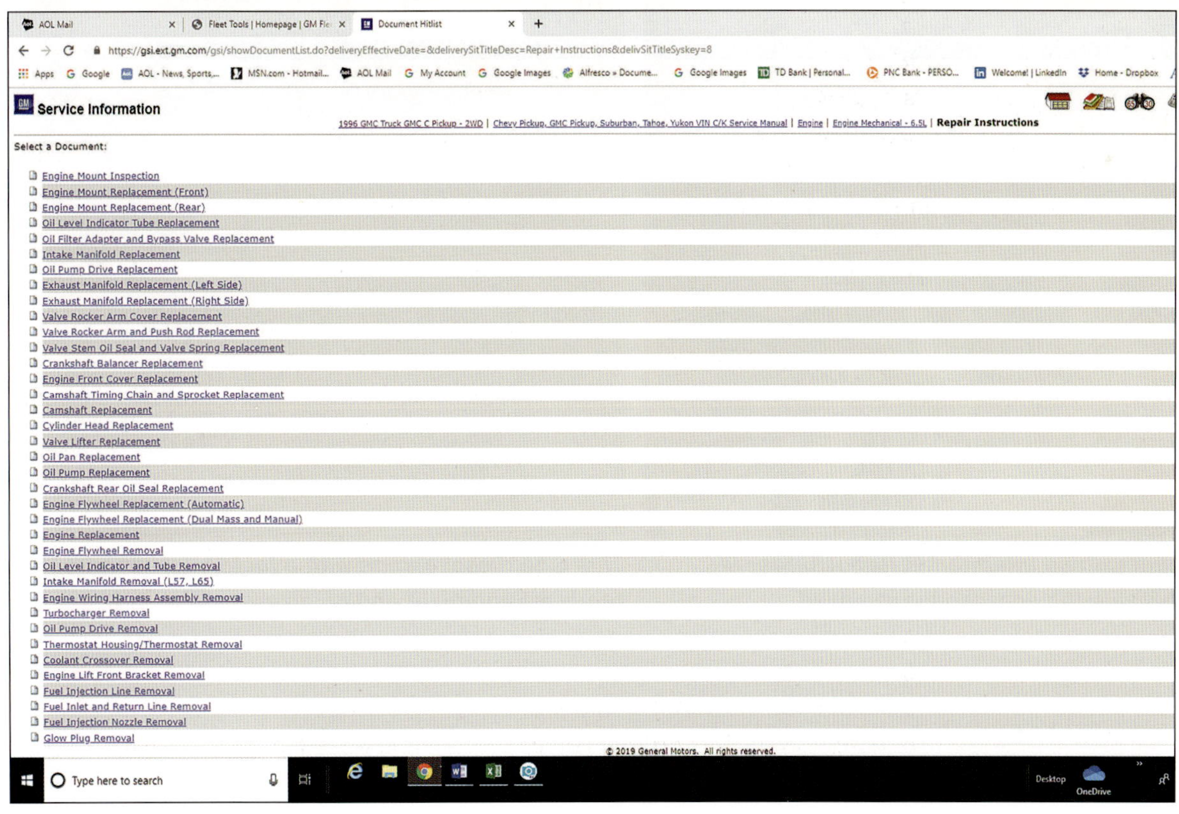

Download the disassembly instructions for either a 6.2L or 6.5L diesel engine from a generic service information website. You can only use the OEM procedures for later-model 6.5L engines after 1997.

---

2 Remove Accessories

Remove the following accessories: serpentine drive belt or all V-belts, drive belt tensioner retaining bolt and belt tensioner, belt-driven vacuum pump retaining bolts and vacuum pump on a belt-driven vacuum pump, right accessory bracket retaining bolts, right accessory bracket retaining nuts, right accessory bracket, left accessory, and the left accessory/lift bracket.

3 Prep for Disassembly

This 6.2L diesel engine with an aftermarket turbocharger is ready for disassembly with the accessories removed.

This 6.5L diesel engine with a factory turbocharger is ready for complete engine disassembly.

4 Remove Crankcase Depression Regulator

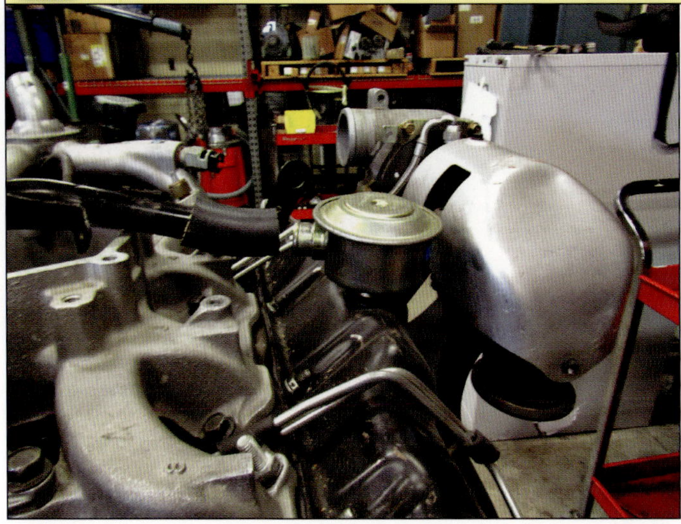

Remove the crankcase depression regulator (CDR) valve from the right rocker arm cover or wherever it is located. Depending on the model year, the CDR can be located in at least three different locations.

The crankcase depression regulator (CDR) valve is used to regulate crankcase pressure and burn up any combustion gases or blowby (gases that blow by the rings) that goes past the piston rings. It depressurizes the crankcase and prevents oil leaks. The CDR meters the flow of crankcase gases or blowby back into the engine through a connection to the intake manifold from the CDR through a connection to the rocker cover.

The blowby travels from the crankcase through the oil passages in the head through the rocker cover to the CDR valve to the intake manifold. The intake manifold vacuum acts against the CDR spring-loaded diaphragm. Higher vacuum (low pressure) at higher engine speeds pulls the diaphragm closer to the top of the outlet tube and restricts the opening, reducing the amount of blowby flow. When engine speed is lower, the spring pushes the diaphragm away from the top of the outlet and increases blowby flow. When engine RPM is low, there is more time for the blowby to leak past the rings, so that is why the CDR allows more flow at lower engine speeds.

The CDR valve and the vent hose could collect condensation and freeze at low ambient temperatures. This could cause the crankcase to pressurize and subsequently lose engine oil.

A new CDR valve is now available that aids in condensation draining back to the engine crankcase. The new CDR valve (part number 25095i84) is designed so that the vent hose forms an angle toward the front of the engine. This new valve is used alone with the G and P model oil fill cap (part number 25060118) to prevent oil loss due to crankcase pressurization. This CDR valve is interchangeable with the former one and is installed in the same location. (Chapter 8 will detail the testing of the CDR).

5 Remove Intake Manifold Cover

Remove the six bolts retaining the intake manifold upper cover on a turbocharged 6.5L engine. The 6.2L engine without a turbo will not have an upper intake manifold cover. The RPO code LH6 or "C" engine will have an exhaust gas recirculation (EGR) valve to be removed before removing the actual intake manifold. The LL4 or "J" 6.2L does not use an EGR valve.

6 Remove Fuel Filter Assembly

Remove the fuel filter assembly from the intake manifold and position the filter aside while discarding the internal filter cartridge.

7 | Remove Turbocharger

Remove the turbocharger from the right exhaust manifold. Remove the turbocharger assembly if equipped. Remove the turbocharger short brace retaining bolts, short brace, long-brace retaining bolt and nut, and long brace. Loosen the turbocharger connection hose clamps. Loosen the turbocharger connection hose and insert a small flat screwdriver between the turbocharger connection hose and the turbocharger. Slide the screwdriver blade along the surface of the turbocharger until the hose twists freely.

Remove the braces from the turbocharger and the upper and lower intake manifold. Some quantity of oil will exist inside the vent system. The crankcase vapor consists of vaporized oil that condenses within the vent and intake system. The inside of the air duct and compressor-wheel housing will have some oil due to the venting of the crankcase vapors. Loosen the clamps on the hose between the air cleaner assembly and the turbocharger. Remove the oil feed line from the turbocharger and position it to the side, then remove the oil return line from the turbocharger.

On EFI engines, disconnect the intake air temperature (IAT) sensor connector, remove the IAT sensor, disconnect the manifold absolute pressure (MAP) sensor connector, remove the MAP sensor retaining bolts, and remove MAP sensor and gasket.

8 | Remove Oil Pump Drive Stalk

Remove the oil pump drive stalk on a 6.5L or late-model 6.2L with a belt-driven vacuum pump or the vacuum pump assembly on a 6.2L diesel.

The oil pump drive stalk provides the connection from the engine oil pump to a gear on this drive that is driven by the camshaft.

All 6.2L and 6.5L diesels use a mechanical vacuum pump. Early engines prior to the serpentine belt used a vacuum pump; it was located at the rear of the camshaft in the back of the engine and is also part of the drive system for the oil pump. It was driven by the camshaft. Later models (due to space restrictions for the fuel filter) relocated the vacuum pump to the accessory drive on the front of the engine, and it became belt driven.

Due to the relocation of the vacuum pump, an oil pump drive stalk was added to drive the oil pump. This pump is necessary because diesel engines do not have a throttle and cannot retain vacuum to operate accessories inside the vehicle and the vacuum modulator used on the THM400 automatic transmission. The oil pump driveshaft is inserted into the lower end of the pump gear. There is a white plastic collar that is used to retain it in the block if the engine is turned over.

Never attempt to run the engine without the vacuum pump installed or the drive stock installed because there will be no oil pump operation.

9 Remove Intake Manifold

Remove the glow plug relay from the lower intake manifold and the nuts on the oil pump that are retaining the heater hose bracket. Remove the lower and main intake manifold along with the intake gaskets that will need to be discarded.

10 Remove Oil Fill Tube

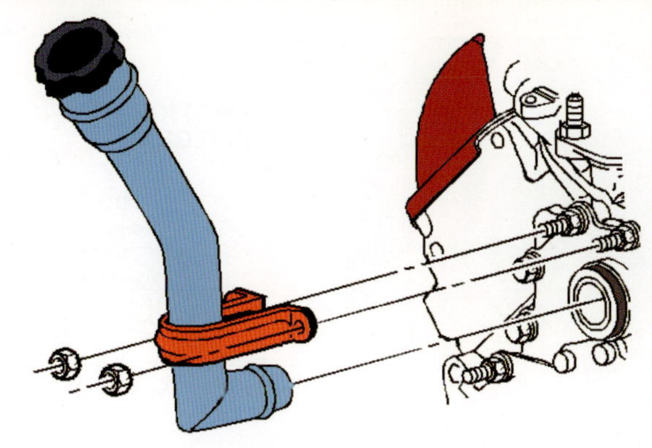

Remove the oil fill tube retaining nuts and use a pry bar to remove the oil fill tube. Be careful not to damage the grommet in the water pump plate when removing the oil fill tube.

Make sure that the sealing surface is in good condition and that the tube is not bent. Vented tube (14071059) was used during 1983 to prevent oil from getting into the air intake.

11 Remove Oil Level Indicator

Remove the oil level indicator, the oil level indicator tube retaining bolt, and the oil level indicator tube O-ring seal. Discard the old seal.

12 Remove Thermostat

Remove the bolts to the thermostat cover and remove the thermostat.

You can remove the thermostat by itself or later remove the entire thermostat housing.

13 Remove Coolant Housing

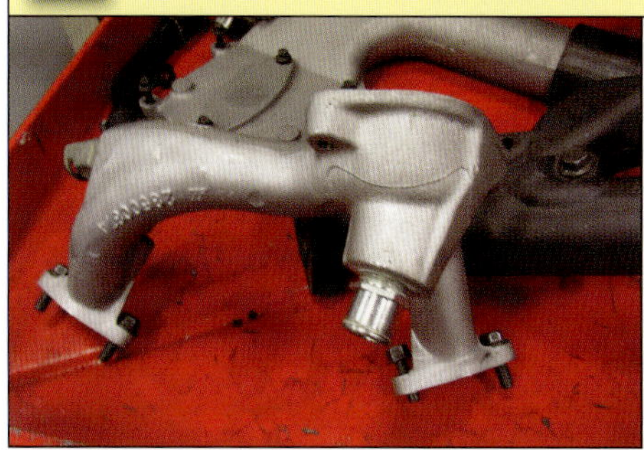

Remove the coolant crossover housing assembly and thermostats, depending on whether it is a 6.2L (one thermostat) or the 6.5L (one or two thermostats). Remove the coolant outlet attached to the crossover housing assembly along with the thermostat bypass nipple.

Disconnect the bypass hose and remove it.

14 Remove Exhaust Manifold

Remove the exhaust crossover pipe bolts from the exhaust manifolds, the exhaust manifold bolts, and the exhaust manifold. Clean the threads on the exhaust manifold bolts and stud/nuts.

15 Remove Gear Retaining Bolts

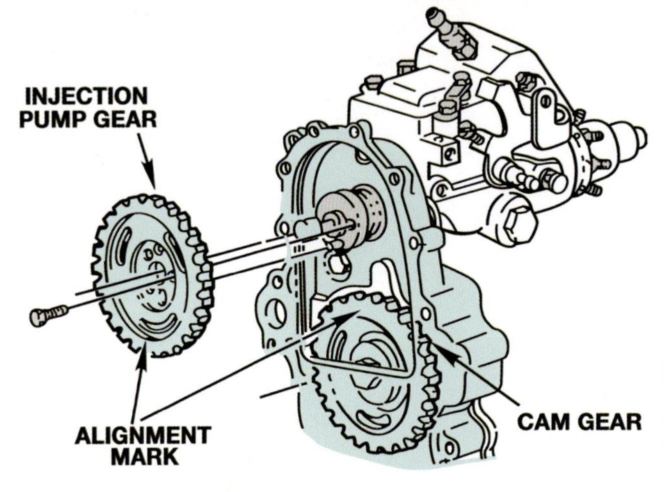

Going through the oil fill pipe opening, remove the three fuel injection pump–driven gear retaining bolts. Do this one at a time while rotating the crankshaft until you see the bolt, which has a 13-mm head. Remove the fuel injection pump fuel feed hose. Never rotate the engine with the starter, with the starter location engine rotation fixture, or with the wrench from the front of the engine with the fuel injection pump removed. The loose fuel pump drive gear could become lodged in the front cover and cause gear tooth distress and shear the camshaft drive gear. Always align the camshaft gear timing marks before installing the fuel injection pump drive gear during reassembly.

16 Remove Fuel Injection Line

As part of the fuel injection line removal, remove the fuel injection pump fuel feed pipe clips at the brackets and the fuel injection pump fuel feed pipe brackets. Loosen the fuel injection nozzle to the fuel return pipe's hose clamps. Remove the fuel injection nozzle to the fuel return hoses and retaining nuts and remove the fuel return pipe. Remove the fuel feed pipe fittings. Cap the fuel feed pipe fittings and the fuel injection pump fittings immediately. Be careful not to bend the fuel injection fuel feed pipes.

Using 30-mm and 19-mm wrenches, loosen the fuel line connectors to the fuel injector nuts and remove the fuel nozzle and fuel injection fuel feed pipe fittings. Wear safety glasses to protect against fuel spray. Loosen the fuel return hose clamps and remove the fuel return hose.

17 Loosen Fuel Injection Pump

Using a special 15-mm wrench, loosen and remove the three nuts holding the fuel injection pump to the engine front cover.

19 Remove Fuel Injection Nozzles

Using a 30-mm socket or the GM special tool J 29873, remove the eight fuel injection nozzles. Store the fuel injection nozzles in a clean place while discarding the metal gaskets. Mark the fuel injection nozzles to return each one to its original location during installation. Failure to use the 30-mm hex socket will result in damage to the injection nozzle.

18 Remove Fuel Injection Pump

Remove the fuel injection pump and fuel injection lines as an assembly.

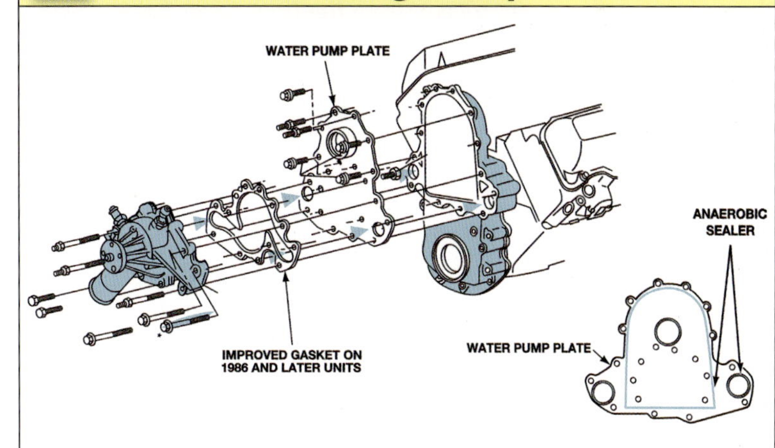

Place the fuel injection pump and lines in a safe place. It was common to call this assembly a Tarantula because it resembles that spider.

20 Remove Cooling Pump

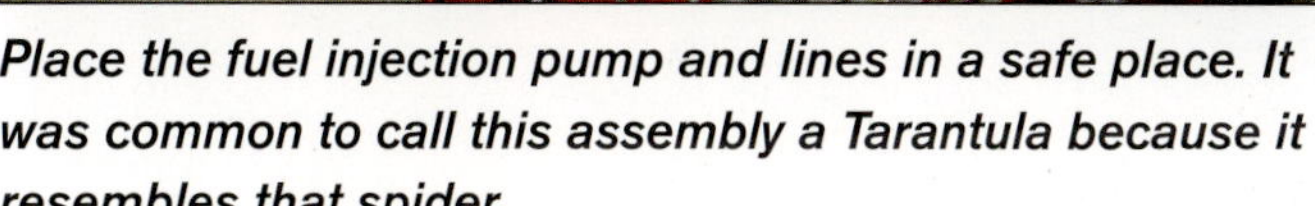

Remove the water pump attaching bolts, studs, and backing plate. The coolant pump will come off as a complete assembly. You cannot remove the water pump by itself until you remove the backing plate.

21 Remove Water Pump

Remove all bolts from the rear of the water pump backing plate.

Once all of the rear backing plate bolts have been removed, the water pump will come off.

22 Discard Water Pump Gasket

Remove the water pump gasket from the front cover backing plate and discard it.

23 Remove Drive Gear

Remove the fuel injection pump–driven gear from the drive gear. The gear will just lift off of the camshaft drive gear, which is bolted to the camshaft sprocket.

24 Remove Balancer Bolt

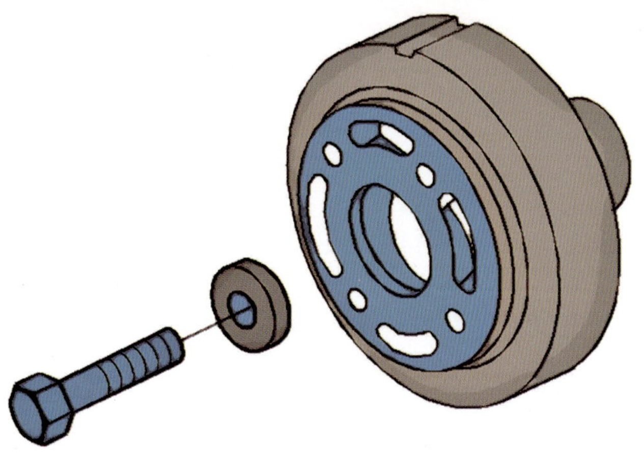

Remove the crankshaft balancer bolt and washer from the crankshaft. The best way to remove it is to use an air or high-powered electric impact gun. Otherwise, you will need to reinstall the flywheel and anchor the gear to remove it using a breaker bar or torque wrench, as I did during this disassembly.

25 Remove Crankshaft Balancer

Use GM special tool J 23523-F or a generic steering wheel puller to remove the crankshaft balancer from the crankshaft.

Using the steering wheel puller, remove the crankshaft balancer from the crankshaft.

26 Remove Front Cover

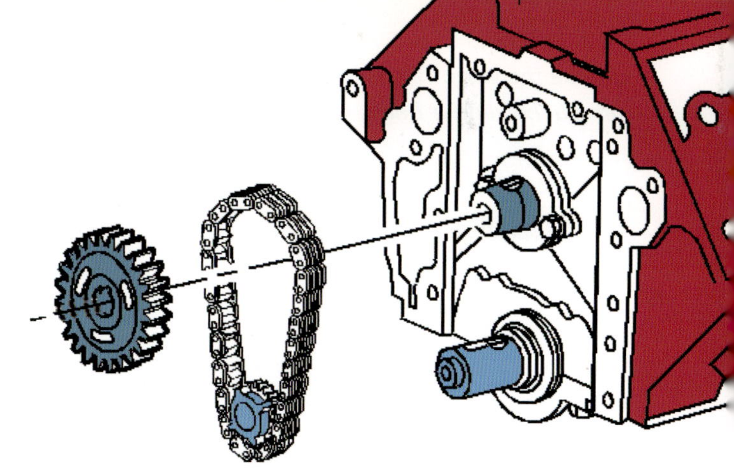

Remove the bolts at the bottom of the front engine cover to the oil pan, all of the remaining front cover bolts, and the front cover from the engine block. Also pry out the crankshaft front cover oil seal and discard it.

27 Remove Camshaft Gears

Remove the camshaft bolt that holds the fuel injection pump drive gear, and then remove the gear. Next, remove the chain, crankshaft timing gear, and camshaft sprocket as an assembly.

Use two pry bars or screwdrivers behind the camshaft sprocket to gently pry the camshaft gears off of the camshaft. Place the assembly in a safe place for inspection and possible replacement. Note the position of the timing marks for reassembly.

Both of these engines use a double roller chain, crankshaft sprocket, and camshaft sprocket. The valve timing on these engines is set on the number-6 cylinder at TDC with the mark on the crankshaft sprocket at 12 o'clock and the mark on the camshaft sprocket at six o'clock and in alignment. The difference from the injection pump is time and the number-1 cylinder.

28 Remove Rocker Cover

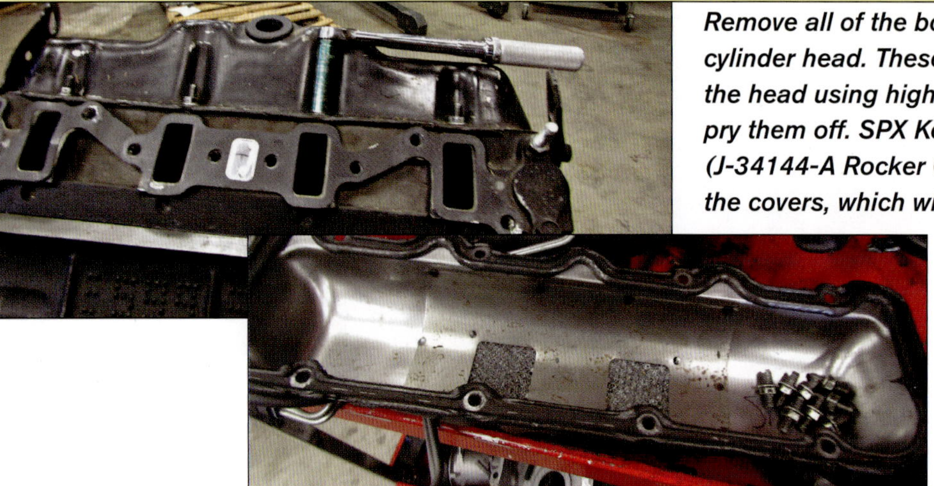

Remove all of the bolts holding both rocker covers to the cylinder head. These rocker covers are basically glued to the head using high-temperature RTV, so you will have to pry them off. SPX Kent-More makes a special lifting tool (J-34144-A Rocker Cover Remover) to assist in removing the covers, which will prevent bending and damaging the sealing surface.

After removal, use the rocker cover to store the fastening bolts.

29 Remove Rocker Arms and Pushrods

This 6.5L turbo engine used the 1985-and-later stamped steel rocker arms. At this point, remove all of the engine pushrods and place them either in a marking tray or on marked cardboard or paper so they are marked for their cylinder location. This is done to preserve any wear patterns to avoid noisy operation after assembly. This step is not necessary if they are going to be replaced. Note that the pushrods have a shiny end, which goes toward the valve lifter and a copper-coated end, which goes toward the rocker.

Remove the valvetrain rocker arms and shaft assembly from each cylinder head, marking them for reassembly.

30 Loosen Head Bolts

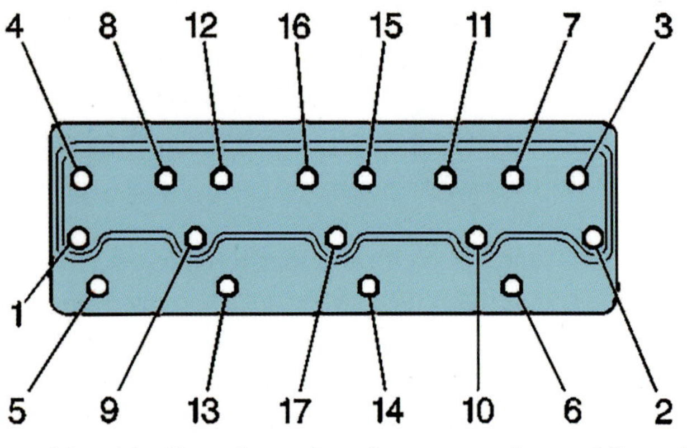

To avoid warping the cylinder head, General Motors recommends an untightening sequence for removing the head bolts or stud nuts. Start from the outside at both ends and work your way toward the middle.

Loosen the number-1 head bolt. The opposite sequence will be used for tightening the head to provide the maximum clamping force.

31 Remove Head Gaskets

The cylinder head is made of cast iron and has several different design features that changed over the years. (Chapter 7 will show the proper way to install the cylinder heads and which ones are the best to use for longevity and performance.)

In 1982, the compression ratio was 21.5:1. Around 1985, Detroit Diesel Division of General Motors (in charge of engine design, engineering, and service from 1983 to 1987) increased the compression ratio from 21.5:1 to 22.5:1 for both the C and J engines, based on service engineering reports. For a 6.2L, the cylinder head that performs the best is part number 14079304, which was the cylinder head for the military applications CUCV and HMMWV. The compression ratio for all 6.5L engines both naturally aspirated (NA) and turbocharged was 21.3:1.

Head Gasket

The 6.2L used two different head gaskets in production: the Fel-Pro Print-O-Seal design (with sealant already applied around the critical sealing areas) and the Victor (or green gasket as it was called).

The cylinder heads have been removed from the block with the help of an assistant because these are very heavy cast-iron heads. Replace the head gaskets with either Fel-Pro or Mahle head gaskets. Mark the heads for reassembly to the same cylinders.

32 Remove Roller Lifters

Loosen the bolts holding the roller lifter locking arm.

Use a magnet to remove the locking arms, lifter guide plates, and roller lifters from both cylinder banks.

33 Remove Valvetrain Components

When removing all valvetrain components that will be returned to the engine, mark their cylinder positions for reassembly. There are special trays made for this operation, but you can improvise as I did and just use a sheet of white copy paper with the cylinder numbers on it and the components placed in their respective positions.

34 Remove Camshaft

Gently remove the camshaft from the block. Try to avoid galling the camshaft bearings. Place it on the bench and then transfer it to V-blocks for measurement and inspection.

35 Remove Pan

With the engine on the engine stand, turn it sideways, or with the pan facing upward for pan removal. Loosen and remove all of the pan bolts. There are quite a few of them, so make sure they are all out before prying on the oil pan. This oil pan is also sealed with high-temperature RTV, so it may be difficult to remove. Use a sharp putty knife or the SPX Kent-More lifting tool J-34144-A to pry the oil pan loose.

36 Remove the Oil Pump Assembly

Remove the flywheel retaining bolts, outer retainer (if equipped), flywheel, and inner retainer (if equipped). Remove the oil pump assembly and drive rod from the engine. Place it in an area for disassembly and inspection. The oil pan is sealed using RTV, so it may be necessary to use a sharp chisel to break it loose.

The 6.2L and 6.5L engines require 7 quarts of oil. The oil pan is a reservoir on the bottom side of the crankcase that is used to hold the oil that is waiting to be circulated through the engine. This lubrication system is a pressure-feed type, which means that the pump forces oil through the galleries to the necessary parts. The pump is mounted to the bottom side of the number-5 main bearing. Extending down from the pump and into the oil is the pickup tube with a screen cover that filters out large foreign particles. Oil is picked up by the pickup tube and screen and sent through the oil pump.

The pump uses meshing gears. As these gears rotate in opposite directions, the space between the gear teeth in the housing fills with oil from the inlet side of the pump. Then, as the teeth match, the oil is forced out the inlet tube. The pump is driven from the engine camshaft using an intermediate shaft that runs from the bottom of either the vacuum pump or the oil pump stalk directly to the oil pump drive gear. Oil is next pumped through the cooler located in the radiator or an external cooler that cools the oil and helps to remove the heat.

From the cooler, the oil then passes through the oil filter. It is a cartridge-type oil filter with the relief valve, so it is a full-flow oil filter. If the oil filter gets clogged, the relief valve will open and allow unfiltered oil to lubricate the engine. From the filter, the oil is pumped through the drill galleries in the crankcase to the various moving parts of the engine.

The rear main crankshaft bearing is fed by a drilling in the rear main cap that comes from the main gallery in the cylinder case. Oil from this gallery feeds the crankshaft Babbitt bearings and other galleries that run the full length of the right-side crankcase. All other engine components are lubri-

36 | Remove Oil Pump Assembly *continued*

cated by these two galleries. Holes are drilled from the camshaft bores to provide oil from the main bearings number-1 through -4. The lifters on the right side receive oil from the right-side main oil gallery, and lifters on the left side receive oil from the left-side oil gallery. Lifters contain a check-all that meters oil through the hollow pushrods and to the rocker arm and valve stems in the cylinder head.

After a small accumulation of oil is in the head, it begins to drain back to the crankcase. The four main bearings receive oil from the vertical holes drilled from the cam bores to the crankshaft. The oil flows into the crankshaft main bearing, which provides lubrication for the crankshaft bearings. The oil also flows around the grooves in each main bearing through holes drilled in the crank-

shaft to the crankshaft journals to provide lubrication for the crankpins and connecting rod bearings.

As the crankshaft rotates, it slings oil off of the crank pins to cover the cylinder walls and piston pin area. Piston ring oil drains back off these parts and back into the engine. On the 6.5L turbocharged engine, there are oil jets that lubricate the bottom side of the pistons to keep them cool.

37 | Remove Carbon Ridge

Inspect the top of the cylinder wall for a carbon ridge, which is common on a diesel engine with mileage run on it.

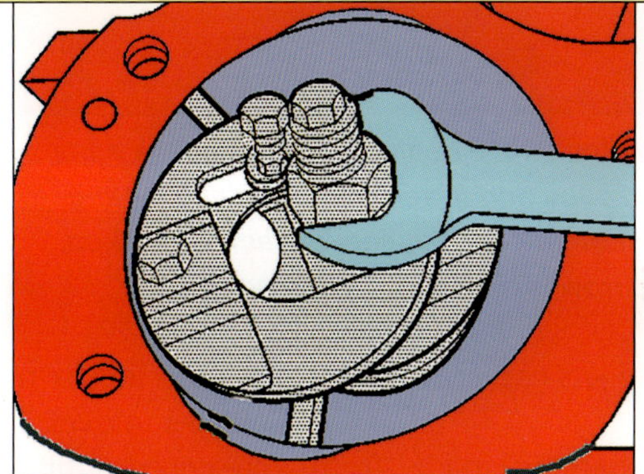

Using a ridge reamer on each cylinder, remove the ridge before attempting to remove the piston and connecting rod assembly.

38 | Remove Cap Bolts

Remove the connecting rod cap bolts for each cylinder along with the cap bottom rod bearing. Check that they are marked for each cylinder. If they are not, mark them for each cylinder and place them on a tray or a cart to be reunited with the piston and rod when they are removed.

39 | Remove Piston and Rod Assembly

Remove each piston and rod assembly from the block. Place them alongside their respective rod cap and bearing on the same cart or tray.

40 Remove Main Bearings

After all of the pistons have been removed, remove all of the main bearing caps and lower main bearings, noting their locations on the block. The cap location is marked, and there is an arrow on the cap to ease assembly.

Once the caps are removed, remove the crankshaft assembly with the help of an assistant. Locate the crankshaft in a vertical position to avid warpage because this is a nodular cast iron crankshaft and can be easily bent if you lay it unsupported. However, you can place it on V-Blocks. The one-piece rear main seal will come out with the crankshaft; discard it. All early 6.2L engines used a two-piece rope seal that was never used on the 6.5L engine.

The oil for these jets comes from the main gallery.

The crankshaft is made from nodular cast iron with ground journals and rolled fillets. The oil holes are drilled from the connecting rod journals to the main journals with no plugs required. The crankshaft has five main journals classified by three different categories of dimensions for an accurate bearing fit. The butt of the shaft is a flange, which is drilled to accept six bolts and one for locating and holding the flywheel or flexplate.

The crankshaft has a natural resonant frequency of vibration, so torsional impulse frequencies are induced by the firing of the cylinders. When the two frequencies are in residence, the magnitude of the combined vibrations could overstress the crankshaft and cause it to break. For these reasons, a vibration damper (or balancer) is used.

The inertia mass of the vibration damper moves freely within certain prescribed limits about a few hundredths of a millimeter because it is bonded and rubber. The inertia mass acts somewhat like a fixed weight and reduces the stresses to within safe limits by absorbing some of the torsional stress. Many rebuilders of these engines use an oil-filled hydraulic vibration damper to replace the factory unit.

Rear Main Seal

The 1982 to 1987 engines used a rope-type rear main oil seal made from asbestos. It was preceded by a series of parallel hashmarks on the shaft that were positioned to draw oil away from the seal. Preceding the hashmarks was a slinger that used a pressure-relief groove in the number-5 main bearing shell. The 1988-and-later 6.2L engines and all 6.5L engines used a single piece of round rubber lip seal.

41 Remove Plugs

Once all components are removed from the cylinder block, remove the freeze plugs and gallery plugs (if needed).

The 6.2L and 6.5L block is made from cast iron alloyed with carbon, silicon, and chromium for good elasticity and thermal expansion. There are five marked main bearings with arrows toward the front of the block. The center bearing is the thrust bearing.

STANADYNE DB2 PUMP SERVICE

The Stanadyne DB2 distributor-type fuel injection pump pressurizes and distributes a metered amount of fuel to each cylinder nozzle at the proper time based on the calibrated needs of the engine. Some parts have surfaces with machining tolerances measured in microns and require extreme cleanliness during any service. This chapter covers the steps to service the Stanadyne DB2.

Pump Operation

This pump uses one pump barrel and a set of plungers to supply all cylinders in a rotation. The pumping element operates eight times because it is used on an 8-cylinder diesel

All 6.2L diesel engines and mechanical-injection-system 6.5L engines use the Stanadyne DB2 fuel injection pump. This is a high-speed injection pump with injection pressures as high as 6,000 psi. The tolerances of the head and rotor are tight and precise to the micron. It uses just one pumping element within a cam ring of eight lobes, where the fuel is distributed to eight cylinders. Timing is controlled by moving the cam ring clockwise for advance or counterclockwise for retard. (Photo Courtesy Stanadyne Diesel Systems)

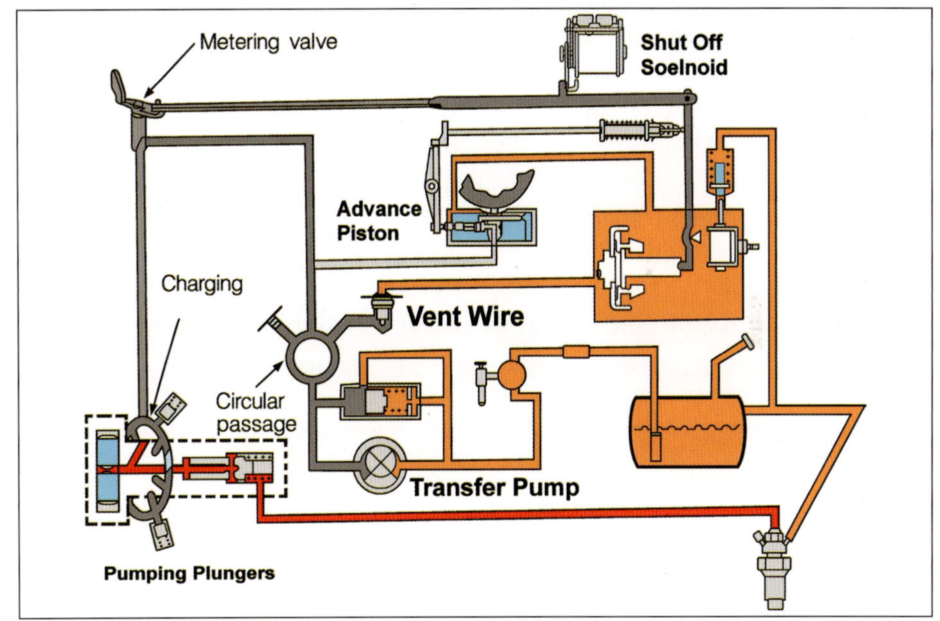

The driveshaft engages the rotor in the head and contains two pumping plungers that are actuated toward each other at the same time by the lobes of the internal cam ring. This takes place by the use of shoes and rollers. The shoes contact the pumping plungers, and the rollers contact the cam lobes. The number of opposing lobes equals eight cylinders. The hydraulic head contains the bore in which the rotor revolves, the metering valve bore, charging ports, trailing port snubber, and the head discharge fittings to the lines and nozzles. This is an inlet metering pump. (Photo Courtesy Stanadyne Diesel Systems)

engine and is provided with a distributor or means of connecting the pump delivery to each of the injection nozzles.

The DB2 pump operation includes metering, pressurization/distribution, lubrication, and timing. The injection pump is a hydraulic fluid pump (not a carburetor) and cannot deliver a rich or lean mixture to the engine. Fuel under lift-pump pressure enters the inlet of the transfer pump.

The driveshaft rotates the rotor, which has slots in its end to operate the blades of the transfer pump inside a stationary cam ring. The transfer pump varies the pressure of the fuel, depending on the speed of the engine. At idle, the transfer pump outlet pressure is approximately 20 to 30 psi. At full engine speed, the transfer pump outlet pressure may be over 120 psi. A transfer pump regulator controls the transfer pressure and has an adjustment made during injection-pump calibration on the test stand.

Diesel fuel under transfer-pump pressure travels through passages to the metering valve. The metering valve is like a spigot that controls how much fuel under transfer-pump pressure enters a circular charging passage in the high-pressure portion of the injection pump. When the valve rotates in a clockwise direction, less fuel enters the charging passage. As the valve rotates in a counterclockwise direction, more fuel enters the charging passage.

A governor mechanism positions the metering valve by balancing the opposing forces of the throttle shaft position and the speed of the injection pump. The governor mechanism includes the metering valve, linkage connected to the metering valve, a governor arm connected to the linkage and pivoting on a pin in the injection pump housing that contacts the governor arm, a governor weight assembly, and a min-max governor assembly.

The governor weight assembly has a weight retainer that is mounted on the rotor and rotated by the driveshaft and six weights that pivot farther outward as the injection pump speed increases. A governor sleeve is moved by the action of the weights and in turn moves the bottom end of the governor arm. The min/max governor assembly mounts in the injection pump housing by sliding on a guide stud and connects the throttle shaft to the upper end of the governor arm.

Min/Max Governor Operation

A fuel shutoff solenoid contacts the metering valve linkage when it is off, blocking fuel from entering the charging passage and stopping engine operation. At any engine speed, the metering valve is positioned by opposing forces of the governor weights. The throttle shaft position acts on the governor arm/linkage with the min/max governor and the tension of its springs at low idle. The injection pump driveshaft speed acts on the governor arm/linkage with force from the rotating weights and the governor sleeve.

Diesel Fuel Pressurizing and Delivery

The circular charging passage in the head of the injection pump has eight ports that align in pairs with the two ports of the rotor pumping chamber. Metered fuel under transfer pump pressure travels through the charging passage and enters the rotor, pushing two pumping plungers outward as it fills the chamber. Two accumulators located in the transfer pressure annulus provide reserve pressure to help maintain a consistent pressure in the charging passage. Each pumping plunger contacts a shoe/roller assembly.

The two shoe/roller assemblies contact the inner surface of a cam ring, which has eight lobes and valleys. During the charging of the pumping chamber, the valleys of the cam ring allow the pumping plungers and shoe/roller assemblies to move outward at a distance controlled by the amount of fuel that fills the pumping chamber.

The DB2 uses a governor that balances the opposing forces of the throttle shaft position and pump speed. It controls minimum and maximum speeds. Parts include a metering valve, linkage to the metering valve, a governor arm, a pivot pin, weights, a thrust sleeve, and min/max springs. The sleeve is moved by the action of the weights.

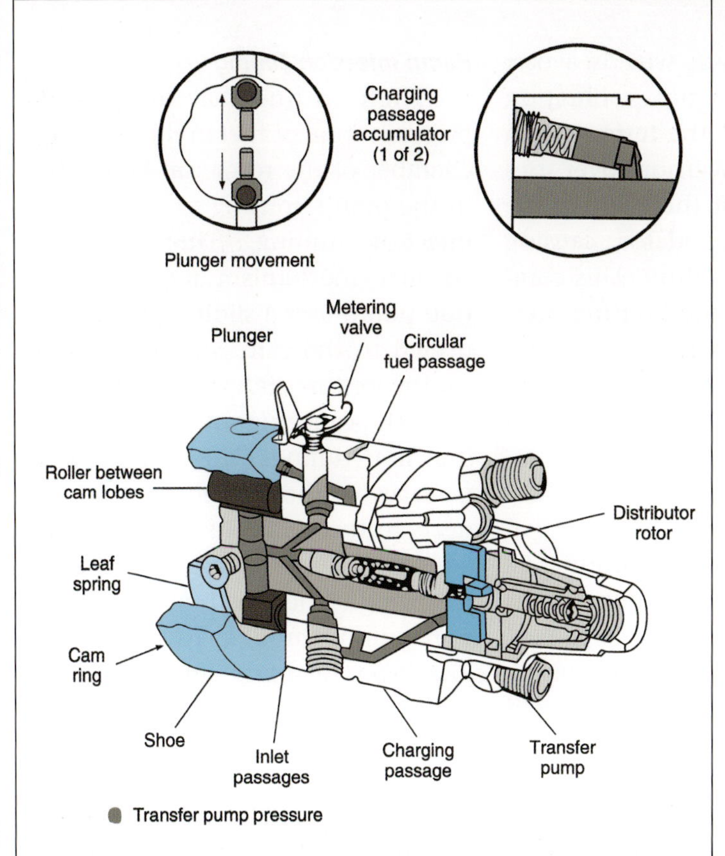

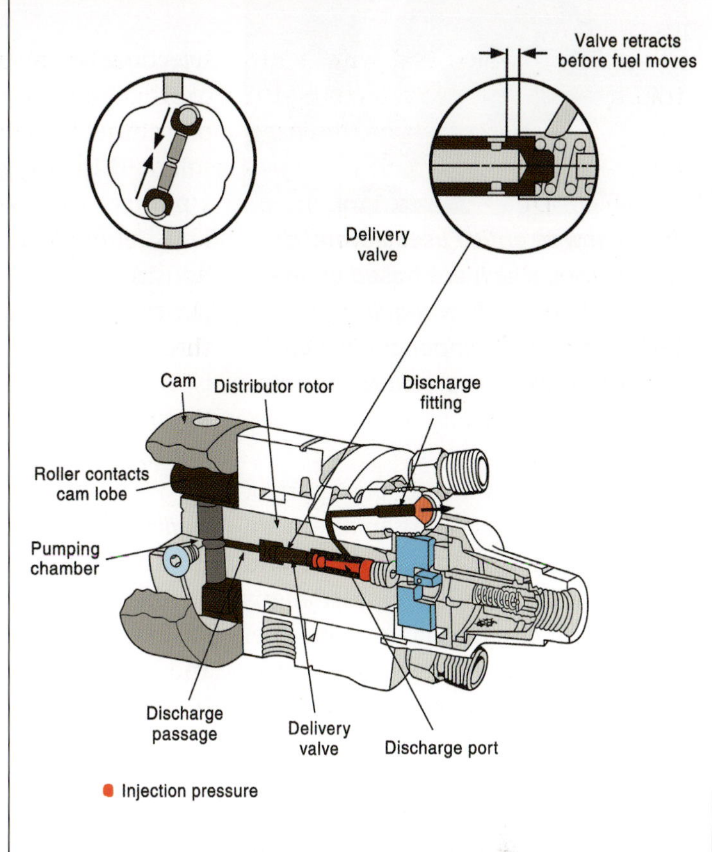

The fuel pressurization process begins when the metering valve allows a quantity of fuel to enter between the two pumping plungers. It will then be pressurized by the action of the rollers and the shoes being pushed by the lobes on the cam ring. The pressurized diesel fuel will then push open the single delivery valve. (Photo Courtesy Stanadyne Diesel Systems)

The fuel delivery process begins at the single delivery valve, where it will retract before it opens as the inlet passages in the head are filled with pressurized fuel. As the rotor continues to turn, the inlet passages move out of registry, ending the charging period. Fuel will exit through one of the eight discharge ports to the injection nozzle. (Photo Courtesy Stanadyne Diesel Systems)

As the injection pump rotor continues its rotation, the two ports of the pumping chamber are blocked from the charging passage. At the same time, two of the cam ring lobes push the shoe/roller assemblies and pumping plungers inward, increasing fuel pressure in the pumping chamber to an amount approximately 100 times greater than the transfer pump pressure.

When the fuel pressure in the pumping chamber rises, a delivery valve is pushed against a spring force. The fuel then moves past the

The vent wire assembly is used to bleed the air out of the pump, and it is the means by which the return flow is regulated through the outlet port. The outlet port has a spring-loaded valve that regulates the flow of fuel from the injection pump housing into the return system. This valve, known as the housing pressure regulator, works with the vent wire assembly to provide a housing pressure of 8 to 10 psi. (Photo Courtesy Stanadyne Diesel Systems)

The vent wire orifice uses several different sizes, which are based on the amount of return flow required. The selection of this component is a part of the injection pump calibration on the test stand.

delivery valve to a discharge port of the rotor. When a port in the head connecting to the injection line and nozzle for a particular cylinder aligns with the rotor discharge port, fuel under a pressure wave exits the injection pump. The process of pressurizing and distributing fuel takes place eight times in one revolution of the injection pump driveshaft and rotor.

The outlet of the transfer pump connects to a restrictor known as the vent wire assembly. This component causes fuel under transfer-pump pressure to undergo a pressure decrease. It also vents the pump of air and uses a wire with hooked ends to assist in this task.

The fuel passing through the vent wire assembly flows inside the pump housing to cool and lubricate most of the injection pump internal parts. An outlet port in the governor cover allows fuel to enter the return system and travel back to the fuel tank. The outlet port has a spring-loaded valve that regulates the flow of fuel from the injection pump housing into the return system. This valve, known as the housing pressure regulator, works with the vent wire assembly to provide a housing pressure of approximately 8 to 10 psi.

The vent wire assembly has several sizes that are based on the amount of return flow required. The selection of the vent wire is a part of the injection-pump calibration procedure done on the test stand. A solenoid in the governor cover uses a plunger to unseat the valve in the housing-pressure regulator, causing housing pressure to drop. This component, known as the housing pressure cold advance (HPCA) solenoid, is on during cold engine operation to cause a change in fuel injection timing.

Trailing Port Snubber

The DB2 pumps on 6.2L and 6.5L engines use a damper orifice that is located right after the discharge port and is called a trailing port snubber.

The trailing port snubber is used to prevent secondary injections and cavitation erosion of a high-pressure system by attenuating the reflected pressure waves. This port trails the discharge port radially and resonates the fuel back into the delivery valve cavity. This cavity is directly drilled into the rotor bore and has a 0.018-inch orifice diameter at the bottom of the hole.

The rotor has a port that is right after the discharge port known as the trailing port snubber, which is radially behind the discharge port. This device acts like a shock absorber to capture high levels of pressurized fuel and absorb it like an accumulator, weaken the pressure wave, and prevent secondary injections. The discharge cycle at each port is about 20 degrees. At the 15-degree point of injection, the snubbing begins for about 22 degrees.

Pump Injection Timing

The cam ring that controls the pressurization of fuel in the pumping chamber of the rotor can be rotated in the pump housing to change fuel injection timing. The automatic advance mechanism for the injection pump uses a sliding piston connected to the cam ring with a pin. As the piston slides in its housing bore, the cam ring rotates to change injection timing. One of the outlet passages of the transfer pump connects to the piston of the automatic advance mechanism, following a passage in the head of the injection pump, through a hollow head locating screw, and into a housing passage. Fuel under transfer-pump pressure pushes the piston, causing the injection timing to advance automatically in relation to engine speed.

The DB2 pump is an inlet-metering pump that has a pumping period with a variable beginning and a constant ending. At minimum throttle positions, the metering valve is only open a small amount, so the plungers only move a small amount. The rollers have to ride a much greater distance up the cam ramp before they can cause the plungers to pressurize the fuel. This course is retarded timing compared to when the throttle is at WOT, which would be the maximum metering valve opening.

At WOT, plunger pressurization begins as soon as the rollers start up the cam ramp and peaks when the rollers are at the cam lobe peaks. Therefore, timing must be advanced at light loads or part throttle to compensate for this injection timing lag. The amount of light load retard is compensated for by the light load advance maintained or obtained from the mechanical light

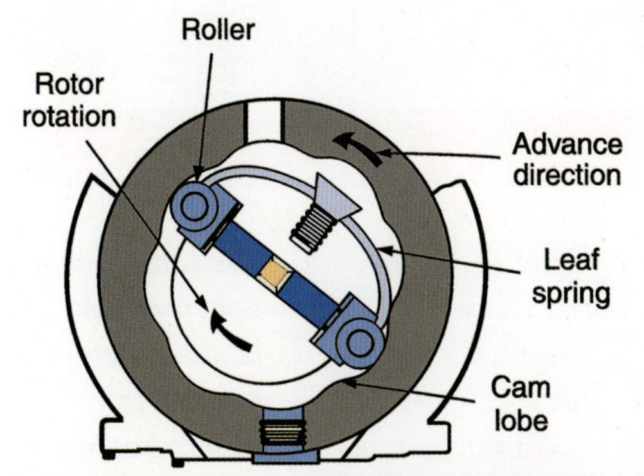

Metering Valve @ WOT/MAX

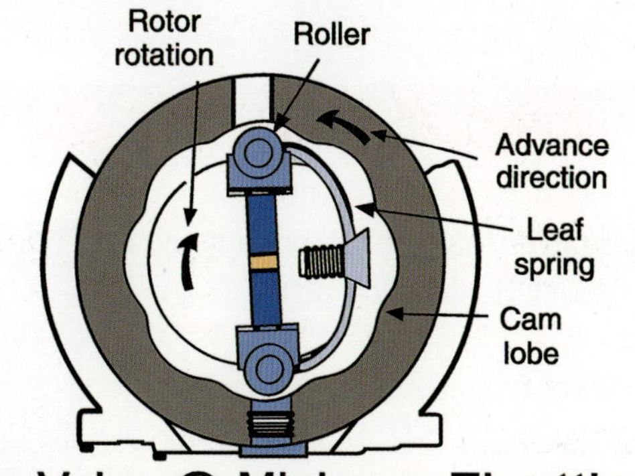

Metering Valve @ Minimum Throttle

At minimum throttle, the metering valve is only open a small amount, so the pumping plungers will need to climb a large distance up the cam ring ramp before fuel will be pressurized. This causes retarded injection timing as compared to wide-open throttle, where the metering valve is wide open and fuel begins to pressurize a lot sooner because fuel will pressurize as the rollers start up the cam ramp. To compensate for this condition, a light load advance rocker lever and face cam are used to push open a service valve in the advance piston, moving it to a more advanced position at light loads or low throttle. (Photo Courtesy Stanadyne Diesel Systems)

load advance system. With this system (having light loads or a nearly closed throttle) the timing would be more advanced because the rocker lever would be moved from the bottom, allowing for the advance piston to move more toward the advance position.

During warm engine operation, fuel under housing pressure pushes on the retard end of the advance mechanism piston, providing lubrication. When the HPCA solenoid is on (during cold engine operation), a drop in housing pressure causes transfer-pump pressure to push the advance piston farther. This results in smoother engine operation during warm-up and combines with the action of the fast-idle solenoid to temporarily increase engine idle speed.

If the HPCA solenoid is off during starting in cold temperatures, white exhaust smoke may result. If the HPCA solenoid is on during warm or hot engine operation, black exhaust during acceleration may result.

Injection Pump Disassembly and Assembly

Performing a complete disassembly and reassembly or making seal replacements on a Stanadyne DB2 pump will require a very clean environment. The reason for this is because the clearance between the head and the rotor in the pump is 1 to 2 microns. One micron is equal to 0.000039 millionths of an inch, one millionth of a meter, or 0.001 mm. This is not a lot of clearance, and a small piece of hard debris from your repair can destroy a head and rotor, necessitating complete pump replacement for $800 to $1,000. However, if you maintain a clean environment and follow the correct service procedures, you can make the proper repair.

You can accomplish the following on-vehicle repairs without removing the pump:

- Governor cover seal replacement
- Guide stud seal replacement
- Throttle shaft seals and governor assembly replacement
- Governor weight retainer checking procedure

HydraClamp

In the fuel injection pump repair business, the Wilton Pow-R-Arm vise is referred to as a HydraClamp. ■

- Sticking advance piston check
- Adjusting fueling by turning the leaf spring screw clockwise 1/16 to 1/8 turn

Pump Terms for DB2 829VP3973

D	Distributor series pump
B	Type of rotor
8	Number of engine cylinders
29	Measured diameter of pumping plungers, 6.2L was 0.290 inch; 6.5L NA was 0.310 inch
VP	Stanadyne accessory code
3973	Pump specification number

Special Wilton Pow-R-Arm Pump Holding Vise

The Wilton Vise Company makes a special vise that you can use to mount the pump. Wilton calls the vise a Wilton Pow-R-Arm (part number 31053). You will need to drill two 3/8-inch holes in the plate and use two 5/16-18 bolts to mount the assembly to the Wilton vise. It retails for about $170. However, you can place the pump in a soft-jaw vise and use shop towels to cushion the soft aluminum parts.

Special Tools

There are several special tools that you will need if you are going to overhaul your DB2 injection pump.

- Synkut oil (GM tool J-33198 or Stanadyne 23451)—Cost $41.16, but you can use Lucas Oil, STP, or Petrogel for about $12.99
- Face cam remember tool (GM Tool J29601, no Stanadyne number)—Cost $29.99 on ebay.com, or you can scribe or paint a line to line up the face cam and throttle shaft
- 1/8-inch Allen wrench
- Stanadyne Support Tool (part number 18332)—You can use a large socket or old sun gear from a GM 350 transmission
- Driveshaft seal installation tool (GM J-29745A or Stanadyne 22727)—Cost $14.17
- Transfer end cap socket (Stanadyne 20548)—Cost $35.73
  The total tool cost estimate is under $100. ■

The total tool cost for what is absolutely needed is approximately $92.88. You will also need a seal kit for around $14 to $25, and if you upgrade to an elastomer insert drive (EID), that costs about $80. The cheapest remanufactured pump that I have seen is around $450 with a core return, but it can be as high at $750. You can find new and used DB2 pumps on the web, but a new pump is generally around $1,063 from GMpartsonline.com.

Pump Servicing

1 Preparation

The Stanadyne DB2 fuel injection pump was used on both the 6.2L and 6.5L diesel engines. The 6.2L used this pump exclusively from the first year of production in 1982 until the end of 6.2L production in 1991. It was used in the non-turbo version of the 6.5L diesel.

When you go through the process of overhauling or resealing a DB2 pump, there are several special tools that you must have to perform an accurate repair. As I go through the overhaul process, I will specifically point out the needed tools.

Stanadyne offers a pump-holding fixture that can mount on the DB2 pump for disassembly and assembly. Due to the nature of this repair, it is a must to ensure accuracy and cleanliness. Of course, you can just mount it in a vise, but due to the delicate nature of this pump, that would be a mistake. The pump-holding fixture assembly (part number 31053) is available from stanadyne.com. This tool and the SPS Kent-Moore version (part number J-29692B) can be used in a vise.

2 Document Injection Lines

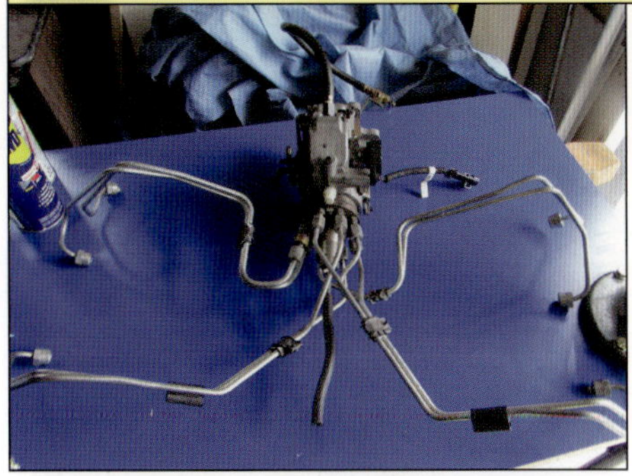

After the pump and lines have been removed from the engine and before mounting the pump in the holding fixture, you will need to remove the injection lines. Take photos of the lines on the pump before removing them to make installation easier and get the right lines connected to the pump. There are a few lines that can be installed in more than one way. If you install the wrong line on for a cylinder, you can get a misfire.

In addition to the photograph, it is also good practice to take a permanent marker and number each line for reassembly. The pump turns counterclockwise, and the firing order is 1-8-7-2-6-5-4-3. The number-1 injection line on later-model engines had an in-line magnetic ring pickup for the magnetic timing meter used in the assembly plant and in the service field with the SPX Kent-Moore Tach-N-Time.

3 Cap Pump Outlets

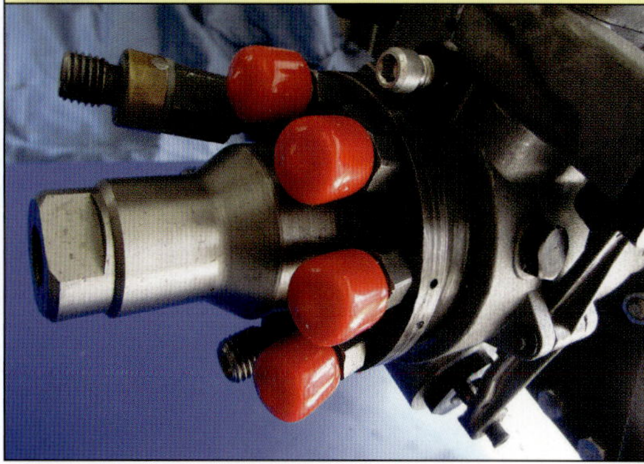

After removal of the injection lines, cap all the pump outlets with rubber caps provided in the Stanadyne injection pump seal kit (part number 24371), which you will need for a total disassembly and reassembly.

4 Remove TPS

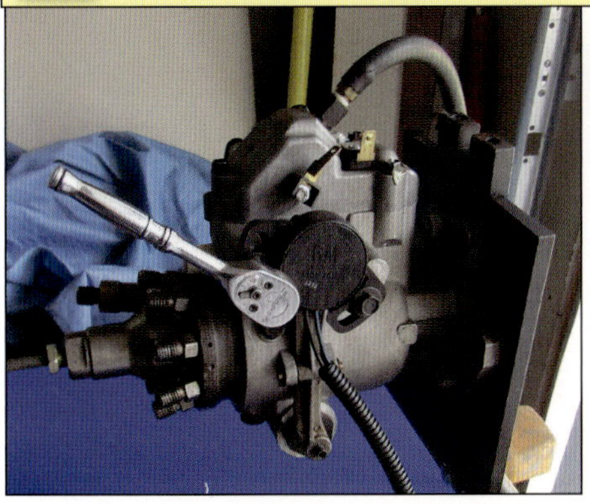

Next, remove the throttle position sensor (TPS). If the pump is used on a truck that has a Turbo Hydramatic 400 automatic transmission, it will have a vacuum regulator valve (VRV) mounted in this location instead of a TPS. The VRV simulates gas engine vacuum to operate the vacuum modulator used as an engine load device.

5 Align Face Cam

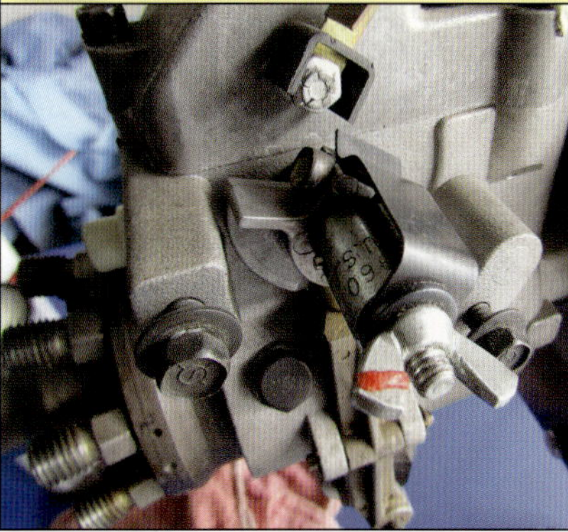

Place the throttle shaft in the low idle position and install SPX Kent-Moore GM special tool J29601 over the throttle shaft with the slots of the tool engaging the pin. Slide the spring clip over the throttle shaft light-load advance face cam and tighten the wing nut. Without loosening the wing nut, pull the tool off of the shaft. This action will provide the right alignment of the face cam to the throttle shaft, which is often done during testing on a test stand. Place the J29601 in a secure place for reassembly.

6 Remove Face Cam

Using a number-27 Torx bit, completely remove the screw holding the face cam and remove the face cam. You will see white or red paint that is used to show if this component has been moved or removed.

7 Remove Shaft Pins and Governor

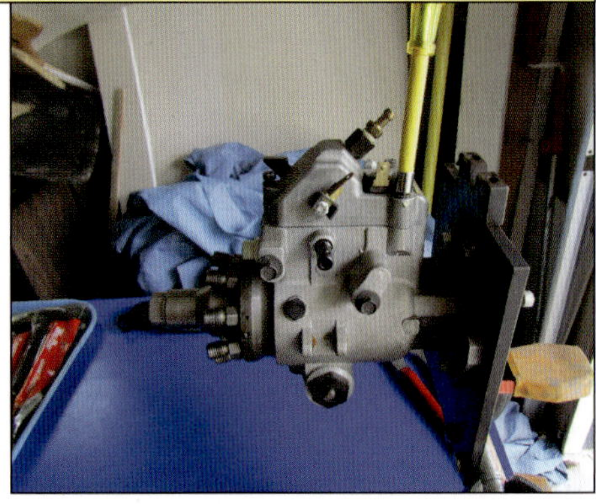

Using a small drift punch, remove the throttle shaft pin and place it in a secure location for reassembly. Some kits may contain a new pin.

Remove the small E-clip from the rocker lever pivot shaft. Then, remove the rocker lever and shaft.

Unscrew the three governor cover screws, and then remove the governor cover and seal. Discard the seal.

8 Remove Electric Shutoff

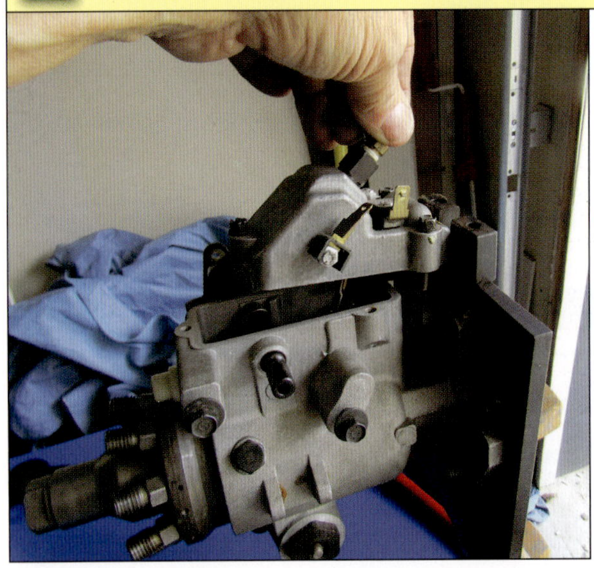

Remove the cover and examine the electric shutoff solenoid and housing pressure cold advance (HPCA) solenoid for damage or debris. Clean out the housing with compressed air. Solenoid plungers should move freely in their bores. You would normally remove these solenoids and replace their seals.

Remove the electric shutoff and cold advance solenoids. Replace the seals and note the position of the washers and seals. The black seal has a lip that goes down (shown at the pointer).

9 Remove Anti-Tamper Plastic Cap

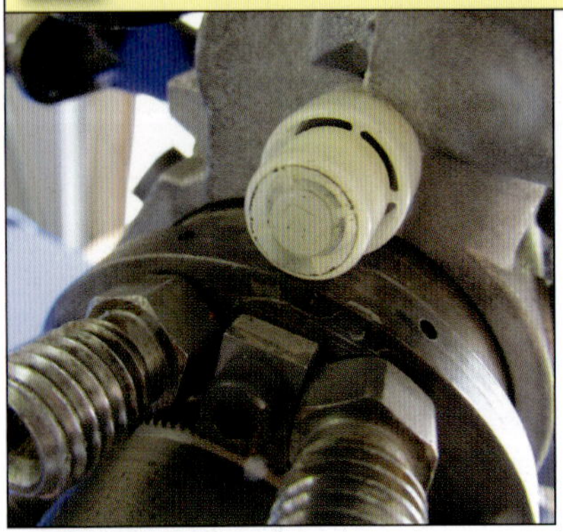

Almost all DB2 pumps use an anti-tamper plastic cap on the guide stud. Use diagonal cutters or a small clip remover to pry off this plastic cap. Because you are not an authorized Stanadyne pump shop, you do not have to reinstall anti-tamper seals. You will find several others in the course of this disassembly.

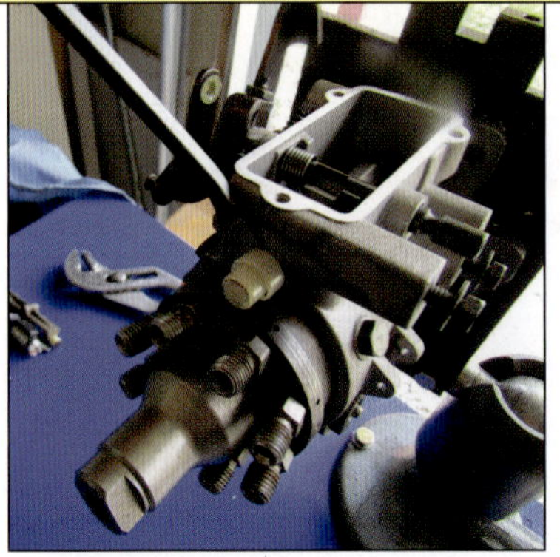

Pry off the anti-tamper plastic cap with a small pry bar and discard it.

10 Remove Guide Stud

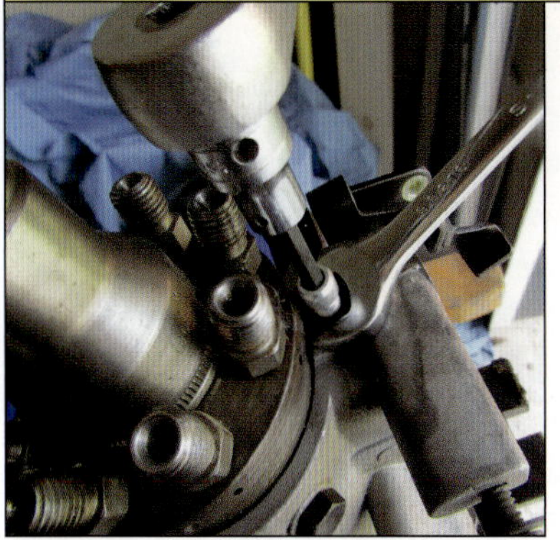

Removing the guide stud usually requires a 1/4-inch Allen wrench on the earlier designs. There are two types of guide studs used. One has a 1/4-inch internal hex that uses a steel washer with a trapped elastomer. The other combination has a 7/16-inch external hex nut and an aluminum washer. This type of washer must be replaced during reassembly. The correct guide stud and washer combination must be used to prevent fuel leakage.

Slowly slide the guide stud out of the min/max governor assembly.

The guide stud is now completely removed from the min/max governor assembly in preparation for the removal of the min/max governor assembly.

11 Remove Governor

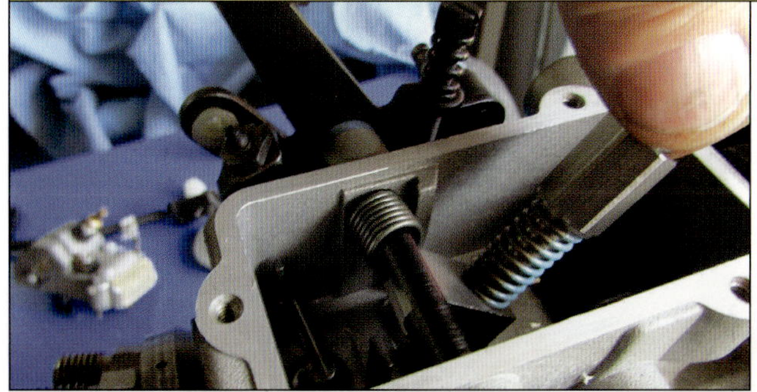

Rotate the min/max governor assembly up and out of the housing and off of the throttle shaft. Late-model pumps have a spring that is wrapped around the throttle shaft and is anchored in the governor block and the housing at the throttle shaft.

Min/Max Governor Note

On 1989-and-later LL4 or J engines with full load, the governor speed was increased to 100 rpm to improve drivability and allow wide-open throttle.

12 Remove Metering Valve

The governor arm and linkage assembly rides up a pivot pin, which is part of the housing.

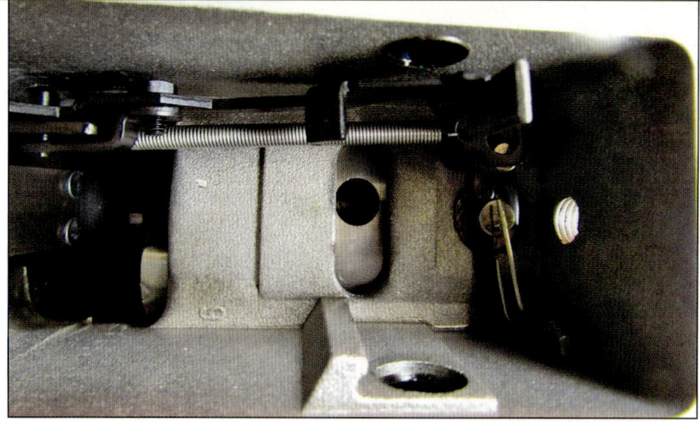

Lift the governor arm off of the metering valve. Shake the governor arm assembly until it releases from the pivot pin that is part of the housing; then, remove the metering valve. Some metering valves have a spring underneath, but most of the 6.2L and 6.5L engines do not use the spring.

13 Remove Vent Wire Orifice

Use a 1/8-inch Allen wrench to remove the vent wire orifice.

The amount of return fuel is controlled by the size of a wire used in the vent wire assembly. The smaller the wire, the greater the flow and vice versa. The vent wire assembly is available in several sizes, which is indicated by a number on the bottom of the orifice body. The higher the number, the thicker the wire and the lower the flow. Pump specification will dictate this flow, which is usually 225 to 375 cc per minute.

Return Oil System

The return oil system provides a controlled flow through the pump housing to maintain a stable condition for the internal pump parts. This fuel flow cools and lubricates the pump and provides automatic air venting of the air that comes through the system by returning it to the tank. This pump will return about 50 percent of the diesel fuel that it pumps.

The return oil vent passage is fed from the transfer pump annulus. This flow is checked and adjusted with the pump on a test stand. However, I am not doing that. The vent passage is located behind the metering valve bore and connects with a short, vertical passage containing the bent wire assembly that leads to the governor compartment or the housing. If some air enters the transfer pump, it immediately passes through the vent passage and flows from the housing to the fuel tank via the return lines. Housing pressure is controlled by a spring-loaded ball check fitting located in the governor cover.

The advance piston that used

14 Remove DB2 Timing Device

This opening is used to mount a timing measuring device, which is used on the test stand.

Remove the DB2 pump timing calibration cover and its gasket. Discard the gasket.

15 Pry out Cam Advance Pin

After removing the advance pin plug, find the cam advance pin, which can be tight in the advance piston. I recommend using a pair of diagonal cutting pliers to grab the head of the cam advance pin and pry it out.

Using a 5/16-inch Allen socket, remove the head-locating screw. You may have to use a large breaker bar or a ratchet with a 1/2-inch drive because this tends to be screwed in tight.

16 Remove Head Locating Screw

Using a 5/16 Allen hex socket, remove the head locating screw. You may have to use a large breaker bar or a ratchet with a 1/2-inch drive because this tends to be screwed in tight.

17 Remove Cam Advance Pin

Remove the cam advance pin using needle-nose pliers. If you find some resistance in removing the pin, use a small pair of diagonal cutters to clamp onto the end of the pin and gently lift it out.

18 Remove Advance Piston

Using a 1-inch socket and a heavy breaker bar, remove the two advance piston plugs on each side of the pump. The plug on the rocker lever side (left side) will have a plunger in it. There will be a spring in the advance piston; be careful not to lose it when you remove the rocker lever side plug.

Push in on the advance piston and slide it out. If there is any significant resistance, the advance piston was likely sticking. Stanadyne does have a procedure for reaming out this bore and installing a 0.008-inch oversized advance piston. This procedure is beyond what we are doing here, so if you encounter this condition, replace the housing with a new standard-size advance piston.

a screw was changed to having the orifice directly machined into the advance piston. The orifice size was 0.030 inch for 1982 and 1983 pumps and was increased to 0.040 inch for 1984 (Stanadyne part number 24433). Some 6.2L diesel engines may experience a loss of power along with erratic engine operation and excessive black or white smoke. If the on-vehicle diagnosis indicates that the injection pump may be at the root of this problem, you should suspect a worn or binding advance piston.

A new nickel-plated advance piston was introduced on the 1980 6.2L engine. This nickel-plated advance piston reduces piston bore wear and

the chance for piston seizure. This piston has been made available as a service part for all 6.2L diesel and DB2 pumps. The part number for the standard advance piston is 27865 and for the 0.008-inch oversize piston is 27869. At the same time as this change was made, a new head-locating screw with the nylon filter (part number 24566) was introduced to prevent contamination from reaching the advance piston.

19 Pull Throttle Shaft Assembly

Now, simply pull the throttle shaft assembly through the housing. Remove the Mylar washer and O-ring seals from the throttle shaft and discard them. Make note of which end of the Mylar washer was on the throttle shaft that the face cam rides against.

19 Pull Throttle Shaft Assembly *continued*

Lift out the throttle shaft return spring that was anchored at the housing to the governor block.

Transfer Pump Service

If the goal of your repair is to replace the governor weight cage or do a resealing that does not involve the transfer pump, the following procedures are optional. They require the replacement of the end seal if it is leaking.

Important!

! If you do not have Stanadyne tool number 20548, do not perform this procedure. The torque on the end cap is critical, and cannot be retorqued without the special socket. Sure you could remove it and reinstall it with an adjustable wrench, but you will not get the proper torque on the end cap or the correct transfer pump pressure.

20 Loosen End Cap

Loosen and remove the transfer pump and locking screw plate and seal from the hydraulic head. Discard the seal.

For this operation, Stanadyne tool number 20548 is needed. It is a special socket that fits over the transfer pump end cap. Loosen the end cap. Do not remove it at this time.

21 Remove Head and Rotor Assembly

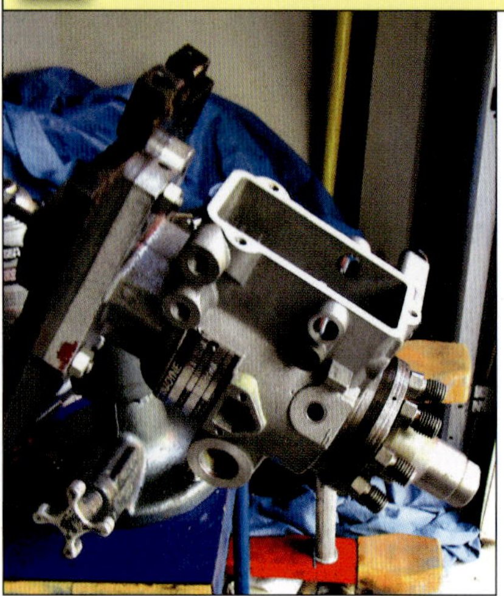

Take a 1/2-inch socket and remove the two locking screws. Rotate the pump housing so that the transfer pump and bases point down (as shown). Now use both hands to grasp the whole head assembly with the transfer pump caps and twist and pull to remove the entire head and rotor assembly with governor weight cage.

Place this entire assembly in the special Stanadyne holding fixture tool (part number 18332) or a large deep-well socket or a standard vise. You can also use a GM 350 transmission sun gear and shell as the holding fixture.

Governor Weight Retainer Ring Failures

In the early days of the 6.2L diesel, Stanadyne used a flexible Pellethane (polyurethane) governor weight retainer ring that connected the governor weight cage to a drive member that connected to the rotor. This was sort of a rag joint coupling that compensated for the torsional twist of the rotor in the pump. These Pellethane rings failed after a number of miles because of the heating and cooling that takes place in the pump.

Failure of the ring is generally heat related and will most likely result in a rough idle condition, and in some cases, the engine may not run. A failed ring will break apart into small black particles, plugging the fuel return check line. If you remove the governor covering and see tiny black pieces inside, you most likely have a failed governor weight retainer ring. Check the cage with the governor cover off by taking a screwdriver and pushing against the weight retainer in both directions. If the retainer moves more than 1/16 inch and doesn't return, the retaining ring has failed. To replace it, remove the pump and follow the procedures in this book.

This problem was resolved in 1986 with the release of the elastomer insert drive (EID) cage. This new drive mechanism by Viton consists of six inserts in a self-contained drive mechanism and is completely interchangeable with all weight retainer rings. The GM part number is 22529991. Always replace the weight retainer with an EID. ■

22 Remove Governor Weight Cage Assembly

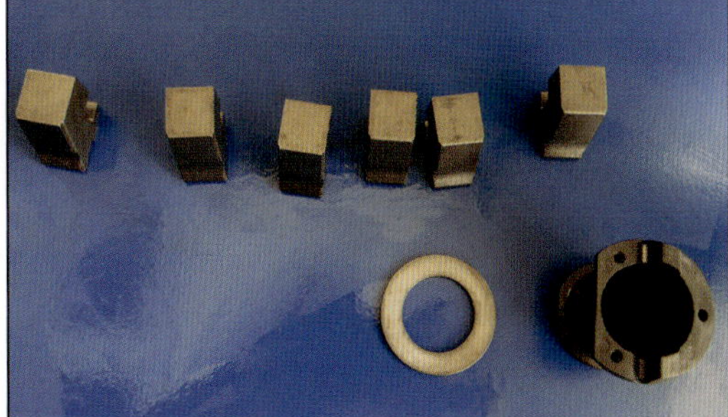

Remove the six governor weights along with the thrust sleeve washer and the thrust sleeve. Place them in a clean and secure location for reassembly.

Take a pair of snap-ring pliers that has tips that are not worn. Remove the snap ring that holds the weight cage to the rotor assembly.

Remove the governor weight cage assembly. The one that we have in this pump is the latest design, which has the elastomer insert drive (EID) cage.

23 Examine Cam Lobes

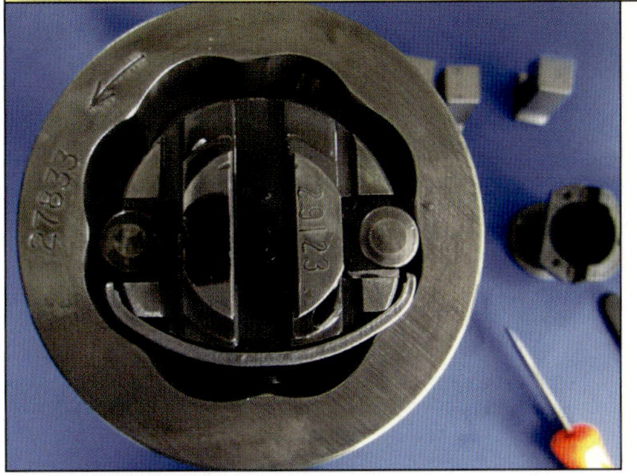

Remove the pump timing cam ring from the rotor assembly and place it in a clean and secure location. Examine the cam lobes for any wear. If wear or scuffing is found on any of the cam lobes, the cam ring must be replaced.

The cam in this pump is Stanadyne part number 27833, which is a wrought cam. This cam design is stronger than this previous design, which was a sintered metal cam. On the 0.290-inch-diameter pumping plunger, the sintered cam can take up to 8,000 psi and the wrought cam can handle up to 9,700 psi. On the 0.310-inch-diameter pumping plunger, the sintered cam is 7,000 psi and the wrought cam is 8,600 psi. Note that the directional arrow on the cam goes in a counterclockwise direction because this is a CCW drive pump.

24 Remove Driveshaft Seals

Remove the driveshaft snap ring from inside the pump with a pair of snap-ring pliers that has tips that are not worn. The snap ring retention of the driveshaft in this pump is the latest design.

There were three driveshaft retention types: Type 1, Type 2, and Type 3. The Type 3 design (shown) uses snap ring part number 10445. The Type 2 design used an elastomer O-ring. The Type 1 (original design) used a wire ring.

With the driveshaft removed, pull off the three driveshaft seals.

Take a photo so that you can remember the positioning of the driveshaft seal. The first black cup seal lip faces the engine side of the pump driveshaft. The center seal is red and made of Viton. Its lip faces toward the pump rotor. The last black seal lip also faces toward the pump rotor.

25 Remove Roller Bearing

The pump housing has a roller bearing at the very end that the driveshaft rides on. Use a standard blindfold puller, like the one here, to remove this bearing.

Using the appropriate-size driver, install a new bearing into the housing.

26 Remove Transfer Pump Liner

The transfer pump is a positive-displacement pump that will discharge a certain amount of diesel fuel for each revolution of the rotating blades.

Remove the rollers and shoes from the rotor (as an option you can remove the pumping plungers, but it is not necessary) and invert the head and rotor assembly. Place it in the Stanadyne rotor support tool (part number 16313).

Remove the transfer pump liner as an assembly with the four transfer pump blades and the two springs enclosed in the liner, not disturbing the position of the pump blades. The blades must have remained in the exact position that they were when you removed them.

27 Remove Transfer Pump Retainers

Remove the transfer pump inlet screen filter pump regulator and seal. Discard the seal.

Remove the transfer pump liner locating spring with a pair of needle-nose pliers.

Using a small screwdriver or a pick, pry out the two transfer pump retainers.

28 Remove Pump Motor

Gently remove the pump rotor from the hydraulic head. Place it in a bath of calibration fluid (not diesel fuel) to keep it free from contamination.

Optional Inspections and Adjustments

The injection pump is designed to deliver a metered amount of fuel at the proper time. Therefore, it is incapable of delivering a rich or lean mixture. **PRO TIP** The procedures in steps 29, 30, and 31 are optional for most 6.2L rebuilders who do not have the special tools to perform these procedures.

29 Measure Driveshaft Tangs

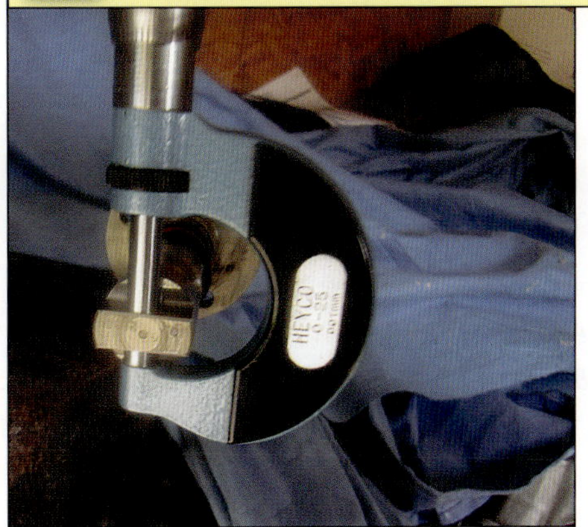

Use a 25-mm metric micrometer to measure the distance across the flats of the driveshaft tang. The measurement must not be less than 7.75 mm. The driveshaft seal area must also be free of nicks and scratches.

The micrometer shows the measurement at exactly 7.820 inches, which is well within the specifications for this pump.

30 Measure Pumping Plungers

Use the micrometer to check the measurement of the pumping plungers. Pumping plungers are sized as A, B, C, or D. Consult the Stanadyne injection pump specifications for the correct replacement parts, which are also available through Amazon.

31 Adjust Fueling Leaf Spring and Rollers

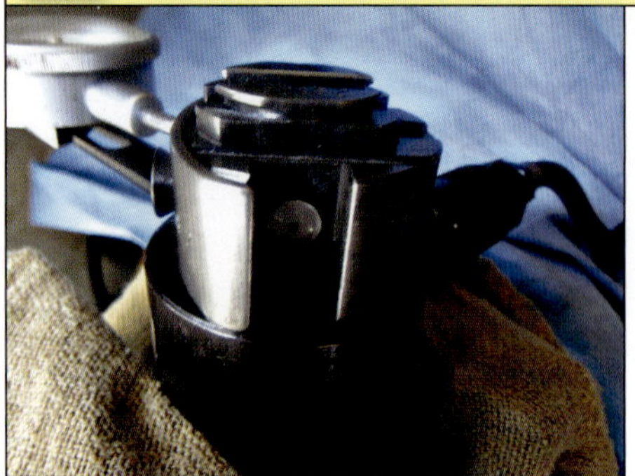

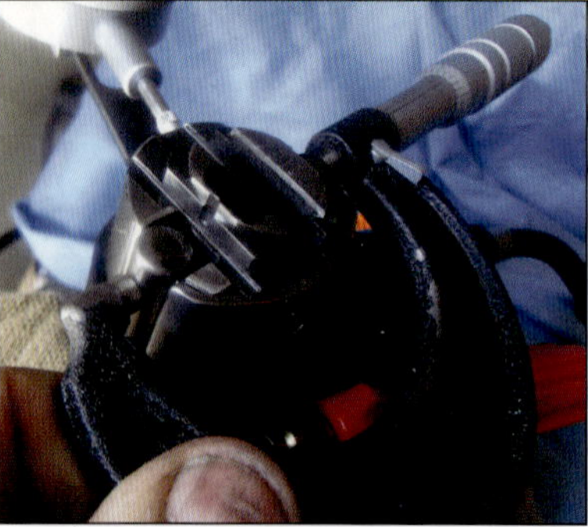

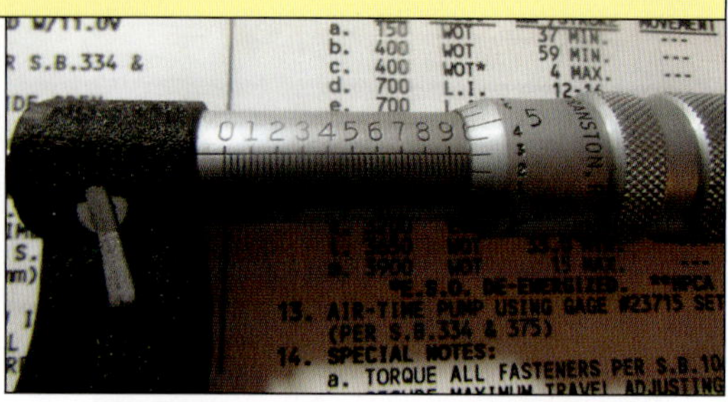

To adjust the fueling leaf spring, a special Stanadyne tool (part number 19969) is needed along with compressed air. This tool also has a built-in dial indicator to check the total indicator runout (TIR) of the rotor.

Using the same tool (part number 19969), check the TIR of the rotor. The maximum eccentricity is 0.008 inch (0.2 mm) TIR.

Install the rotor into the tool assembled with the pumping plungers, rollers, and shoes to make the roller-to-roller adjustment. Apply 30 psi of air pressure to the tool to expand the pumping plungers, rollers, and shoes. Use a 2-inch English micrometer to adjust the fueling with the leaf spring to specifications.

This is pump number DB2831-4927 for a late-model 6.5L turbocharged mechanical pump engine. The roller-to-roller dimension is 1.978 inch (plus or minus 0.001 inch). Turn the leak spring clockwise to increase this dimension and counterclockwise to decrease it.

32 Examine the Rotor

Examine the rotor for any scratches or pitting on the running surfaces. Make sure that the pumping plungers move freely in the rotor.

Injection Pump Rotor

The heart of the diesel injection pump is the rotor. Due to the extremely close tolerances of the head and rotor assemblies, a thermal relief group has been incorporated into the rotor design. Thermal shock can cause a head assembly to contract, resulting in seizure of the head and rotor. To lessen this possibility, a reduction in the rotor diameter at the center between the ports was added. The rotor in 1984 pumps use residual pressure balancing ports. The small ports operate by simultaneously registering with the discharge outlets right after each injection. This operation allows a balance of the residual pressure between the lines and helps smooth out the operation and sounds of the engine.

A rotor seizure can occur due to a loss of clearance between the head and rotor during the transient warm-up condition. Heat generated by the shearing oil film at the hydraulic head-to-rotor interface causes heating of the head and rotor. Because the mass of the rotor is much less than that of the head, it heats up and expands at a faster rate. The clearance at the interface of the head and rotor is thereby reduced, and the possibility of rotor seizure is possible. A relief group was added to the diameter of the rotor to minimize rotor seizures.

Pump Reassembly

I cannot emphasize enough the importance of cleanliness during the reassembly of this DB2 fuel injection pump. Any particles of dirt or debris can damage the pump. During reassembly, use calibration fluid as a lubricant to clean parts. As a last resort, WD-40 or diesel fuel can be used, but diesel fuel is not recommended due to its higher volatility and evaporation rate compared to calibration fluid and WD-40. What this means is that as the fuel evaporates, it leaves a residue that can cause parts to stick and rotors to seize. You will also need Synkut oil special tool J-33198 or Stanadyne tool 23451 for reassembly.

33 Prep Transfer Pump

If you made or did not make the roller-to-roller adjustment, install the rotor into the head and remove the rollers and shoes. Place the head and rotor assembly back on the Stanadyne rotor support tool (part number 16313) in preparation for reassembly of the transfer pump.

34 Oil the Housing

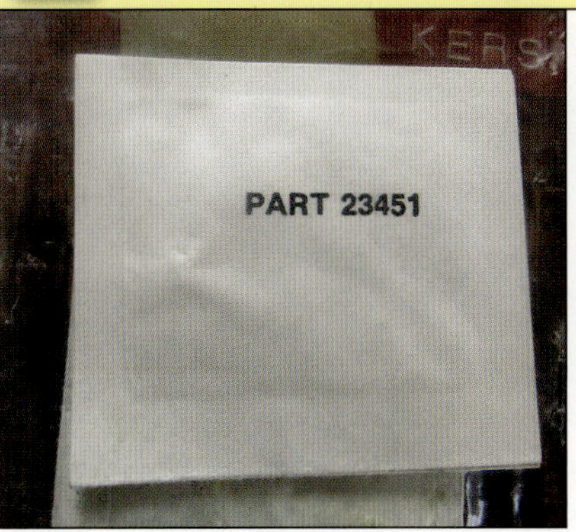

Obtain a packet of Synkut oil (part number 23451) or a bottle of J-33198 and coat the inside of the housing, where the head and rotor assembly will be installed. Also make sure a complete new seal kit is available for your pump, such as seal kit 33814 that is available from Stanadyne, Amazon, or most automotive parts suppliers.

35 Install Driveshaft

Using Special Tool J-29745A or Stanadyne Tool 22727, apply a liberal amount of Synkut oil to the driveshaft seals. Install them on the driveshaft with the first black seal lip toward the engine end of the pump driveshaft, followed by the red Viton seal lip in the opposite direction toward the tang end of the driveshaft, followed by the second black seal lip also toward the driveshaft tang.

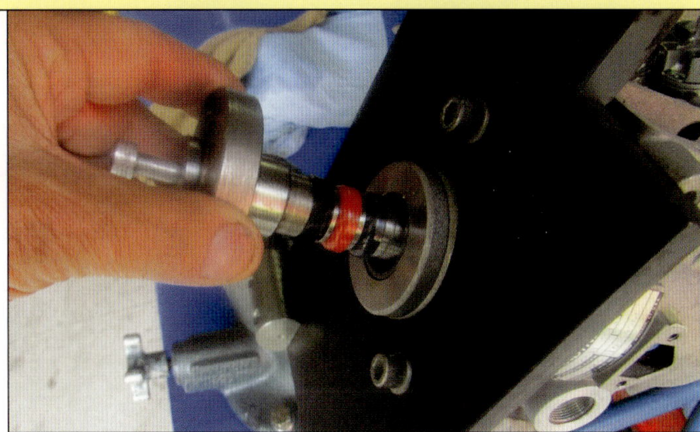

Using a liberal amount of the Synkut oil, install the driveshaft into the pump housing with a slow twisting motion.

36 Install Snap Ring

Install the snap ring using a pair of snap-ring pliers that do not have worn tips. This snap ring does not have a right side up, so install it in either direction.

After installing the driveshaft retention snap ring, look down in the housing to make sure that it is fully seated in the groove.

37 | Install Pump Blades and Springs

Install the two transfer pump retainers with the aid of a small screwdriver. You will need to maneuver these retainers around a little bit before they will slip into place.

Make sure to line up the hole in the head between the two square cuts in the transfer pump retainers.

Install the transfer pump liner retainer spring around the two transfer pump retainers.

Line up the hole and then install the pump liner, the four transfer pump blades, and the two springs between them. If you followed the procedure at the beginning of the disassembly, you should have the liner blades and springs as an undisturbed assembly so that you can install them as an assembly. Remember that utmost cleanliness is required during this procedure. The blades must have remained in the exact position that they were when you removed them.

38 | Install End Caps

Install the transfer pump pressure regulator, making sure that the pin fits into the hole in the head between the transfer pump retainers.

Install the transfer pump inlet filter and a new seal. It will fit directly on top of the transfer pump pressure regulator seal.

Install the transfer pump end cap using Stanadyne tool 20548 hand tight. Do not torque it until the head and rotor have been installed in the pump housing and secured with the head-locking screws and head-locating screw.

39 | Install Cam Ring

Flip the head and rotor over and install the transfer pump end cap end into the Stanadyne holding fixture tool (part number 18332) or a large deep-well socket or a standard vise. Install the rollers and shoes into the rotor and the pumping plungers if you did not already install them.

Install the cam ring with the part number facing upward and the directional arrow in the counterclockwise position. Pump rotation is expressed as viewed from the drive end of the pump. This is the wrought cam used for higher pumping pressures.

40 Install Governor Weight Cage

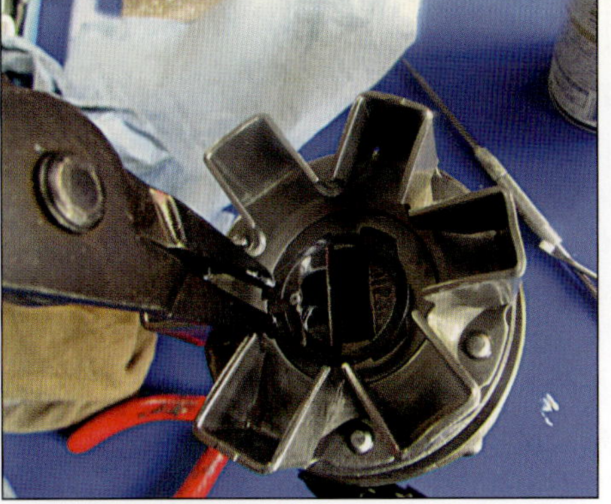

Inspect the governor weight cage to make sure it is tight and has no movement. Do not use the older governor weight cage with a Pel-lethane ring; only use the EID type.

Install the governor weight cage onto the rotor using unworn Truarc snap ring pliers. The snap ring can be installed in either direction.

Install the governor weight cage drive ball in the hole that connects the weight cage to the rotor. In this photo, you will notice a piece of blue fuzz from a shop towel. It is critical that you wash away any debris (such as this) and prevent it from entering your pump.

41 Place Thrust Washer

Place the six weights in the cups of the governor weight cage and place the thrust washer on top of the tang ends of the weights. Place the thrust sleeve on top of the thrust washer.

Push down on the governor thrust sleeve and the thrust washer will fall into the tang grooves of the governor weights.

42 Prep Pump Housing

Locate the pump housing in the down position so that the governor weights do not fall out on installation of the head and rotor assembly. If not already done, lubricate the inside of the pump housing with Synkut oil where the head and rotor will be placed.

43 Align Tangs

Inside the housing, line up the dot on the tang end of the drive-shaft at the 6 o'clock posi-tion to line up with the dot on the rotor also at 6 o'clock.

44 Insert Head

Install a new seal on the head assembly lubricated with Synkut oil. Grasp the entire head and rotor assembly with the governor weight cage at the top with the rotor dot lined up with the drive tang dot and the head-locking screw holes on the top. Insert the entire assembly into the housing and use a slight twisting motion until you see the head-locking holes in the holes of the pump housing. Never force it. If it jams, remove it and start over. Be very careful not to insert the head assembly too far into the housing because if it goes in too far past the locking bolt holes, the seal will tear in the vent wire opening and cause a leak.

Once the head and rotor assembly is in the pump housing, install the head-locking screws finger tight. Check through the timing tool opening to make sure that the timing line on the cam ring is on top of the hole in the cam.

45 Torque Head

Looking inside the top of the pump housing, make sure you can see the hole in the cam ring where you can view the 5/32 Allen head screw used to adjust the leaf spring for fueling. This is where 6.2L owners can turn up the fueling amount.

Install the head-locating screw into the pump and torque it to 20 to 25 Nm (120 to 180 in-lbs).

Torque both head locking screws to 20 to 25 Nm (120 to 180 in-lbs).

46 Install Vent Wire Orifice

Install the vent wire orifice, using a 1/8-inch Allen wrench into the head inside the governor area of the pump housing.

Torque the vent wire orifice to 2.8 to 3.4 Nm (25 to 30 in-lbs).

47 Install Advance Piston

Install the nickel-plated advance piston in the bore with the feed-channel pressure port facing toward the head-locating screw and head.

Install the cam advance pin into its bore, making certain that it engages the cam ring, which you can view from inside the governor area of the housing. Install the timing window cover with a new gasket.

48 Install Servo Valve and Spring

Install the servo valve and spring into the advance piston bore with spring facing outward.

Install the left-side advance hole plug and torque it to 34.7 to 42.4 Nm (307 to 375 in-lbs).

Install the spring or right-side advance hole plug with the light load advance push pin and torque it to 34.7 to 42.4 Nm (307 to 375 in-lbs).

49 Torque Timing Cover

Torque the timing cover to 2.8 to 3.4 Nm (25 to 30 in-lbs).

Install the cam advance pin and cap with a new seal and torque it to 8.5 to 11.3 Nm (75 to 100 in-lbs).

50 | Install Governor Arm

Install the governor arm onto the pivot pin in the housing using a rocking motion. Make sure that the tangs of the governor arm contact the governor thrust sleeve.

Lubricate the metering valve with calibration oil and install it in the head; then, place the arm of the governor assembly onto the metering valve.

51 | Install Governor Assembly

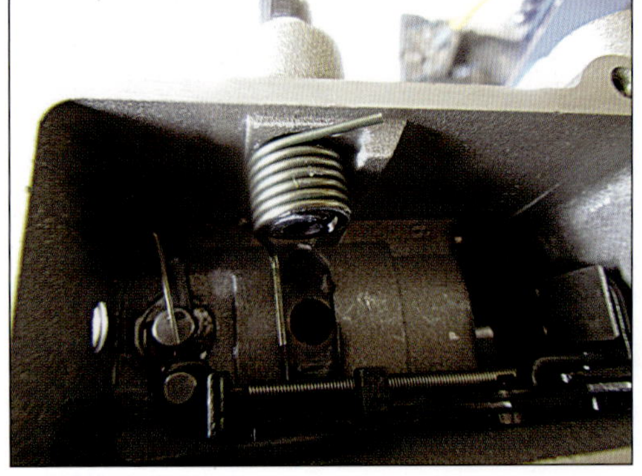

Install new seals on the throttle shaft and make sure the spacer is installed near the throttle lever end. Push the throttle shaft inward about 1/2 inch so that the governor thrust return spring can be placed on it.

Push the throttle shaft all the way into the housing through the spring and rotate the throttle shaft to the left while installing the min/max governor assembly. Place the bottom of the spring into the groove in the governor block.

52 | Install Spring Tang

Make sure that the long link of the governor thrust return spring bottom is in the groove in the governor block and the top spring tang is in position for installation into the housing.

Using a pair of needle-nose pliers, bend the top spring tang downward into the housing groove.

53 Install Guide Stud

Install the guide stud seal and washer and insert it into the governor block. Make sure that the guide stud is under the metering valve spring.

Check the movement of the governor and metering valve on the guide stud.

Torque the guide stud to 9 to 10 Nm (80 to 90 in-lbs) with the locking nut loose; then, tighten the locking nut.

54 Install Rocker Lever

Install the Mylar washer on the throttle shaft followed by the face cam. Then, install the number 27 Torx screw into the face cam.

Install the rocker lever onto the pump housing.

Install a new E-clip that holds the rocking lever pivot pin. Snap-on makes a tool to install these very small E-clips.

55 Torque Transfer Pump End Caps

Torque the transfer pump end cap to 41 to 50 Nm (360 to 440 in-lbs) using the Stanadyne special tool (part number 20548) at a cost of $35.73. It is a must-have item because this torque will maintain the original transfer pump pressure, which is only adjusted on a calibration stand.

Install a new seal onto the transfer pump end cap lock screw and tighten it to 8 to 9 Nm (70 to 80 in-lbs).

56 Tighten Governor Cover Screws

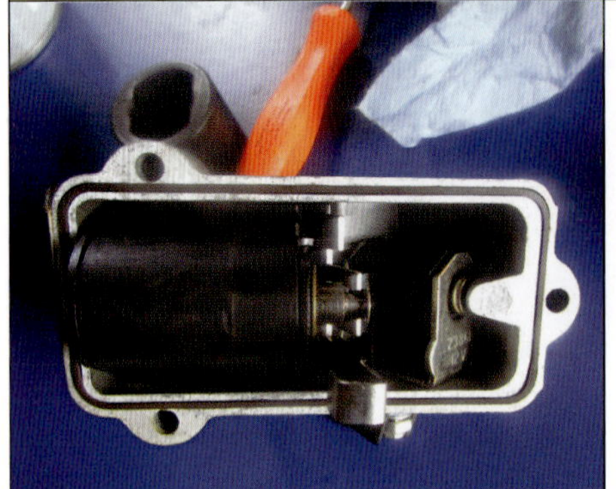

Reassemble the shutoff and HPCA solenoids into the governor cover. Install a new seal onto the governor cover.

Place the governor cover slightly toward the drive end of the pump and slide it forward toward the head of the pump until it lands on the pump housing. Stanadyne makes a special tool (part number 26528) to lock the shutoff solenoid in the retracted position that will allow an easy installation of the governor cover.

Tighten the governor cover screws to 4 to 5 Nm (35 to 45 in-lbs).

57 Install Face Cam

Install a new drive pin into the throttle shaft and place the face cam placement tool (J-29601) onto the face-cam drive pin. Insert a 0.005-inch feeler gauge between the throttle shaft Mylar washer and the housing. Push the throttle shaft into the housing and squeeze the advance cam to remove any clearance.

Using a number 27 Torx bit, tighten the face cam to 3 to 4 Nm (28 to 32 in-lbs).

58 Install TPS or VRV

Install the TPS or VRV onto the injection pump and hand tighten the adjusting screws because these devices will be adjusted to the correct position using either a DMM or a mity-vac with the right gauge block between the throttle stop and the pump housing stop. (This adjustment will be covered in chapter 8).

Install the number-1 cylinder magnetic pickup (if equipped).

Injection Pump Test Stand

Accurate fueling adjustment testing requires a test stand, which is also called a pump calibration stand. The test stand uses a 2- to 15-hp electric motor to drive the injection pump. This motor simulates the diesel engine with the RPM controlled on the machine by the operator and not by the engine's throttle opening. Various tests and adjustments are performed, such as shutoff solenoid pull-in voltage, housing pressure cold advance solenoid operation, face cam positioning, min/max governor operation, return oil volume, housing pressure, transfer pump pressure, and automatic advance adjustments. Actual calibration of the fuel delivery is not adjustable within the head and rotor assembly, but it is affected by some of the adjustments that I just mentioned. Various RPM ranges and throttle openings are used to check the output of the fuel injection pump.

59 Place on Test Stand

In the service field, this pump would be placed on a test or calibration stand to test fueling and make timing and return fuel adjustments. They are adjustable within the head and rotor assembly, but it is affected by some of the adjustments that have been mentioned. Various RPM ranges and throttle openings are used to check the output of the pump.

60 Install Fuel Injection Lines

The final procedure before installation back on the engine is to install the fuel injection lines based on your markings or the photo taken prior to removal.

ENGINE INSPECTION, CLEANING, AND MACHINING

At this stage, the 6.2L/6.5L engine should be completely disassembled. Several clean workbenches should be available to tag and organize parts for a proper inspection and measurements. Document your disassembly by using photographs, tags, or arranging the components in the order of disassembly. Then, examine and measure all of the component parts to determine what needs to be replaced in the engine.

Engine Block Inspection and Service

The engine components are in four groups:
• Group 1: The cylinder block assembly
• Group 2: The intake and exhaust components, including the intake manifold, exhaust manifolds, emission components, and turbocharger (if equipped)
• Group 3: The top end of the engine, which includes the cylinder heads and the valvetrain, which includes poppet valves, roller lifters, roller lifter retainers, and rocker-arm assemblies
• Group 4: The bottom-end components, which includes the crankshaft, connecting rods, pistons, harmonic balancer, and the flywheel or flexplate

Most DIYers are capable of visually inspecting and cleaning most of the components in groups 2 and 3. Group 1 and Group 4 may require the use of the machine shop for some of the inspection. In Group 3, the cylinder heads may also require the use of a machine shop for pressure testing.

The 6.2L or 6.5L engine inspection procedure will require several precision measuring tools, such as a digital vernier caliper, different-size micrometers, a precision straight-edge, a dial bore gauge, feeler gauges, a dial indicator set, and some GM special tools (covered in chapter 2). Perform the inspection work using the proper OEM methods and tools. Using components worn beyond the acceptable limits will decrease the performance of your rebuilt 6.2L or 6.5L diesel engine.

Cylinder Block Cleaning

1 Determine Level of Cleaning Necessary

Start with Group 1, which is the cylinder block. Inspect and evaluate the cylinder block for the level of cleaning needed. The tools needed include various bristle brushes, a gasket scraper, and a degreasing solvent.

Important!

Whenever using cleaning solvents for cleaning parts, follow the solvent manufacturer's recommendations and all safety precautions. Always wear protective clothing when using cleaning solvents. Also wear safety glasses with side shields throughout the cleaning, inspection, and repair process. A source of compressed air set at the US Occupational Safety & Heath Administration (OSHA) safety pressure will be helpful.

The block and most likely the cylinder heads will need to be sent to a local machine shop to be pressure tested because you most likely do not have the proper equipment to do pressure testing. While the machine shop has the block, have them check for cracks at the crankshaft main bearing webs.

Continue the cylinder block inspection and check for cracks.

Clean the cylinder bores with hot water and detergent. Then, using a fingernail, check the cylinder bore for fine vertical scratches. You should not be able to feel fine vertical scratches. They can cause minor oil consumption. Honing is used to remove fine vertical scratches if found.

If doing an immersion cleaning in a hot tank, remove all of the oil gallery plugs and core plugs (freeze plugs) before immersing the block into the cleaning tank. You can use a small-bore rifle-cleaning wire brush to clean out the oil gallery bores if the gallery plugs have been removed.

The 6.2L and 6.5L engines have an electric heater that is installed in one of the core plug holes, and it will need to be removed if the block is going to be placed in a hot tank. This is commonly referred to as a block heater.

Depending on the age and the condition of the cylinder block, it may need to be immersed in a cleaning tank, and preferably a heated one, to clean out all of the core passages. After the block comes out of the tank, perform a visual check before further testing or measurements. During engine disassembly, internal components should have been removed so there is a bare block.

Cast-iron blocks use a core box with a liner that shapes the outside of the cylinder block. Oil or sand cores shape the internal openings and passages in an engine block. The cores are supported within the core box. Cast iron is poured into the core box and flows between the cores and the core box liner. As the cast iron cools, the core breaks up. When the cast iron has hardened, it is removed from the core box. The pieces of sand core are removed through the openings in the block, and these openings are plugged with core plugs.

1 Determine Level of Cleaning Necessary *continued*

If the block was placed in a heated cleaning tank, most gasket material would have fallen off or dissolved. If you did not, clean the block gasket surfaces and cylinder bores. Check the coolant passage in the front of the block for any visual signs of damage or erosion. Inspect the valve lifter bores for deep scratches and varnish deposits.

Clean scale deposits from all the coolant passages. Note that this is a 6.5L block, where the coolant passages going to the cylinder head are much larger than on a 6.2L diesel. Use a bent wire coat hanger or a piece of welding rod to clean out the coolant passages through the core plugs around the water jackets that cool the cylinders.

2 Inspect Main Bearing Webs for Cracks

Inspect the crankshaft bearing webs for cracks with either the Magnaflux electromagnetic tester or the Magnaflux red-dye penetrant method process. The red-dye penetrant typically has the following steps, depending on the product you use:

1. Thoroughly clean the block main bearing web area and spray the areas close to the main bearing caps with a Spotcheck cleaner to allow total visibility of the possibly-cracked area.
2. Apply the dye penetrant by spraying or brushing the web area. Allow time for the area to dry completely, fully absorbing into the surface of the web. This can take anywhere from 1 to 3 hours, depending on the dye product being used.
3. Carefully remove any excess penetrant with a solvent or a water wash.
4. Apply the developer.
5. Inspect the main bearing web area for red lines, which will indicate a cracked area.

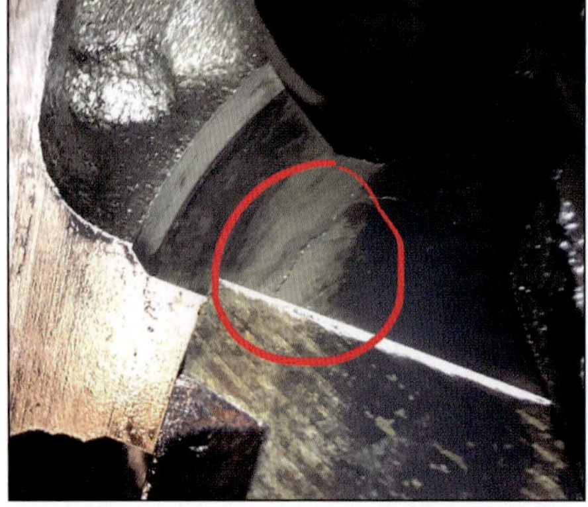

The engine block crankshaft support webs are very prone to cracks on the 6.2L diesel, and this problem could also plague the 6.5L. If cracks are found in the main web, it is best to replace the cylinder block or, in most cases, look for another engine.

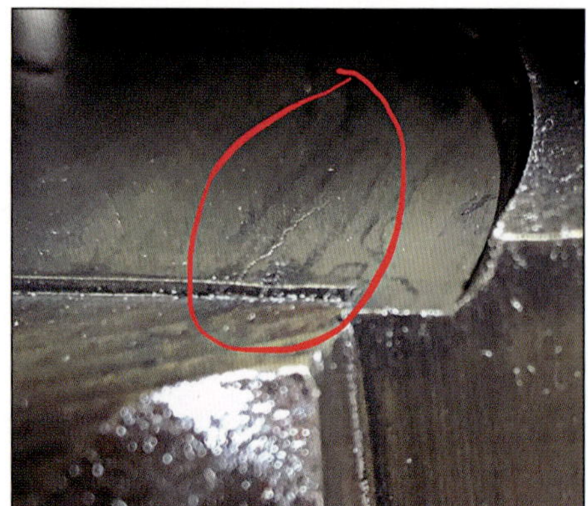

Check both sides of the main bearing web. If it is cracked on one side, it will most likely be cracked on the opposite side. To locate cracks, use the magnetic particle or red-dye method.

3 Magnetic Particle Testing

An alternative to magnetic particle testing is fluorescent-penetrant testing, which requires a black light and can be used on iron, steel, or aluminum parts. Cracks will show up as bright lines when viewed with a black light. A last resort is pressure testing, where a machine shop uses air to check the cylinder heads and block for leaks.

Magnetic particle testing can be used when you have the equipment and surface area that can accommodate the size of your magnetic probe. The process creates a magnetic field by applying a magnetic probe to the component's surface, which attracts any particles to the magnet ends or poles. An accumulation of these particles indicates a crack. (Photo Courtesy Jim Halderman)

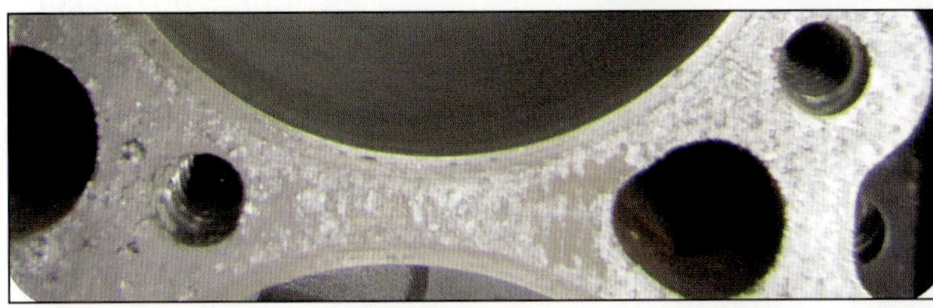

Continue the inspection of the cylinder block by looking down the top of the block into the coolant holes and coolant jackets for any signs of excessive corrosion. Also inspect the cylinder walls for any signs of cracks or leaks. The cylinder bores can be checked for cracks using the red-dye penetrate method. If excessive corrosion is found in the coolant passage, the block should be cleaned in a hot tank. If the corrosion is really bad and/or you find any cylinder-wall cracks, the block will need to be replaced or you will need to find another engine to rebuild.

4 Inspect Crankshaft Main Bearing Bores and Caps

The crankshaft bends as it rotates, so when the main bearing housing bores are not in alignment, they can cause a broken nodular cast-iron crankshaft. If the main bearing bore is found to have taper or an out-of-round condition beyond specifications, you will need to line bore the main caps and install undersized bearings, which is a machine shop project. The other option is to replace the engine.

A precision-ground straightedge and a feeler gauge can be used to determine the amount of warpage. The amount of variation along the entire length of the block should not exceed 0.0015 inch (0.038 mm). When the block bores (saddles) exceed 0.0015 inch of distortion, then align honing is required to restore the block. When the block saddles are straight, the bores should be measured to be sure that the bearing caps are not distorted.

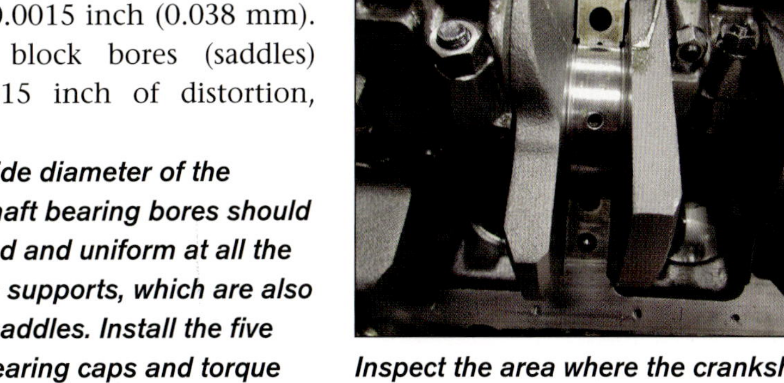

Inspect the area where the crankshaft bearing inserts contact the crankshaft bearing bore. This can be done with the crank in or out of the block. This area must be free of burrs and scratches.

The inside diameter of the crankshaft bearing bores should be round and uniform at all the bearing supports, which are also called saddles. Install the five main bearing caps and torque them in place to specifications. Then, check the main bearing bores for size, taper, and out-of-round using a dial bore gauge. The main bearing journals of a straight crankshaft are in alignment when the crankshaft turns freely in its bearings.

4 Inspect Crankshaft Main Bearing Bores and Caps *continued*

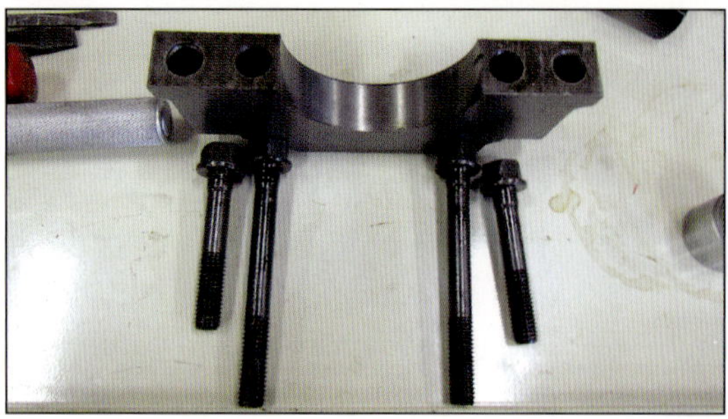

Inspect the cap for any burrs, check that the bearing inserts fit snug in the cap, and make sure that the bearing has crush where each end of the bearing shell is slightly above the parting surface of the cap. When the bearing cap is torqued, the ends of the two bearing shells touch and are forced together. This force is called bearing crush. Crush holds the bearing in place and keeps the bearing from turning when the engine runs. Crush must apply a force of at least 12,000 psi.

5 Inspect Mounting Hole Threads

Inspect the engine mount bosses for good thread contact for the motor mounts.

On each side of the engine block, there are three mounting holes at the front for the motor mounts. Inspect the threads by chasing them with the right-size tap to be sure they can support the mount that will hold the engine.

6 Inspect Gasket Mating Surfaces

Inspect the cylinder head gasket mating surfaces on the block for pitting or damage. Inspect the engine block to cylinder head gasket surface area by placing a new head gasket on the block. Check the block deck or cylinder head mounting surface for flatness with a feeler gauge and a precision straightedge. Replace the block if it is warped more than 0.006 inch (0.15 mm) longitudinally or more than 0.003 inch (0.08 mm) transversely across the cylinders. This will be the same procedure used later on the cylinder heads. You can check the block-to-head guide dowel pins by placing the cylinder head on the block without the head gasket and running a 0.005-inch feeler around the edge of the head. If there is no clearance, this indicates that the dowel pins are okay and not holding the head off the block.

7 Inspect Camshaft and Bearings

For camshaft bearing inspection, you need a dial bore gauge, a magnetic base dial indicator, and V-blocks. Inspect the camshaft bearings and replace them if any of these conditions exist: scratches, pits, or a loose fit in their bores. Inspect the camshaft bearings' inside diameter using a dial bore gauge against OEM specifications (see appendix). If the bearings are worn beyond specification, replace the bearings.

7 Inspect Camshaft and Bearings *continued*

Wear safety glasses with side shields to avoid eye damage while using compressed air to dry the camshaft. Using a soft cloth and solvent, clean the camshaft bearing inserts. Do not scratch the camshaft bearing inserts. Inspect camshaft bearing journals for scoring or nicks; worn camshaft lobes; damaged sprocket bolt threads or sprocket pin; damage caused by lack of lubrication; inserts having scoring, nicks, or damage caused by a lack of lubrication; and damage to the camshaft retainer plate and oil pump drive gear.

Using a digital vernier caliper or micrometer, measure the camshaft lobe against specifications. Also measure the camshaft journal diameter and taper in several places, about 90 degrees apart.

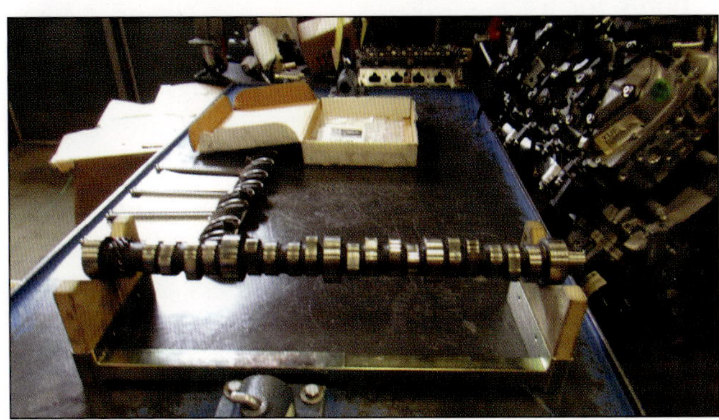

Mount the camshaft in V-blocks at camshaft journals 1 and 5 to measure for a bent camshaft or excessive camshaft runout using a dial indicator.

Using a magnetic base dial indicator, first zero the indicator and place the button on one of the camshaft journals. Then, rotate the camshaft to measure the runout. Replace the camshaft if runout exceeds 0.0039 inch (0.1000 mm).

8 Camshaft Bearing Removal

You must use a camshaft bearing service set for removal. Cam bearings are numbered 1 through 5, from front to rear. The number-1 cam bearing is the largest and the number-5 cam bearing is the smallest. To allow the tool to remain centered, it is recommended that the number-5 (rear) cam bearing be removed with the tool installed through the front of the block and the number-1 (front) bearing be removed with the tool installed from the rear. This will allow the guide cone of the tool surface to center itself on the block.

1. Remove the rear camshaft plug.
2. Insert the driving bar of the camshaft bearing removal tool with the correct expanding driver into the camshaft bearing (collet four for camshaft bearings 1 through 4, and collet three for camshaft bearing 5).
3. Turn the tool until the collet has tightened the bearing.
4. Push the guide cone against the block and into the first bearing bore to center the tool.
5. Drive the bearing from the block.
6. Repeat this procedure to remove the remaining bearings.

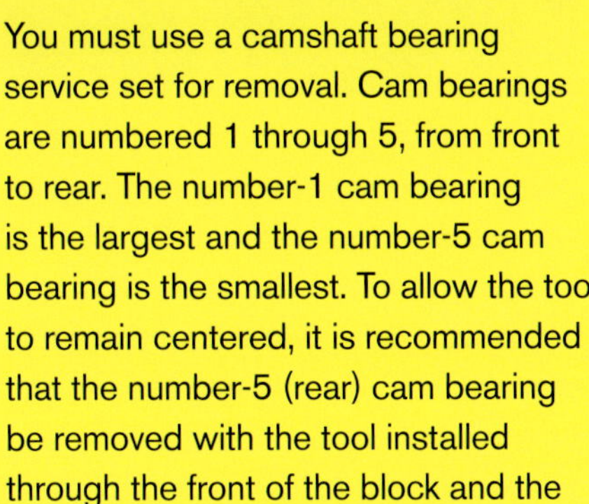

9 Remove Piston Oil Cooling Nozzle

The piston oil nozzles are made of aluminum and are press fit into the block. Certain cleaning solutions can damage the nozzles, so be careful to use only the GM-recommended cleaning solvents.

1. Do not damage the nozzle bore when removing the nozzle.
2. Do not damage the cylinder bore or deck surface.
3. Remove the piston oil nozzles.
4. Discard the used piston oil nozzles.
5. Using a brass drift, drive the piston oil nozzles out of the block.
6. Do not reuse the nozzles.

10 Check the Cylinder Bores

The 6.2L and 6.5L engines in production used different bore sizes and size designation codes along with different piston-selection methods. So, I will cover them separately during the process of inspection.

6.2L Cylinder Bores

If the bore measurements indicate taper or out-of-round, bore the cylinder out to 0.750 mm (0.030 inch oversize) to accommodate a 0.030-inch piston or 0.50 mm (0.020 inch oversize) for a 0.020-inch piston, depending on the amount of wear. In production, the 6.2L pistons were match fitted to the bores for a total standard bore range that was divided into six size ratings and coded A-B-C-D-E-G. (The letter *F* is not used because if not stamped properly, it can look like an *E*.)

The 6.2L pistons were also size marked A-B-C-D-E-G, so an A piston would be installed into an A bore to control the piston-to-bore clearance. The size codes were stamped on the case. Service pistons are currently available in standard, high-limit standard 0.50 mm OS (0.020 inch), and 0.750 mm (0.030 inch) OS.

6.5L Cylinder Bores

The 6.5L diesel engine cylinder bores number-7 and -8 are slightly larger than cylinders-1 through -6. This difference in bore sizes allows for more piston expansion in the rear two cylinders (numbers -7 and -8).

Each piston will have a size identification mark on its face and the piston boss surface. The cylinder block

Check the cylinder bores for taper, out-of-round, and size for piston selection. You can use an inside telescopic gauge with an outside micrometer or a dial bore gauge to measure the cylinder bore. You can also use the GM Special Tool J-8087 cylinder dial bore gauge. (Photo Courtesy Jim Halderman)

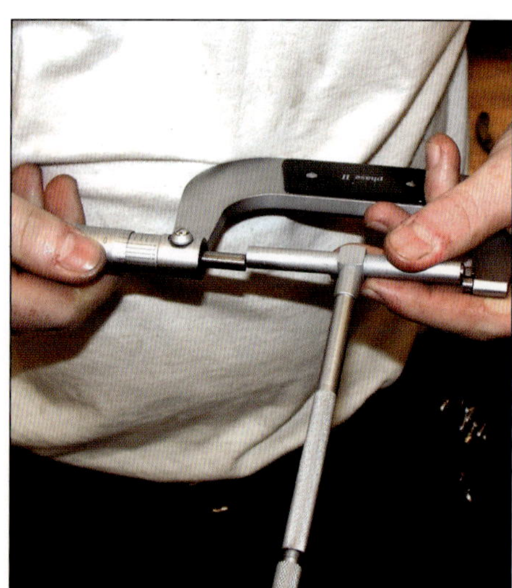

When using a telescoping gauge to measure the cylinder bores, after expanding the gauge in the bore, remove it. Then, take a 5-inch outside micrometer and measure the expanded telescoping gauge. (Photo Courtesy Jim Halderman)

The letter designating the cylinder bore and corresponding piston size is stamped on the pan rail. On the 6.5L, an S stamped on the pan rail next to any reworked cylinder identifies that cylinder as production oversize. A J piston will also be stamped in a single place on the oil pan rail to represent a J or standard-size cylinder. It is always best to measure the pistons to be sure they are replaced with the right size.

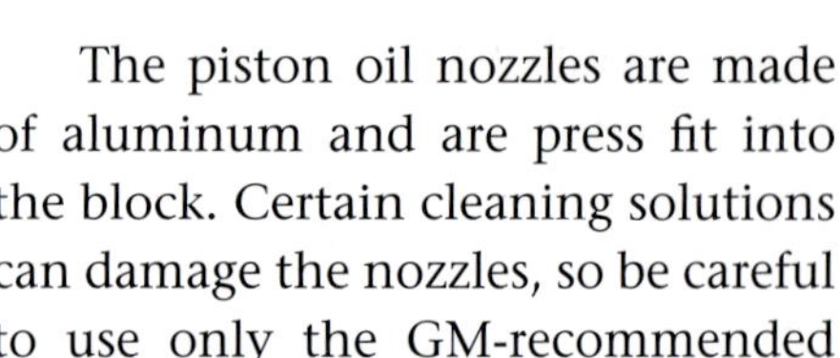

10 Check Cylinder Bores *continued*

or case will have the piston size identification mark for each bore next to the bore. There are five different size codes: production standard marked J or JT, production standard marked S or ST, service standard marked JT, service high-limit marked GT, and service 0.50 mm marked OS that all remaining cylinders are production standard. There is only one production standard piston grade size.

When using production standard grade size pistons in all eight cylinder bores, a *J* is stamped in a single place on the cylinder block oil pan rail. A 0.13-mm oversize production piston was available for a plant rework of cylinders that do not meet the production standard specification.

Important!

! Record all cylinder and clearance measurements for the engine reassembly process covered in chapter 7 to include bearings and pistons.

11 Cylinder Boring and Honing

Note that it is not absolutely necessary to hone the cylinders when replacing the rings or doing an overhaul, but it is recommended and is just a good engine rebuild practice. You generally should not change the rings without first honing the cylinder walls because changing the rings without honing may not solve the problem that caused the rings to wear originally. If there are scratches or any sort of disruption in the cylinder wall finish, that can cause premature wear of piston rings and possibly even cause one to break.

During disassembly, I reamed the ridge from the top of the cylinder bores to make the pistons easier to remove. This ridge is the area that the rings do not reach, so it's unworn. Also, if this ridge is left in place, it could break the top compression rings. Honing removes many surface imperfections when done correctly, plus it generates a crosshatch pattern of scratches that helps hold oil onto the cylinders and break in the new rings to provide a good sealing surface.

The honing process is as follows:

1. Visually check the cylinder bore for smooth, shiny, polished areas through the hone marks. If present, hone the cylinder lightly with a finish hone.
2. Repeat steps 3 through 10 for the remaining cylinders.
3. All crankshaft bearing caps must be in place and tightened to the proper torque to avoid bore distortion.
4. Make sure that the specified clearance between pistons, rings, and the cylinder bores is maintained.
5. Make full strokes of the hone in the cylinder bore.
6. Move the hone up and down at a sufficient speed to obtain very fine uniform surface finish marks in a crosshatch pattern at the specified angle of 45 to 65 degrees. The finish marks should be:
   a. Smooth
   b. Free of imbedded particles
   c. Free of torn or folded metal
7. Check the measurement at the top, middle, and bottom of the cylinder bore regularly, using the dial bore gauge. Any abrasive material remaining in the cylinder bores will cause premature wear to the piston rings, cylinder bores, and bearing surfaces.
   a. When using coarse- or medium-grade stones, leave sufficient metal to allow all stone marks to be removed with the fine stones used during the finishing process.
   b. The surface roughness specifications for cylinder bores are: RA (Minimum) = 0.40 micrometer (16 microinch) RA (Maximum) = 0.90 micrometer (32 microinch)
8. Clean cylinder bores with hot water and detergent.
9. Clean dry cylinder bores with a power-driven fiber brush.
10. Apply a light coating of clean engine oil or Marvel Mystery Oil to cylinder bores or GM Engine Oil Supplement.

12 Inspect the Roller Lifters

All valvetrain components will need to be carefully inspected and in some cases measured. These include roller lifters, lifter guide plates, rocker arms and shafts, and pushrods.

12 Inspect Roller Lifters *continued*

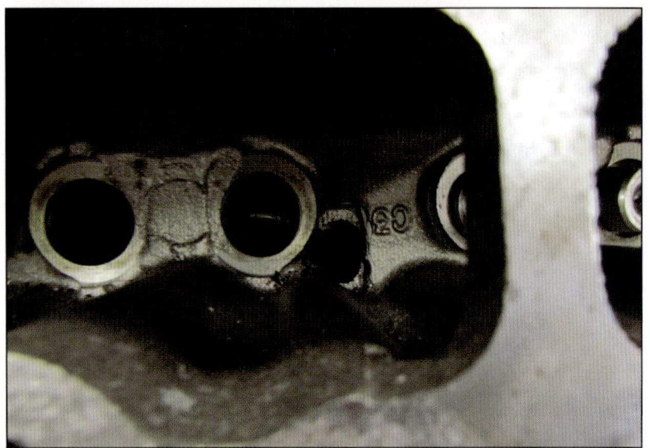

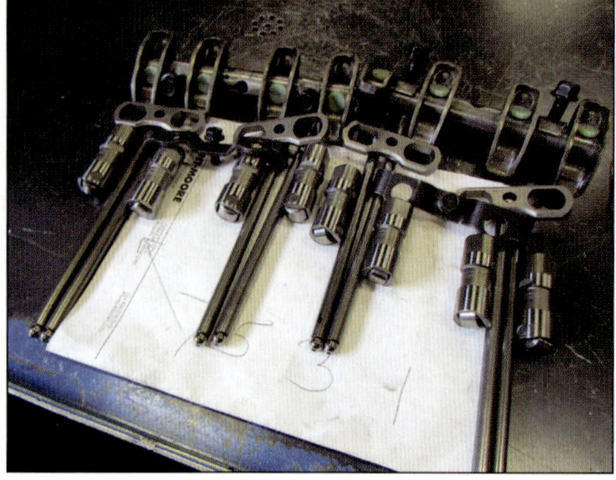

Inspect the roller lifter bores for scoring and clearance by moving the lifter in and out of its bore and side to side using a dial indicator. Lifter-to-bore clearance is 0.04 to 0.08 mm (0.0015 to 0.0031 inches). Some engines can have both standard and 0.010-inch oversize valve lifters. The oversize lifter will have a "10" etched on the side. Stamped on the cast pad next to the lifter bore and on the top rail of the cylinder case above the lifter bore will be the letters "OS."

When disassembling the engine, the rocker arms, pushrods, roller lifters, and retainers were placed in a marking tray or on paper showing their original operating position. Inspect the valve lifter rollers for fatigue or pitting. Replace the valve lifter as an assembly if one is found to be defective. Clean the roller lifters, guide plates, and retainers in solvent while wearing protective safety glasses and gloves. Blow-dry the parts with compressed air and inspect the valve lifter guide plates and clamps for damage. Inspect lifter guide plates for burrs that may interfere with up-and-down movement. If there are burrs, it can cause a lifter noise during operation. Replace any damaged parts.

13 Clean and Inspect Rockers and Pushrods

Place the pushrods on a piece of glass and see if they roll without any wobble. If there is any wobble, they are bent and must be replaced.

The pushrods have a shiny end, which goes to the valve lifter. It is the hardened portion of the pushrod due to it rising in the lifter and receiving direct lubrication from the lifter.

Check the rocker arms on the shaft for any wear and the retaining button for excessive discoloring or looseness. If any of these conditions are found, replace the rocker arm assembly as a unit, including all components. If removing the rocker arms from the shaft, drive a screwdriver through the shaft to brake off the button ends and pull out the buttons using pliers.

The rocker-arm end of the pushrod has a copper coating that is a wear item due to its softness, so you need to carefully examine it for wear. Pushrods are not expensive, so it is a good idea during a rebuild to replace them.

14 Clean and Inspect Oil Pump

Inspect the oil pump drive stalk or vacuum pump gear for any signs for wear and that the oil pump–driven gear turns freely in the housing. The drive stalk has an RPM sensor at the top. During oil pump installation, install a new oil pump driveshaft retainer.

Remove the four screws holding the oil pickup tube and oil pump cover and remove the gears as an assembly. Mark them with paint or a scribe so they will be installed back in the same position if the pump is not replaced. Clean all oil pump parts in clean solvent and dry them for inspection.

Inspect the oil pump for:

- *Scoring, damage, or casting imperfections to the housing*
- *Damaged gears (chipping, galling, or wear)*
- *Scoring on top of gears*
- *Damaged or scored gear shaft*
- *Damaged bolt threads*
- *Worn driveshaft housing bore*
- *Damaged or sticking pressure relief valve*
- *Collapsed or broken pressure relief valve spring; if the oil pump is to be reused, install a new pressure-relief valve spring*
- *Reinstall the gears (if not replaced) in their original position and all other removed components and tighten the cover bolts to 16 Nm (12 ft-lbs).*

Check the oil filter seal matting area on the block for any deep grooves that might prevent a good filter seal. If any damage is found, you will need to replace the block or engine.

15 Clean and Inspect Crankshaft and Bearings

The 6.2L and 6.5L crankshafts are made from nodular cast-iron casting with ground journals and a rolled fillet radius. Oil holes are drilled from the connecting rod journals to the main journals using no plugs. The crankshaft has a natural resonant frequency of vibration.

Torsional impulse frequencies are induced by the firing of the cylinders, and when two frequencies are in resonance or harmony, the magnitude of the combined vibrations could overstress the crankshaft and in time cause it to break. For this reason, a torsional damper or harmonic balancer is used. The inertia mass of this balancer moves

Crankshaft inspection begins with a thorough cleaning. Also inspect the crankshaft for damage cracks or excessive scoring. Inspect the timing sprocket for damage and/or wear. Check the harmonic balancer bonding to make sure it is secure and has not been damaged from contact with fuel or lube oil.

freely because it is bonded in rubber. Its inertia mass acts like a flywheel and reduces the stresses by absorbing some of the torsional stresses.

1. Using a soft cloth and clean solvent, clean the crankshaft. Be careful not to scratch the crankshaft bearing journals.

15 | Clean and Inspect Crankshaft and Bearings *continued*

Important!

Wear safety glasses with side shields to avoid injury when using compressed air or any cleaning solvent. Bodily injury may occur if fumes are inhaled or if skin is exposed to chemicals.

2. Using compressed air, clean the crankshaft oil passages; then, use a soft cloth and clean solvent to clean the crankshaft bearing inserts. Do not scratch the crankshaft bearing inserts.

3. Inspect the crankshaft for cracks using the Magnaflux red-dye method.

4. Inspect the crankshaft bearing journals and thrust surfaces for the following conditions:
   a. Scoring
   b. Nicks
   c. Damage caused by lack of lubrication

5. Mount the crankshaft in V-blocks and check the runout to be within 0.005 mm (0.0002 inch) on a new crank or 0.025 mm (0.001 inch) on a worn crankshaft.

6. Inspect the crankshaft bearing inserts and thrust surfaces for the following conditions:
   a. Scoring
   b. Nicks
   c. Damage caused by lack of lubrication

7. Using a digital vernier caliper or micrometer, measure the crankshaft journal diameter and taper in several places, approximately 90 degrees apart.

8. The connecting rod and the crankshaft journal sizes are color coded with paint markings.
   a. Connecting rod journal markings are yellow or green.
   b. Crankshaft journal markings are blue, orange/red, or white.

9. Record all measurements for bearing fitment during reassembly.

16 | Inspect Main Bearings

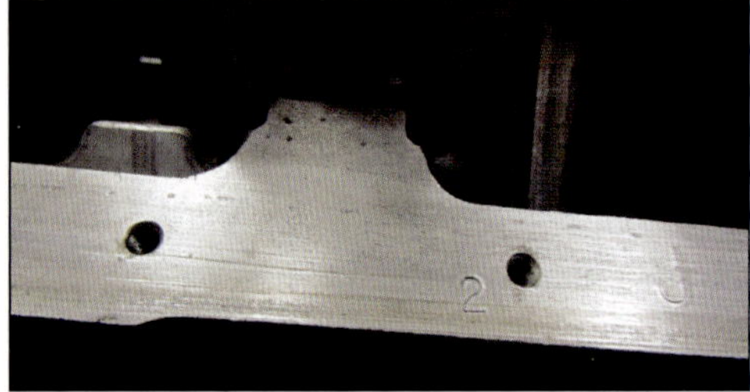

The size code is also stamped on the pan rail at the corresponding main bearing location. The total diameter size range of the main bearing bores number-1 to -5 is 78.826 to 79.850 mm on both engines. The spread of 0.024 mm is divided into three sizes. The sizes were stamped either 1, 2, or 3 on the pan rail and matched to the corresponding size of the split bearing insert in the case half only. The split bearing insert for the main was match fitted to the crankshaft main journal. Three bearings will be used for service or rebuild to get the proper clearance. Note that when the specification says undersize, it means that the crankshaft journal is undersized but the actual bearing insert is thicker.

Bearing Replacement

According to the factory, it is not necessary to replace all main bearings in a 6.2L or 6.5L engine when one or more need to be replaced. However, for any overhaul, you should replace all main bearings. Chapter 2 contains a specific chart of main bearing sizes. ■

17 | Inspect Cylinder Head for Warpage

These 6.2L and 6.5L engines use 38-, 39-, or 42-mm-diameter Stellite-faced exhaust valves and intake valves that are 46 or 50 mm in diameter. Intake and exhaust valves with oversize stems are available in 0.03 inch or 0.09 mm and 0.153 inch and 0.39 mm.

Inspect the cylinder head for warpage using a precision straightedge first longitudinally. The warpage cannot exceed 0.15 mm (0.006 inch), and if it does, replace the cylinder head.

17 Inspect Cylinder Head for Warpage *continued*

Inspect the cylinder head for warpage using a precision straightedge transversely. The warpage cannot exceed 0.08 mm (0.003 inch). If the clearance is greater than this value, replace the cylinder head. Cylinder head thickness (valve cover gasket rail to head gasket surface) must be at least 97.87 mm (3.853 in).

Head Replacement

General Motors does not recommend resurfacing the cylinder head due to the extremely close valve-to-piston clearances, although it is done in the field with some success. If you do it, install 0.010-inch-thicker head gaskets, which are available. However, I always recommend following the OEM recommendations. ■

18 Remove and Inspect Valve Assembly

Remove all of the intake and exhaust poppet valves and their components. Compress valve springs with a valve spring compressor and remove the valve keepers (keys) and the following components:
- *Caps from intake valves*
- *Rotators from exhaust valves*
- *Shields and O-rings*
- *Valve springs with dampers and shims*
- *Exhaust valve seals*

Place the valves in a rack so you can return them to the original positions during reassembly.

Examine each component of the poppet valve system by laying it out in order of removal. In this case, for an intake valve: keepers, cap, shield, spring, seal, and the valve. Note the position of the valve spring and make sure to reinstall it in the same position. If it were an exhaust valve, you would have a rotator. Every time the exhaust valve opens, the valve rotator turns the valve slightly and prevents the valves from sticking due to carbon buildup. They are used on the exhaust valves because they run hotter and rotators reduce thermal gradient and stress.

Check the valve springs for pressure, squareness, and installed height. Place the spring on a valve-spring tester that is used to measure the compressed force of valve springs. On a new spring, at 80 pounds, the length should be 1.811 inches. On a worn or used

When you first compress the valve spring, the first valve component you remove will be the valve keeper. This is a wedge-shaped device that retains the poppet valve mechanism together inside the spring cap.

spring at 70 pounds, the length should be 1.811 inches. The installed height should be 46 mm (1.8110 inches). Squareness is checked by measuring spring length, and it should not vary more than 1.59 mm (0.0626 inch) when being rotated in a free state. Consult the specifications section for further details.

19 | Valve Guide Measurement, Reaming, and Valve Grinding

Measure the valve stem-to-guide bore clearance using the following procedure:

- Attach a dial indicator on one side of the cylinder head valve rocker arm cover gasket rail. Zero-in the dial indicator. Place the indicator pad on the valve just above the valve guide bore and observe the dial indicator movement while moving the valve from side to side (crosswise to the head).
- Drop the valve head about 1.6 mm off the valve seat.
- Move the stem of the valve from side to side using light pressure to obtain a clearance reading. If the clearance exceeds specifications, it will be necessary to ream the valve guide bores for oversize valves. This process is best achieved by sending the head out to an automotive machine shop or replacing the head.

If you have the necessary valve grinding equipment, follow the factory procedure listed here. This is what a machine shop will do:

- Ream the valve guides for oversize valves if the clearance exceeds the specifications.
- Recondition the valve seat after reaming the valve guide bores or installing the new valve guides.

Valve Stem-to-Guide Bore Clearance

Excessive oil consumption and component damage may result from excessive valve stem-to-guide bore clearance. Insufficient clearance may cause noisy and sticky functioning of the valve and disturb the smoothness of the engine. ■

- The valves must seat perfectly for the engine to deliver optimum power and performance.
- Cooling the valve heads is another important factor. Good contact between each valve and its seat in the cylinder head is necessary to make sure that the heat in the valve head is properly carried away.
- Regardless of what type of equipment is used, it is essential that the valve guide bores are free from carbon or dirt to ensure the proper centering of the pilot in the guide.
- The valve seats should be concentric to within 0.05 mm (0.002 inch) total indicator reading.
- Reface pitted valves on a valve refacing machine to make sure they have the correct relationship between the head and the stem.
- Replace the valve if the stem is warped or if the stem shows signs of excessive wear.
- Replace the valve if the edge of the head is less than 0.79 mm (0.031 inch) thick after grinding.
- Clean the valve stems and the heads on a wire wheel.
- Clean carbon and old gasket material from the cylinder head gasket surface.
- Clean the valve guides using a valve guide cleaner.
- Inspect the valves for burning, pitting, or warpage.
- Grind or replace the valves as needed.
- Check the valve stems for scoring or excessive wear. Stems must not be bent.
- Inspect the valve seats for pitting or other damage. Grind or reface as needed.

- Inspect the exhaust valve rotators. The rotators should rotate smoothly without binding.

Valve Seat and Face Inspection

Examine the valve seats and valve faces to see if grinding the seat or face is required. The face and seat angle on both engines and both intake and exhaust valves is 45 degrees. An interference angle is not used. If you determine that grinding is needed, I recommend sending the heads out to an automotive machine shop for this job because they will have the tools and know-how to perform this service. ■

Grinding Valves

The valves can be ground to achieve some performance benefits, although this is not recommended by General Motors. Set the valve-grinder angle to 30 degrees for the 45-degree face angle and grind a 30-degree transition between the 45-degree valve face and the valve stem area of the valve. This may reduce some desirable swirling of the air/fuel mixture at lower engine speeds and can increase cylinder filling, especially at times when the valve is not fully open.

Chamfer or round the head of the valve between the top of the valve and the margin on the side. By rounding this surface, additional airflow into the cylinder is achieved. Again, I would leave this kind of machining to the professionals at the automotive machine shop. ■

20 Clean and Inspect Cylinder Head

Remove the fuel injection nozzle and glow plug. Drive out the prechambers with a small nylon or brass drift inserted through the injection nozzle hole. The prechambers use high-temperature super nickel alloy materials. Note that it is possible to deform the narrow throat of the prechamber. If this happens, the prechamber must be replaced. Replace the prechambers with the correct part number for that engine.

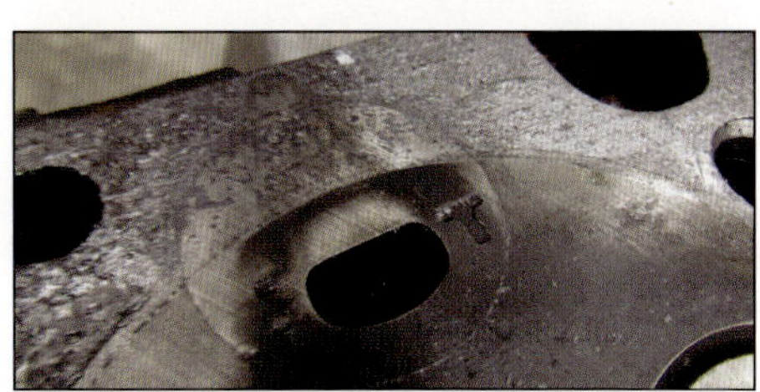

The 6.5L has two dots and the letter T stamped on the prechamber. The latest and best prechambers are those with a diamond stamped on them.

Clean the head by soaking the combustion chamber area with GM Top Engine Cleaner, which contains Carbon-X and will help soften and melt the carbon. Clean the carbon from the combustion chambers using a wire-brush drill bit.

21 Inspect Cylinder Head for Cracks

There are several factors that relate to the cracking, including the use of induction-hardened seats (the seat is an integral part of casting), temperature range, rate of expansion and contraction in the valve seat area, and the type of vehicle use. It is possible that these cracks can eventually form on every 6.2L/6.5L diesel engine. The point at which this occurs in the life of the vehicle is directly affected by truck use, horsepower, torque output of the engine, and the temperature of operation.

During inspection, examine the prechambers for excessive cracks into the fire ring area. Prechamber inserts are replaceable. Prechambers only need to be replaced if there is a crack that exceeds 3/16 inch (5 mm) in length. Cracks in the prechamber inserts that are shorter than 5 mm are not an issue. Service prechambers are available in standard and 0.25 mm (0.010 inch) oversize.

Inspect the cylinder head for surface cracks that may be found between the valve seats on both engines. You will most likely find some surface cracking between the intake and exhaust valve seats on either engine.

Minor surface cracks in the valve port area of the cylinder head, especially between the intake and exhaust ports, are not a normal condition. Give close attention to the exhaust ports. If these cracks are just on the surface, they may be okay, but they may go deeper and cause coolant loss that leads to engine damage. I would not use any 6.2L or 6.5L head with a crack in the valve port area because it will only get worse. Use the Magnaflux red-dye or magnetic particle method to see if these cracks are severe and to check for cracks in the combustion chamber and external cracks to the coolant chamber. Any crack that is visible with the red dye or magnetic particles requires a head replacement. Make sure the gasket surfaces are free of damage.

Head Bolt Replacement

Always replace all 17 head bolts with new bolts that have the Teflon coating on about 3/4 inch of thread area. If they do not have sealer on them, coat about 3/4 inch of the thread with the white Teflon sealer. I recommend using Automotive Racing Products (ARP) studs on your 6.2L or 6.5L builds. You also need to seal the bottom threads of the stud that go into the block with the Loctite sealer provided by ARP in the kit. This is done because these fasteners go into cooling system passages. Failure to do so can result in coolant loss and overheating. ■

22 Clean Crankshaft Balancer and Pulley

Use a mild cleaning solvent to clean the crankshaft harmonic balancer. Then, use compressed air to dry it off. Inspect the front oil seal area for grooves and finish condition that will cause leaks. Make sure that the outer ring separated by the rubber insert is tight. If the seal area is compromised or the outer ring is not tight, replace the balancer. Most

rebuilders of these engines replace the balancer with an aftermarket performance product, such as the Dayco PB1492DP harmonic balancer.

Inspect the crankshaft pulley for cracks. There are two rubber inserts to check on the pulley: one around the hub and one between an outer ring and the belt rim. If these rings are not tight, replace the pulley.

23 Clean and Inspect Piston, Connecting Rod, and Bearing

The connecting rod is not serviceable for the following repairs:
- Straightening
- Bushing replacement
- Connecting rod bearing bore enlargement

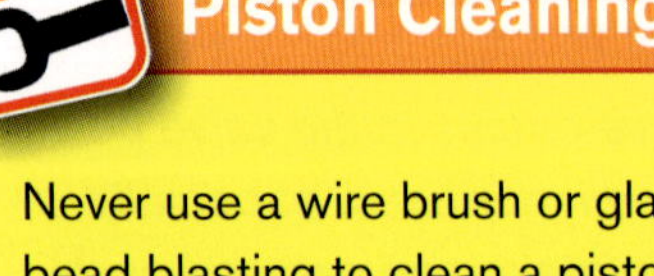

Clean the piston by removing all of the varnish and carbon deposits. Inspect the piston for the following conditions: ring land cracking or wear, ring groove burrs or nicks, cracking of skirts or pin bosses, dome cracking (Magnaflux spot-check dye method to check), skirt scuffing or deep scratches, bore scuffing, and wrist pin wear in the retaining ring or grooves.

Inspect the connecting rod for the following conditions: cracks or nicks on the connecting rod (Magnaflux spot-check dye method), scuffing or scratching of the piston pin bushing, nicks or scoring of the bearing bore, and bent or twisted rods.

Piston Cleaning

Never use a wire brush or glass-bead blasting to clean a piston. Use a cleaning solution that will dissolve the carbon deposits, and remove the carbon in the ring grooves with a ring-groove cleaner. ■

24 Clean and Inspect Timing Chain and Sprockets

Inspect the sprockets for chipped teeth and wear and the reluctor wheel's four square bosses for nicks or dings on 1994-and-later 6.5L engines with electronic fuel injection. Handle the reluctor wheel carefully because damage to the machined bosses will directly affect engine timing. Also inspect the timing chain for damage and wear, and replace worn sprockets and chains. For a major rebuild such as this one, replace the timing chain and sprockets.

24 Clean and Inspect Timing Chain and Sprockets *continued*

Inspect both the drive and fuel injection pump gears for broken teeth and wear.

26 Clean and Inspect Front Cover

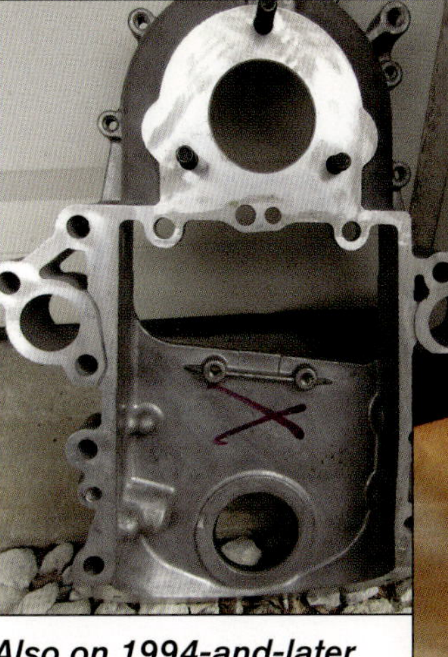

Clean the old sealer from the sealing surfaces on the front cover. Then, inspect the front cover for cracks and damage to the sealing surfaces.

Also on 1994-and-later EFI 6.5L engines, inspect the hole for the crankshaft position (CKP) sensor by placing the sensor in the hole and making sure that there is no play.

25 Check Timing Chain Wear (Optional)

Examine the double-roller timing chain, camshaft sprocket, and crankshaft sprocket. Then, measure the assembly freeplay. While it is important to always replace the chain and both sprockets during an overhaul, it is also a good idea to know how to check for wear. Follow these steps:

1. Attach a magnetic-base dial indicator to the front of the engine cylinder block.
2. Position the dial indicator to allow the plunger to contact the timing chain. The dial indicator plunger should contact the timing chain centered between the two sprockets.
3. Using finger pressure on the inside radius of the timing chain, push the timing chain outward (parallel to the front face of the block) to the maximum deflection.
4. Set the dial indicator to zero and use finger pressure on the outside radius of the timing chain to push the timing chain inward (parallel to the front face of the block) to the maximum deflection.
5. Record the deflection of the timing chain (total travel of the dial indicator plunger). For used parts, the deflection must not exceed 20.3 mm (0.80 inch) and for a new chain and sprockets, the deflection must not exceed 12.7 mm (0.50 inch).

27 Clean and Inspect Valve Cover

Clean the valve cover in a solvent tank, removing all sludge and varnish. Use a gasket scraper to clean the old sealer from the sealing surfaces. Inspect the valve cover for bent or damaged sealing flanges and any deterioration of the rubber grommets used for the CDR valve.

Locate the correct tap and chase all of the thread in the holes in the cylinder head that are used to attach the valve cover.

28 Clean and Inspect Oil Pan

Clean the oil pan in a solvent tank, removing all sludge and varnish. Use a gasket scraper to clean the old sealer from the sealing surfaces and inspect for the following conditions: bent or damaged sealing flanges, damage to oil pan caused by rocks, loose fit of the oil pan baffle, and stripped oil pan drain plug threads.

Both of these engines use a windage tray in the oil pan. A windage tray is a baffle installed under the crankshaft to help prevent aeration of the oil.

Where does the wind come from? The pistons push air down into the crankcase as they move from TDC to BDC. The pistons also draw air and oil upward when moving from BDC to TDC. At high RPM, this causes a lot of airflow, which can aerate the oil. So, the windage tray helps prevent this movement of wind from affecting the oil in the pan.

29 Clean and Inspect Intake Manifold

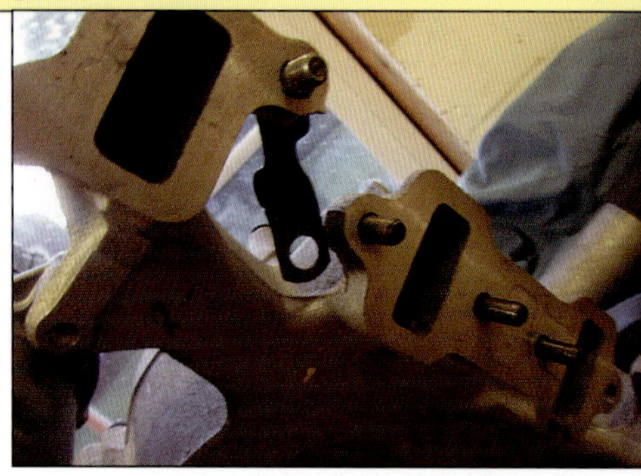

Remove the manifold absolute pressure (MAP) and intake air temperature (IAT) sensors from the intake manifold (1994-and-later 6.5L EFI). Clean the old pieces of gasket from the gasket surfaces and clean the soot deposits. Inspect the manifold for the following conditions: cracks, broken flanges, and gasket surface damage.

30 Clean and Inspect Water Pump

Never immerse the water pump in solvent because it will dissolve the lubricant supply for the permanently lubricated bearings, which will cause premature bearing failure. Clean the old gasket off of the gasket surfaces on the water pump and the water pump backing plate. Note that this is a 6.5L water pump built prior to 1997 and has a 4-inch scroll impeller with a flow rate of 87 gpm. The 1997 to 2000 (2005) 6.5L water pump has a 4.25-inch impeller with a flow rate of 130 gpm. The 6.2L flowed at 70 gpm.

Replace the water pump when these conditions exist:

- Excessive end play in the pump shaft (0.20 mm/0.008 inch end play is normal)
- Pump driveshaft will not rotate smoothly (binding or roughness)
- If the pump has been dry for a while, it may be difficult to turn the shaft on the first try
- If the pump does not turn smoothly after a few attempts
- Coolant leakage at water pump weep hole
- Damage to water pump sealing surface
- Damage to water pump pulley

Replace the water pump backing plate if the following condition exists:

- Damage to water pump backing plate sealing surface
- Damage to oil fill tube seal flange

Water Pump

The water pump used with the serpentine belt system rotates counterclockwise. Replace the pump only with the proper part number. Otherwise, engine overheating may occur, damaging the engine. The 1997 to 2005 6.5L pump has the best cooling system performance for these engines due to its larger impeller and 130-gpm flow rate. ■

31 Inspect Thermostat Housing

Inspect the inside of the thermostat housing and water crossover for any signs of erosion dues to cavitation and also for any cracks. Check the fit of the full-blocking single or dual thermostats and check the flange areas for any damaged or broken ears.

32 Clean and Inspect Flywheel

Inspect the flywheel for loose or improperly installed balance weights (manual transmission only). A properly installed balance weight should be installed until flush with or below the face of the flywheel. Inspect the manual-transmission flywheel for these conditions, and if found replace it:

- Pitted surface, scoring, or grooves
- Rust or other surface damage
- Stress cracks around the flywheel-to-crankshaft bolt hole locations
- Loose or improperly positioned ring gear. The ring gear has an interference fit onto the flywheel and

Check the welded areas that retain the ring gear onto the flexplate for cracking on an automatic transmission truck. If any cracking is found, replace the flexplate.

should be positioned completely against the flange of the flywheel on a manual transmission truck. Never repair the welded areas that retain the ring gear to the flywheel plate.

ASSEMBLY AND INSTALLATION

In the course of any engine rebuild, it is customary to begin with the engine block reassembly, which includes the bottom-end components of the crankshaft, bearings, pistons, and connecting rods. We will start with the block. Because this is a pushrod engine, I will be installing the camshaft bearings and the camshaft before the bottom-end components. The engine used in this rebuild was a 1993 6.5L diesel.

Installing camshaft bearings may be difficult for the first-time engine rebuilder and will require special tools. It is recommended to farm this out to a local automotive machine ship.

During any major engine reassembly, begin the build at the bottom end of the engine, which on a cam-in-block engine includes the block, camshaft, timing gears, crankshaft, pistons, and connecting rods.

The 6.2L red block, as it is called by the 6.2L and 6.5L Facebook community, was the original 6.2L engine block used in the beginning of 1982–1983 production and had a casting number of 14022660. The original 1982–1983 block casting was called a 660 RED block and had high nickel content. They were originally painted red from the factory.

Engines from General Engine Products

New engines were made by General Engine Products (GEP)/AM General in Moraine, Ohio, which is the same factory that originally made them as part of Chevrolet in 1982 and then on to Detroit Diesel from 1983 to 1987. GEP still makes them as replacements and upgrades and also supplies the US military with them for all HMMWVs.

The block casting number is a way of identifying certain 6.2L and 6.5L blocks. The casting number is located on the back of the transmission bellhousing. The blocks were called red blocks because the 1982 and 1983 engines were designed by Chevrolet and painted Chevrolet Red. The last three digits of the casting number can be used to identify the block.

The 6.2L and 6.5L 599 block that had a high nickel content introduced the one-piece round rear man seal. The 6.5L 2555506 block was the first to use 10-mm-diameter outer main bearing cap bolts and piston oil cooling nozzles. ■

Bottom-End Build

1 Install All Previously Removed Block Plugs

If any of the oil gallery or core-out block plugs were removed during the rebuild, they need to be reinstalled.

Install the front camshaft oil gallery plugs using Loctite thread-locking compound on the threads and tighten them until they are completely seated. Install the oil cooler line fittings using thread-locking compound on the threads and tighten to 43 ft-lbs. Install the side oil gallery plugs and tighten them to 25 ft-lbs. An oil gallery plug is located inside the rear main bearing cap land. Tighten it using thread-locking compound on the threads. Install the engine oil pressure sensor switch and tighten it to 9 ft-lbs. Install the core-out (freeze) plugs and the block heater and use red Permatex to seal them. Install the coolant drain plugs using thread-locking compound on the threads and tighten them to 18 ft-lbs.

2 Install Oil Filter Adapter

Install the oil cooler bypass valve using a socket the same size as the outside diameter of the valve. Drive the valve into the bore until the valve seats on the shoulder in the bore. The cup plug has an orifice hole that prevents an air lock from occurring and blocking the oil flow. Install the cup plug for the oil cooler bypass valve and the oil filter bypass valve using a socket the same size as the outside diameter of the valve. Drive the valve into the bore until the valve seats on the shoulder in the bore. Install the oil filter fitting and tighten to 31 ft-lbs.

Next, install the oil filter adapter.

3 Install Camshaft Bearing

All bearing locations are viewed from the front of the block (with the block in an upright position in the engine stand).

There are two oil holes in the front camshaft bearing. Using the seam in the 12 o'clock position and the notch facing the front of the block as reference points, one oil hole will be in the 1 o'clock position and the other oil hole will be in the 4:30 position. Make sure that both oil holes in the camshaft bearing line up with the oil grooves in the block. There is one oil hole in the center camshaft bearings. Using the seam in the 11 o'clock position as a reference point, the oil hole must be in the 1 o'clock position. Be sure that the oil hole in the camshaft bearing lines up with the oil groove in the block.

Install the rear camshaft bearing using the camshaft bearing installer. Insert the driving bar with the correct expanding driver into the camshaft bearing (collet 4 for the camshaft bearing number-1), and turn the tool until the collet has tightened in the bearing. Push the guide cone against the block and into the fifth bearing bore to center the tool and drive the bearing into the block.

Install the front camshaft bearing using the camshaft bearing kit. Insert the driving bar with the correct expanding driver into the camshaft bearing (collet 3 for camshaft bearing number-5). Turn the tool until the collet has tightened in the bearing and push the guide cone against the block and into the first bearing bore to center the tool. Drive the bearing into the block.

1. Install the inner camshaft bearings using the same camshaft bearing installer.
2. Insert the driving bar with the correct expanding driver into the camshaft bearing (collet 4 for

Install the camshaft bearings (if you removed them).

camshaft bearings 2–4).
3. Turn the tool until the collet has tightened in the bearing.
4. Push the guide cone against the block and into the first bearing bore to center the tool.
5. Drive the bearing into the block.
6. Repeat this procedure to install the remaining camshaft bearings.
7. Install a new rear camshaft plug and seal it with Permatex #2.
8. Install the plug flush or to a maximum of 0.03 inches (0.80 mm) deep.

4 Install Piston Oil Nozzle

Use a brass drive pin that has the same outer diameter as the piston oil nozzles to install them into the block. Remember that excessive force can crush the piston oil nozzle. Be careful not to damage the piston oil nozzle bore. Do not damage the crankshaft bearing bore. Gently tap the piston oil nozzles into their bores and make sure that the piston oil nozzles are fully seated in their bores.

5 Install Camshaft

Coat the camshaft lobes with GM Engine Oil Supplement or Marvel Mystery Oil and lubricate the camshaft bearing journals with engine oil. Install the camshaft sprocket key and the camshaft sprocket spacer with the ID chamfer facing the camshaft; then, gently insert the camshaft into the block.

Roller Valve Lifters

Always replace the roller valve lifters when a new camshaft is installed. ■

6 Install Thrust Bearing

Install the thrust bearing and install the thrust bearing bolts. Torque them to 17 ft-lbs.

7 Install Main Bearings

There are five crankshaft bearings numbered 1 through 5, as viewed from the front of the engine. They are fastened to the block with four bolts, hence the term four-bolt mains.

the thrust bearing.

An arrow on each bearing cap points toward the front of the engine. The center crankshaft bearing, number-3, is

All of the upper crankshaft bearing inserts have an oil groove, and in the center of the groove is an oil gallery hole from the block. The upper crankshaft bearing inserts also have additional holes in the oil groove at 10 o'clock and 2 o'clock to provide oil to the oil spray nozzles on the 6.5L engine. The 6.2L engine does not have oil spray nozzles. The oil spray nozzles are mounted in the crankshaft bearing bulk heads. The lower bearing inserts do not have oil groove or holes.

During initial assembly at the Moraine, Ohio, engine plant, the crankshaft bearings are select fitted to each of the five crankshaft bearing bores. The total diameter size range of crankshaft bearing bores 1 through 5 is 79.826–79.850 mm (3.145–3.146 inches). This range divides into three sizes, represented by the numbers 1, 2, or 3. The proper size number is then stamped on the pan rail at the corresponding crankshaft bearing bulkhead.

7 Install Main Bearings *continued*

The crankshaft is color-marked in red/orange, blue, or white near each crankshaft bearing journal. Cross-referencing the size number on the pan rail with the color on the crankshaft indicates the proper bearing selection. Crankshaft bearings are available in standard 0.013 mm (0.0005 inch) and 0.026 mm (0.0010 inch) undersized for select fitting to attain proper crankshaft bearing clearance. Undersized refers to an undersized or smaller crankshaft diameter, not the size of the bearing insert thickness. (Chapter 2 contains a table showing the pan rail numbers 1-2-3 that correspond to the main bearing inserts).

8 Check Main Bearing Clearance

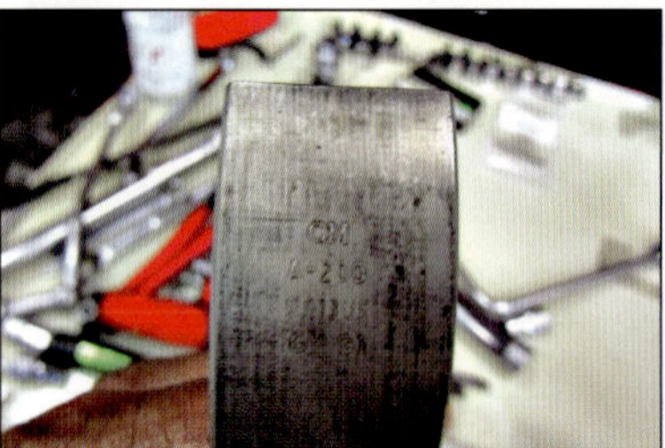

Check the clearance on main bearing journals 1 through 4, which should be 0.045 to 0.083 mm (0.0018 to 0.0032 inches). Check the clearance on the number-5 journal, which is 0.055 to 0.093 mm (0.0022 to 0.0037 inches). Main bearing shells are available in the standard size 0.013 mm (0.0005 inch) and 0.026 mm (0.001 inch) undersize. Main bearings are select fitted to each of the five main bearing bores.

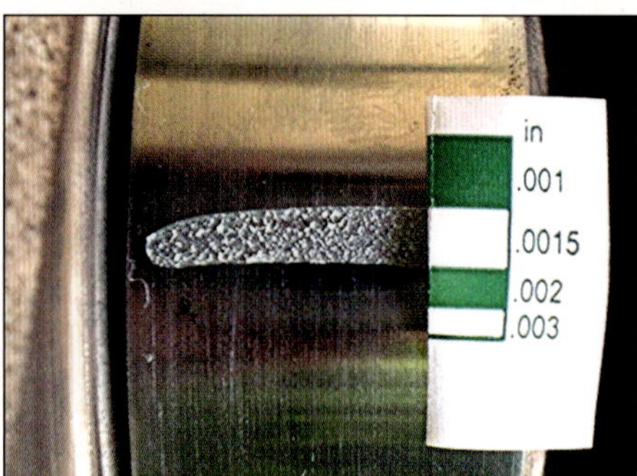

The rear main bearing on all 6.2L engines up to 1988 used a two-piece rope rear main seal, which was later replaced by a one-piece lip seal. The upper crankshaft bearing inserts must have holes for the piston oil nozzles

Bearing size combinations should provide the following clearances, which you check using Plastigauge: Crankshaft bearing numbers 1, 2, 3, and 4: 0.045–0.083 mm (0.0018–0.0033 inch) and crankshaft bearing number 5: 0.055–0.093 mm (0.0022–0.0037 inch).

(jets) used on 6.5L turbocharged engines. The 6.5L turbo engines were assembled with three-hole upper crankshaft bearing inserts in positions 1, 2, 3, and 4 and with a two-hole upper crankshaft bearing insert in position. Replace the upper crankshaft bearing inserts with the same type as originally installed for proper lubrication to the piston oil nozzles. The 6.2L engine does not have these three-hole upper bearings.

9 Install Crankshaft

Coat all main bearings with Permatex Ultra Slick engine assembly lube. Install the upper crankshaft bearing inserts to the block and the lower crankshaft bearing inserts to the crankshaft bearing caps. Then, apply engine oil to the crankshaft bearing inner surfaces.

Install the crankshaft, then apply a 1/8-inch bead of RTV gasket maker (GM part number 1052942) or Permatex Red on each side of the rear crankshaft bearing cap area.

Install the upper half of the rear main rope seal into the block and the bottom half of the rope seal into the engine, if used.

10 Tighten Main Bearing Cap

All 6.2L and 1992–1997 6.5L engines use 12-mm-diameter inner and outer cap bolts. Apply engine oil to the crankshaft bearing cap bolt threads and tap the caps into place with a brass or leather mallet before the bolts are installed. Do not use the bolts to pull the crankshaft bearing caps into their seats because this could damage the cap and/or block. First, torque all inner bolts to 110 ft-lbs (150 Nm). Next, tighten all outer main bearing cap bolts to 100 ft-lbs (136 Nm). When doing CUCV military training, I had a student misinterpret the specs and torque it to 150 ft-lbs instead of 150 Nm and break the inner main bolt. If using aftermarket bolts, such as those from ARP, refer to their specs before applying torque.

Main Bearing Stud Kits

The Heath Heavy-Duty Main Stud Kit replaces all 20 main bearing cap bolts with studs. The Heath Main Stud Kit fits 1997-and-earlier 6.5L turbo engines and 6.2L engines.

For 1998 to 2001 6.5L engines, double-check your block casting number to see if it is a 506 block (using the last three digits of the casting number).

If your block is a 506 block, you need the 506-specific main stud kit because this version of the 6.5L used 10-mm-diameter outer bolts and had a passage for the oil jet to cool the pistons. The 506 block also used three oil holes in the upper main bearing insert. The main bearing cap stud kit greatly decreases cracking in the main webbing due to stress risers caused by the bolts. These studs are a must for higher-horsepower turbocharged 6.2L engines. ■

TECH TIP — Crankshaft Bearing Cap Bolt Sizes

1998–2005 6.5L crankshaft bearing cap bolt sizes are as follows:
• All inner crankshaft bearing cap bolts on crankshaft bearing caps 1, 2, 3, 4, and 5 are long 12-mm bolts.
• All outer crankshaft bearing cap bolts on crankshaft bearing caps 1 and 5 are short 12-mm bolts.
• All outer crankshaft bearing cap bolts on crankshaft bearing caps 2, 3, and 4 are 10-mm bolts.
• The main bearing bolts on the 6.5L are torque-to-yield, and you must use new bolts. These bolts will be tightened using the torque turn method. I also recommend replacing all main bearing bolts, and you have the option to use the torque turn method on your 6.2L engine. ■

On all 1998-and-later 6.5L engines, apply engine oil to the crankshaft bearing cap bolt threads. The crankshaft bearing caps are to be tapped into place with a brass or leather mallet before the bolts are installed. Never pull the crankshaft bearing caps into their seats using the bolts because this could damage the bearing cap and/or block. Install the number 1, 2, 4, and 5 crankshaft bearing caps and bearing by tapping into place with a brass or leather mallet, then apply engine oil to the cap bolt threads and install all the crankshaft bearing cap inner 12-mm bolts for the 1, 2, 4, and 5 main bearings and torque them to 55 ft-lbs.

11 Install Thrust Main Bearing Number-3

Install the number-3 (center) crankshaft thrust bearing cap and the thrust bearing by tapping it into place with a brass or leather mallet. Install the number-3 crankshaft bearing cap inner 12-mm bolts and torque them to 10 ft-lbs. Tap the end of the crankshaft first rearward then forward with a lead hammer to line up the crankshaft bearing and the crankshaft thrust surfaces. Then, retorque the inner 12-mm bolts to 55 ft-lbs. Measure the crankshaft end play with the crankshaft forced forward. Measure at the front end of the number-3 crankshaft bearing with a feeler gauge. The proper clearance is 0.10 to 0.25 mm (0.004 to 0.0010 inch).

12 Tighten Remaining Caps

Tighten all crankshaft main bearing cap bolts in the following sequence: Tighten all main bearing cap inner 12-mm bolts to 55 ft-lbs and then turn the inner 12-mm bolts an additional 90 degrees or a quarter torque turn.

Tighten the outer 12-mm bolts (crankshaft bearing caps 1 and 5) to 48 ft-lbs. Retighten the outer 12-mm bolts (crankshaft bearing caps 1 and 5) to 48 ft-lbs and then turn the outer 12-mm bolts an additional quarter turn. Tighten the outer 10-mm bolts (crankshaft bearing caps 2, 3, and 4) to 30 ft-lbs. Do not torque turn the outer 10-mm bolts (crankshaft bearing caps 2, 3, and 4) an additional 90 degrees. Try turning the crankshaft to check for binding. If the crankshaft does not turn freely, loosen the crankshaft bearing cap bolts, one pair at a time, until the tight bearing is located. A lack of clearance at the bearing could be caused by burrs on the crankshaft bearing cap, foreign matter between the insert and the block or the crankshaft bearing cap, or a faulty insert.

13 Install 6.5L/Late-Model 6.2L Crankshaft Rear Main Seal

To install the one-piece rear main seal, use the J 39084 Rear Main Seal Installer or tap it in place with a plastic hammer. Coat the crankshaft surface with engine oil and coat the lip of the new oil seal with engine oil or lithium grease before installing the new oil seal. Do not scratch or nick the sealing edge of the oil seal. Install the oil seal with the spring cavity facing the engine, onto the crankshaft. Using the J 39084, drive the seal into the crankshaft until the tool bottoms against the block and the rear crankshaft bearing cap.

14 Piston Size Identification

Pistons are available in standard, high-limit standard, and 0.030-inch oversize. Each piston will have a size identification mark on its face and the piston boss surface. Using service oversized pistons does not affect engine balance. The 6.5L bores for number 7 and 8 were larger than 1 through 6. There is only one production standard piston grade size on the 6.5L engine. When using production standard grade size pistons in all eight cylinder bores, a *J* is stamped in a single place on the cylinder block oil pan rail like the 6.2L.

A 0.13-mm (0.005-inch) oversize production piston is available in a plant rework of cylinders that do not meet the production standard specification. An *S* stamped on the pan rail next to any reworked cylinder identifies that cylinder as production oversize. A *J* will also be stamped in a single place on the oil pan rail to represent that all remaining cylinders are production standard.

The 6.2L engine used six matching cylinder bore sizes. Size codes A, B, C, D, E, and G are used to match the piston and cylinder bore. The size codes are stamped on the cylinder block pan rail.

15 Piston Selection

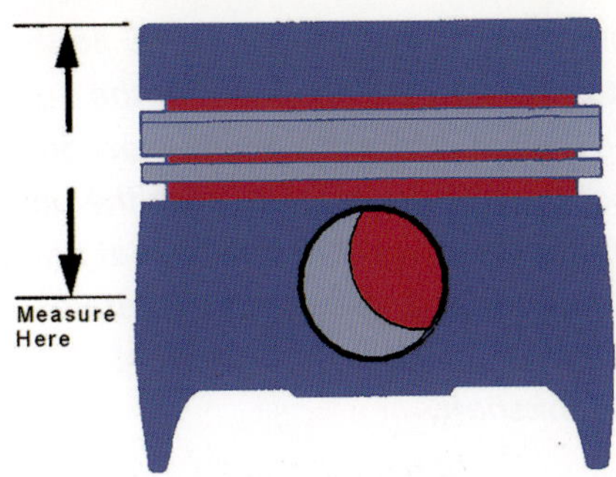

The piston skirts are barrel-shaped. To accurately determine the piston diameter, the piston must be measured at a specific gauge point. The piston measuring point is 2.575 inches from the top of the piston. The cylinder bore measurement and honing was done in chapter 6. Recheck that measurement at this point with the dial bore gauge or telescoping gauge and outside micrometer for each cylinder. Subtract the piston diameter from the bore measurement and you will have the piston-to-bore clearance. The specification for the 6.2L cylinders 1 to 6 is 0.0035 to 0.0045 inch and for cylinders 7 and 8 is 0.004 to 0.005 inch.

This 6.5L piston measures 4.052 inches and the specification for the 6.5L cylinders 1 to 6 is 0.0035 to 0.0049 inch and for cylinders 7 and 8 is 0.004 to 0.0054 inch. Mark the pistons for the specific cylinders that they will be installed into for reassembly below.

Professional Mechanic Tip

Surplus Pistons   PRO TIP

If you check eBay, you will find a lot of military surplus pistons for sale from the HMMWV. ■

16 Measure Floating Piston Pin and Bushing Clearance

1. Measure the piston pin-to-piston pin bushing.
2. Measure the piston pin diameter.
3. Measure the piston pin bushing inside diameter with an inside micrometer. Subtract the piston pin diameter from the piston pin bushing inside diameter to obtain the clearance. If the clearance is excessive, replace the piston and

piston pin. Piston pins are available only with new pistons.

4. If the clearance is excessive with a new piston and piston pin, replace the connecting rod. Piston pin bushings are available only with new connecting rods.
5. Measure the piston pin-to-piston clearance.
6. Measure the piston pin diameter.

7. Measure the piston pin hole inside diameter using an inside micrometer.
8. Subtract the piston pin diameter from the piston pin hole diameter to obtain the clearance.
9. If the clearance is excessive, replace the piston and piston pin. Piston pins are available only with new pistons.

17 Install Piston and Connecting Rod Assembly

Install the selected piston for the correct cylinder to the connecting rod with the Ricardo Comet V flame slot on the same side as the connecting rod bearing tang slots. When installing the piston in the cylinder, the Ricardo Comet V flame slot must face the outside of the cylinder toward the exhaust manifold. Apply engine oil to the surface of the piston pin and install the piston pin to the piston and the connecting rod. The piston, piston pin, and connecting rod assembly must be held firmly with no side-to-side movement during piston pin retaining ring installation.

17 Install Piston and Connecting Rod Assembly *continued*

Install the piston pin retaining rings; use the piston retaining ring installer OTC 4845 wrist pin installer and remover available from Amazon. Align the open end of the retaining ring toward the bottom of the piston. Use a small screwdriver and start one end of the ring in the groove. Install the special tool through the ring and into the piston pin and press down on the ring with the pin on the tool. Turn the tool-to-seat ring in the groove. Check the retaining rings for proper assembly and inspect the retaining ring to make sure that it is seated in the ring groove. The opening in an installed retaining ring should face downward, toward the crankshaft.

18 Measure Piston Ring Gap

Install the keystone top compression ring into the cylinder, using the piston to square it up in the bore at the lower quarter of the cylinder and measure the piston ring end gap with a feeler gauge. The top ring specification is 0.3 to 0.550 mm (0.0118 to 0.0216 inch). Install the second compression ring into the cylinder, using the piston to square it up in the bore at the lower quarter of the cylinder and measure the piston ring end gap with a feeler gauge. The second ring specification is 0.750 to 1 mm (0.0295 to 0.0394 inch).

19 Install Piston Rings

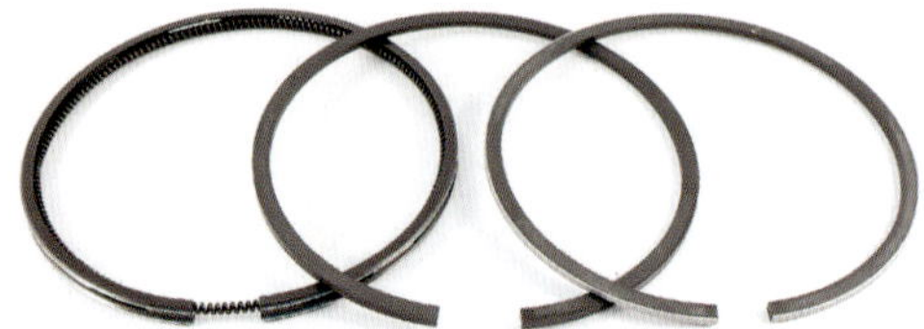

Slip the outer surface of the second compression ring with the dot facing up into the respective piston ring groove to make sure the ring does not bind. If the ring groove causes binding, dress the groove with a fine-cut file. Replace the distorted rings. The oil ring is a two-piece ring, consisting of an expander and a scraper ring. Earlier LH6 or C engines used a three-piece ring set. All LL4 or J engines and all later 6.2L and all 6.5L engines used the two-piece ring set. Install the oil expansion ring in the oil ring groove and the oil ring over the oil expansion ring.

When installing the top keystone barrel-faced compression rings, make sure that the marked side is facing the top of the piston. While assembling the rings onto the piston, rotate the rings to check for binding. When binding occurs, inspect the ring grooves for dirt or damage, such as nicks caused by improper installation.

20 Install Piston and Rod Assembly

Piston, Connecting Rod,
and Bearing Installation

You will need an adjustable piston ring compressor for the 6.5L engine or a fixed 4-inch-diameter piston ring compressor from Summit Tools for the 6.2L engine. The connecting rod bearings are precision insert connecting rod bearings and do not require shims for adjustment. Do not file the rods or the rod caps.

If the engine has excessive clearances, install a new bearing. Service bearings are available in standard size (with yellow color for identification) and 0.026 mm undersized (with green color for identification).

Use half of a 0.026-mm (0.0010-inch) undersized insert, which will decrease the clearance by 0.013 mm (0.0005 inch), rather than using a full standard bearing. When using selective fit rod bearings, always use the standard bearing in the connecting rod, and the undersized bearing insert in the rod cap.

The color coding for selective fit rod bearings is different from the color coding for the crankshaft bearings. Connecting rod bearings are available in 0.026 mm (0.0010 inch) undersized for select fitting. Theses engines may have both standard

20 · Install Piston and Rod Assembly *continued*

and 0.08-mm (0.0010-inch) oversize connecting rod bearings. The oversize connecting rod cap's lower end is stamped with OS.

Place the selected pistons in position to be installed into their respective cylinders and remove the connecting rod cap from the piston and connecting rod assembly. Make sure that the cylinder walls are clean, lubricate the cylinder walls with engine oil, and have your pistons ready to go into their measured cylinders by letters. Install two 3/8-inch rubber hoses onto the connecting rod studs or use special tool protectors. Locate the piston ring end gaps with the piston swirl indent facing up in the following way:

- *Oil ring expander gap at 45 degrees left of the flame slot*
- *Oil control ring gaps at 180 degrees opposite the oil expander ring*
- *Second compression ring gap at the piston top and under the flame slot*
- *Keystone top ring 180 degrees opposite the second ring*

Tap the piston down into the bore using light blows with a dead-blow hammer piston installation tool or a hammer handle while guiding the connecting rod to the journal from beneath the engine. Hold the ring compressor against the block until all rings have entered the cylinder bore. Remove the rod bolt protector hoses from the connecting rod bolts. Apply engine oil to the connecting rod bearings and check the rod bearing clearance with Plastigauge material. The rod bearing clearance should be 0.045 to 0.100 mm (0.0018 to 0.0039 inch).

Lubricate the piston and rings with engine oil and without disturbing the ring end gap location, install the adjustable piston ring compressor or use the 4-inch fixed cone on the 6.2L pistons. (Photo Courtesy Jim Halderman)

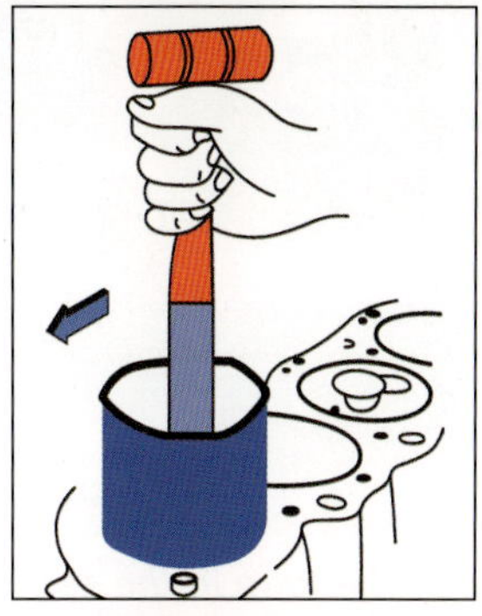

Install the piston so that the flame slot is down toward the exhaust manifold.

TECH TIP · Connecting Rod Bearings

Each connecting rod and bearing cap should be marked, beginning at the front of the engine. Cylinders 1, 3, 5, and 7 are the left bank and 2, 4, 6, and 8 are the right bank. The numbers on the connecting rod and bearing cap must be on the same side when installed in the cylinder bore. If a connecting rod is moved from one cylinder to another, new connecting rod bearings should be fitted and the connecting rod should be numbered to correspond with the new cylinder number. ■

21 · Tighten Rod Cap Bolts and Check Side Clearance

Install the connecting rod cap and the nuts with the bearing and tighten the nuts to 48 ft-lbs.

Measure the connecting rod side clearance. Using a feeler gauge between the connecting rod and the crankshaft, measure the side clearance, which should be between 0.17 and 0.63 mm (0.007 and 0.025 inch). (Photo Courtesy Jim Halderman)

22 Install Oil Pump Assembly

Install the oil pump drive, the idler shaft, and the drive gear with the shaft. Align the marks made during disassembly and install the spacer plate and cover; then, torque the bolts to 12 ft-lbs. Install the pickup tube and screen assembly, if necessary. Align the tube in the same location as it was removed from. Prime the oil pump by filling the cavity with clean engine oil or pack it with Vaseline. Turn the driveshaft by hand and check for smooth rotation. If it does not rotate smoothly, check for proper assembly. Install the oil pump with the driveshaft with a new clip to the oil pump drive stalk or vacuum pump. Install the oil pump bolts and torque to 65 ft-lbs.

23 Install Oil Pan

Apply a 2-mm bead of high-temperature RTV sealant to the oil pan rear seal at the inside corners where the seal meets the rear crankshaft bearing cap on the engine block. Make sure the RTV is wet to the touch and not skinned over when you install the pan. Install the oil pan rear seal to the rear crankshaft bearing cap before the sealer starts to dry. Install the oil pan to the block and the oil pan bolts to the engine block; tighten the bolts in the following order: the two rear bolts to 23 ft-lbs and all the other bolts to 89 in-lbs.

24 Install Timing Chain and Sprocket

Install the front crankshaft oil seal using the J 22102 special service tool with the open end of the seal facing the inside cover or tap it in using a large socket.

Install the keyway in the crankshaft and do not damage the reluctor wheel square bosses on the 6.5L EFI engine. The 6.2L and the 6.5L mechanical injection engine does not use a reluctor wheel.

Place the chain and the two sprockets on the bench. The camshaft sprocket 0 is at 6 o'clock and the crankshaft sprocket 0 is at 12 o'clock. Install the crankshaft sprocket with the 6.5L EFI reluctor wheel square bosses facing the front of an EFI engine and the camshaft sprocket with the timing chain as a unit with the timing marks facing each other. You may have to rotate the camshaft so the woodruff key is at 3 o'clock to line up with the camshaft sprocket 0 at the 6 o'clock position.

24 | Install Timing Chain and Sprocket *continued*

The two timing mark positions set the valve timing at TDC for the number-6 cylinder, not number-1. Both the number-1 and -6 pistons will be at TDC.

Install the fuel injection pump camshaft drive gear, the washer, and the bolt. Tighten the bolt to 125 ft-lbs.

25 | Install Engine Front Cover

Clean the old sealer from the sealing surfaces and inspect the front cover for cracks and damage to the sealing surfaces. Make sure the sealing surface is free from oil.

Coat the seal lips with grease and apply a 2-mm bead of anaerobic sealant to the front cover sealing area. Install the front cover to the engine with the cover bolts; tighten the front cover bolts to 33 ft-lbs. On the 6.5L EFI engine, you will need to do the TDC Off-set Recovery procedure with a factory-level scan tool when the timing chain, timing gears, engine front cover, crankshaft position sensor, crankshaft, or other components affecting the timing are replaced. Replacing any of the following will affect timing: timing chain or gears, front cover, crankshaft position (CKP) sensor (6.5L EFI engine), or crankshaft.

Install the injection pump-driven gear onto the drive gear attached to the camshaft. Align the two timing marks and place some mechanic's wire to hold it in place while you install the harmonic balancer.

26 Install Crankshaft Balancer

The harmonic balancer should always be replaced on a 6.2L or 6.5L engine because it is prone to failure that causes noise and eventual crankshaft breakage. Many engine builders use a fluid-filled balancer due to its superior performance, but it can cost in excess of $400.

Apply a small amount of clean engine oil to the inner diameter of the crankshaft balancer and lightly tap the balancer into the crankshaft. You can use the GM balancer installation tool if you have it to install the balancer. If not, you can use a hammer and a block of wood to drive the balancer on most of the way and then use the bolt to pull the balancer in the rest of the way onto the crankshaft.

Install the crankshaft balancer bolt and washer. Make sure that the curved part of the washer is pointed away from the engine, and tighten the bolt to 200 ft-lbs. Install the crankshaft pulley to the crankshaft balancer, install the crankshaft pulley bolts, and torque the bolts to 30 ft-lbs.

27 Set/Check Cover Timing Mark

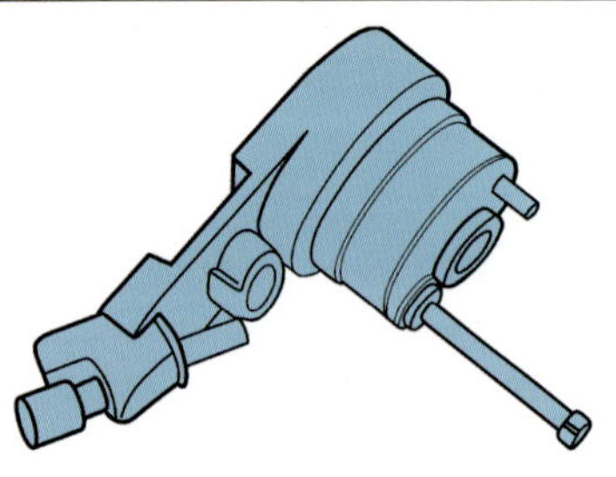

Tool J-33042.

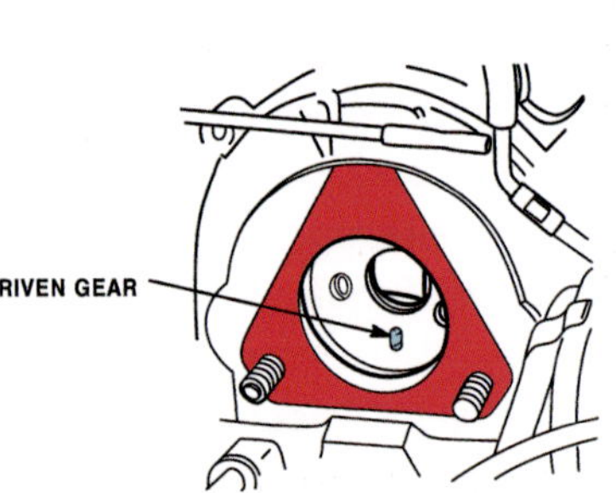

Turn the crankshaft one revolution, which brings it to the number-1 cylinder at TDC, and the slot in the balancer lines up with the 0 mark on the timing bracket.

Using a torque wrench and an 18-mm socket on the tool's hex nut, turn the nut with 50 ft-lbs of torque counterclockwise and tighten the 10-mm nut on the top stud so the tool does not move. Make sure that the crankshaft did not turn during this procedure. Push down on the scriber with hand pressure and check the mark. If it does not line up, file down the old mark and make a new one by hitting the scribe with a mallet. If you are installing a new cover, just strike a new mark with the scribe and mallet.

Special Tool

GM Special Tool J-33042

Remove the 8-mm bolt from the GM special tool J-33042 and install it in place of the injection pump without the gasket. If the timing gear is on right, the pin goes into the elongated hole in the driven pump gear at the 6 o'clock position. Place the 8-mm bolt back into the J-33042 in the threaded hole above the pin and lightly tighten it. Place one 10-mm nut on the front cover top stud and lightly tighten it. It needs to be finger tight. ■

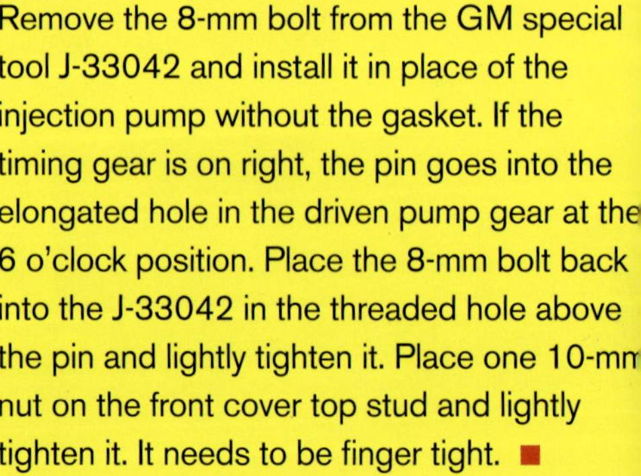

This procedure is done to check an existing timing mark or make a new one if the front cover is being replaced. Turn the crankshaft bolt and note the position of the timing slot to move the engine to the number-1 cylinder position. The engine was timed at number-6, so turn the crankshaft one revolution, which brings it to the number-1 cylinder at TDC, and the slot in the balancer lines up with the 0 mark on the timing bracket.

28 Install Valve Lifters

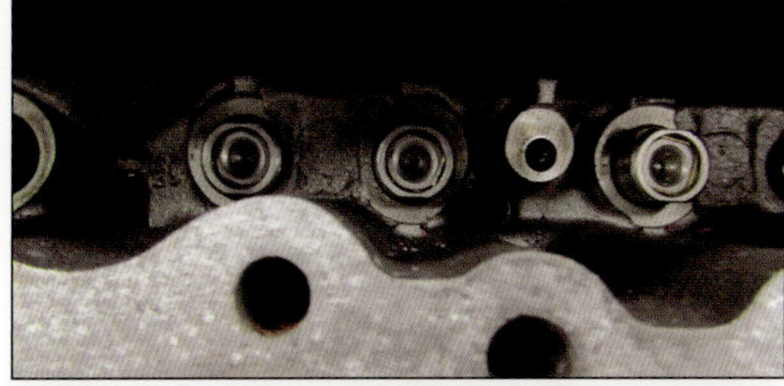

Always replace the lifters when you install a new camshaft. Prime any new valve lifters before installation by working the lifter plunger while submerged in clean kerosene or diesel fuel. Some engines can have both standard and 0.25-mm (0.010-inch) oversize valve lifters. The oversize lifter will have the number 10 etched on the side. The block will be stamped OS on the cast pad adjacent to the lifter bore and on the top rail of the cylinder case above the lifter bore. Coat the lifter roller and the bearings with GM Engine Oil Supplement, install the lifters in their original location, and make sure the straight edge of the guide plates and the clamps face away from the cylinders.

Install the guide plates and clamps. Make sure there are no burrs on the guide plates, which will create a lifter-type noise when running. Tighten the clamp bolts to 20 ft-lbs. If the engine will not turn over by hand, one or more of the lifters may be binding in the guide plates. After installing the clamps, turn the crankshaft by hand 720 degrees, two full turns, to confirm the free movement of the lifters in the guide plates.

29 Cylinder Head Assembly

Reassemble the valves into the head.

Lubricate the valve stems with engine oil and install the valves, valve spring shims (if required), and exhaust valve stem seals. Seat the valve stem seals against the valve guides and use a spring compressor to install the valve springs, valve spring dampers, valve spring shields, intake valve spring caps, exhaust valve spring rotators, valve stem O-ring seals, and valve stem keys.

Measure the valve spring installed height of each valve spring using a narrow thin scale. Measure the valve installed height from the spring seat in the cylinder head to the top of the valve spring cap. The measurement should be 46 mm (1.8110 inches). If valve spring measurements exceed specifications, inspect for the following: proper assembly, excessive wear at the valve keys, worn retainers, and worn valve key area on the valves.

Install or remove the valve spring seat shims between the spring and the cylinder head to obtain the desired measurement. Install the prechambers (if removed) by aligning the locating notch. The prechamber should be flush to a maximum of 0.05 mm (0.002 inch) protrusion. The prechamber must not protrude out of the cylinder head more than 0.05 mm (0.002 inch) and must not recess into the cylinder head.

30 Head Gasket

Do not use a sealer, such as Permatex Spray-A-Gasket on Fel-Pro Print-O-Seal head gaskets because they already have sealer on them and the Permatex sealer can react with this sealer and cause a leak. Early 6.2L and some 6.5L engines used the Victor head gasket that was green and had good sealing characteristics for internal combustion leaks. Make sure that the block gasket surfaces are clean. The head gasket material is soft. Handle the gasket with care. Make sure the gasket surface is not creased or dented.

30 | Head Gasket *continued*

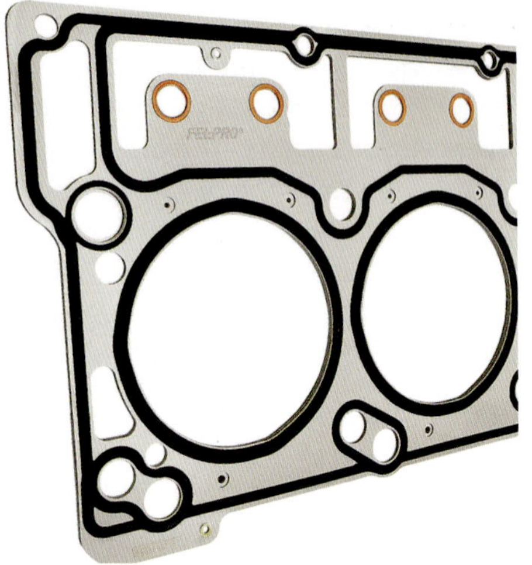

The other head gasket used was the red Fel-Pro that was better at preventing external coolant leaks. The new and improved Print-O-Seal Fel-Pro head gasket is the preferred choice and is made with sealant on the gasket surface. Additional sealer may cause leakage or malfunction on the Fel-Pro gasket. In addition, some sealers may attack the initial sealant on the gasket. Use the head gaskets for the 6.5L diesel to prevent fire ring interference.

31 | Install Cylinder Head Studs

One 6.2L/6.5L building technique that helps to prevent head gasket failure, prevent warpage, and improve head clamping action is the use of a stud kit available from ARP or other racing and parts suppliers. The best way to install these studs is to install about three of them into the holes and seal them with the Loctite sealer that comes in the kit, then install the head and the remaining studs sealing them in the bottom threads with the Loctite sealer. The advantage of installing the stud in this manner is to prevent binding that has been experienced by some rebuilders.

32 | Install Head

Install the cylinder head gaskets to the block, over the cylinder head dowel pins. Install a brass contour plug using Loctite on 1982 and 1983 engines with the core-out hole. Install the cylinder heads to the block, over the cylinder head gaskets and the cylinder head dowel pins. Apply the white Teflon thread sealant to the 17 new head bolts' threads three-quarters of the way up the threads and under the bolt heads. Install new cylinder head bolts using the installation and tightening sequence.

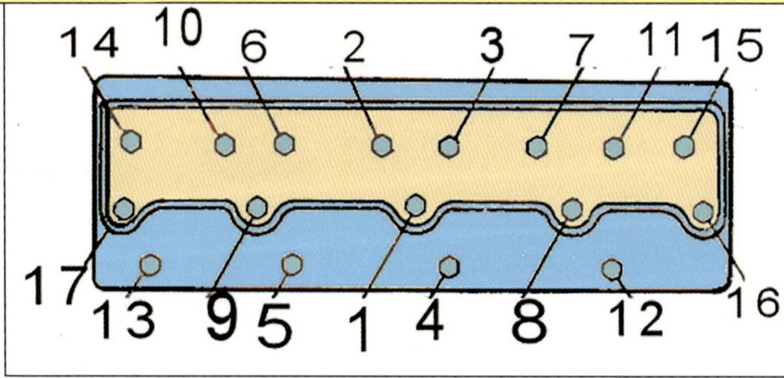

Tighten all of the head bolts in sequence (1 through 17) to 20 ft-lbs. Tighten all of the head bolts again in sequence to 55 ft-lbs starting at number 1.

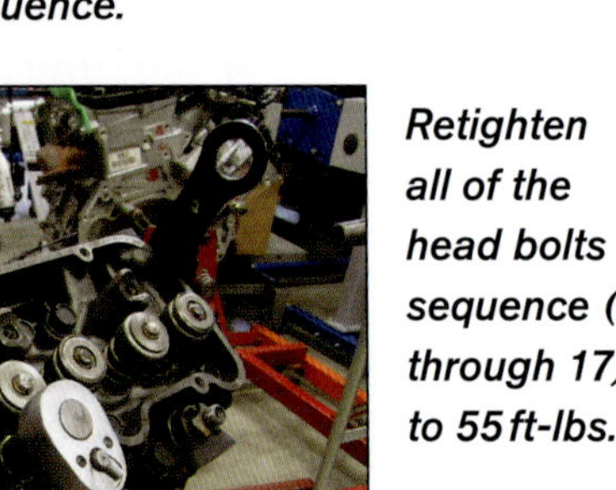

Retighten all of the head bolts in sequence (1 through 17) to 55 ft-lbs.

Tighten in sequence (1 through 17) all head bolts an additional 90 to 100 degrees or a quarter turn. On ARP studs, the fourth step is to tighten the nuts in sequence to 90 ft-lbs, not 90 degrees.

33 Install Valve Rocker Arm, Shaft, and Pushrod

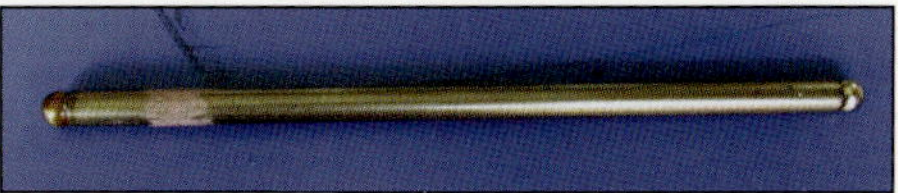

Make sure that the copper-colored ball ends of the valve pushrod seats are in the top position to seat into the rocker arms. The shiny hardened end of the pushrod goes into the roller lifter.

Install the valve pushrods with the copper-colored, painted, or marked end up to avoid damage or premature wear.

Install the valve rocker arm shaft assembly. Improper installation of the valve rocker arm shaft bolts may cause valve rocker arm shaft breakage and piston-to-valve contact. Install the bolts and rotate the crankshaft until the mark on the crankshaft balancer is at the 2 o'clock position. Rotate the crankshaft counterclockwise 88 mm (3.5 inches), aligning the crankshaft balancer mark with the first lower water pump bolt at approximately the 12:30 position. This procedure will position the engine so that no valves are close to a piston crown. Finger-tighten the bolts and tighten the bolts alternately to 40 ft-lbs. Rotate the crankshaft to make sure that there is free movement of the valvetrain.

34 Install Valve Rocker Arm Cover

Clean the sealing surfaces on the cylinder head and the valve rocker arm cover so that the surfaces are free from oil and foreign material. Never allow the RTV sealant to enter any blind-threaded hole. RTV sealant that is allowed to enter a blind-threaded hole can cause hydraulic lock of the fastener when the fastener is tightened. Hydraulic lock of a fastener can lead to damage to the fastener and/or the components. It can also prevent the proper clamping loads to be obtained when the fastener is tightened. Improper clamping loads can prevent proper sealing of the components, allowing leakage to occur. Preventing proper fastener tightening can allow the components to loosen or separate, leading to extensive engine damage.

Apply a 5-mm bead of RTV sealant to rocker arm covers inboard of the bolt holes. The sealer must be wet to the touch when the bolts are tightened. Install new valve rocker arm cover grommets and use new valve rocker arm cover bolts if they are serviced with the grommet. Install the valve rocker arm cover, cover the bolts, and tighten them to 20 ft-lbs.

Install the rocker arm covers.

35 Install Water Pump and Oil Fill Tube

Clean the sealing surfaces on the water pump plate and the block, and install the water pump and the gasket to the water pump plate using the bolts from the engine side. Apply high-temperature thread adhesive to the bolt threads and install the bolts. Tighten them to 20 ft-lbs.

35 Install Water Pump and Oil Fill Tube *continued*

Apply a bead of anaerobic sealer (GM part number 1052942) to the water pump plate. The sealer must be wet to the touch when installing the plate. Apply Teflon sealant to the threads of the bolts and studs, install the bolts and studs, and tighten the water pump to the front cover bolts to 32 ft-lbs.

Tighten the top water pump plate bolts to 20 ft-lbs. Install the oil fill tube grommet to the front cover and install the oil fill tube to the front cover and tighten the nuts to 17 ft-lbs.

36 Install Engine Coolant Thermostat and Water Crossover

Install the correct new thermostat and new gasket into the water crossover housing and tighten the bolts to 31 ft-lbs. (See chapter 2 for the thermostat selection table.) This engine uses a single full-blocking vertical-position thermostat.

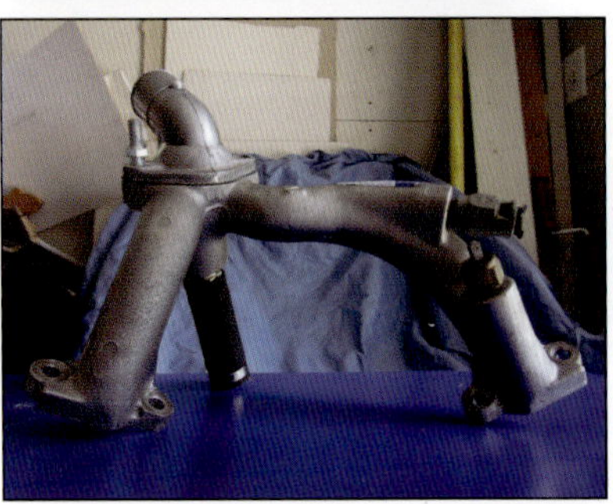

Install a new water crossover gasket and the coolant crossover housing assembly. Install the studs and the bolts, tighten them to 31 ft-lbs, and connect the bypass hose.

37 Install Pump and Lines

Before installing the lower intake manifold, assemble the fuel injection pump and lines and install the assembly onto the engine. Line up the line on the pump with the line on the front cover and tighten the three bolts to 20 ft-lbs (42 Nm).

38 Install Lower Intake Manifold

Install the lower or main intake manifold with new gaskets, bolts/studs, and fuel line clips. Use white Teflon sealer to seal the four bolts (numbers 9, 11, 13, and 15) that are exposed to the crankcase. Apply thread-locking compound to the threads of the bolts and the studs that are not numbered (numbers 9, 11, 13, or 15). Tighten the intake manifold bolts/studs, in sequence, to 31 ft-lbs. Install the hoses and the clamps to the fuel filter assembly. Install the fuel filter assembly and the engine wiring harness bracket. Tighten the fuel filter mount bolts to 31 ft-lbs.

39 Install Upper Intake Manifold

Apply the silicone sealant to the turbocharger outlet and install the upper intake manifold gasket. Slide the intake into the turbocharger outlet hose. Install the intake manifold bolts and tighten to 17 ft-lbs. Install the clamp for the turbocharger connector hose and tighten the connector hose clamps to 50 in-lbs. Install the crankcase depression regulator valve.

40 Install Fuel Injection Nozzle

Install eight new or rebuilt fuel injection nozzles and tighten them to 50 ft-lbs (70 Nm).

Connect all eight fuel injection lines and tighten them to 31 ft-lbs. Install all-new rubber return lines on the fuel injection nozzles.

41 Install Turbocharger and CDR

If your rebuild is equipped with a factory or aftermarket turbocharger, install it in the reverse order of removal.

Install a new CDR valve with new hoses.

42 Install Oil Pump Drive

Install a new gasket to the oil pump drive and install the oil pump drive to the engine. Index the drive with the camshaft gear and the oil pump driveshaft. Make sure the drive seats fully. Install the clamp and the bolt and tighten the bolt to 31 ft-lbs.

Installation

At this point in your rebuild project, you now have a completed 6.2L or 6.5L engine ready for installation into your truck. Follow the photos taken during engine removal and the tags placed on the connectors as a guide for reinstallation.

43 Install Engine

Install the lifting device to the engine assembly and remove the engine assembly from the engine stand. Install the flywheel or flexplate to the crankshaft, and then install the engine assembly in the vehicle using the tags and photos taken as a guide for installation.

Install the left and right engine mount bracket and tighten the engine mount bracket bolts to 40 ft-lbs. Install the left and right engine-mount through bolts and tighten to 44 ft-lbs. Lower the engine into the truck.

43 Install Engine *continued*

Use the following steps to install the engine:
- Raise the vehicle and support it with safety stands.
- Install the bellhousing bolts from the engine block to the transmission.
- Install the starter on the engine block.
- Install the transmission cooler lines to the radiator and the auxiliary transmission cooler.
- Install the bolts from the flywheel to the torque convertor.
- Install the exhaust pipe from the turbocharger to the catalytic convertor.
- Install the oil filter adapter and filter to the engine block.
- Install the power steering lines to the power steering pump.
- Install the front propeller shaft in the vehicle (4WD only).
- Reconnect the electrical connector for the block heater.
- Install the engine oil cooler lines to the engine assembly.
- Install the ground strap in the right front corner of the engine.
- Remove the safety stands and lower the vehicle.
- Install the inner splash shields on the vehicle.
- Install the ground straps at the right rear cylinder head.
- Install the fuels lines to the fuel manager/filter.
- Install the heater lines in the vehicle.
- Install the radiator hoses on the engine block.
- Install the radiator in the vehicle.
- Install the generator to the right accessory mounting bracket.
- Reposition the air-conditioning compressor on the left accessory mounting bracket.
- Reconnect the engine wiring harness.
- Whenever the cooling system is serviced or drained for service procedures, two cooling system sealing pellets (GM part number 3634621 or equivalent) can be added to the cooling system. Cooling system sealing pellets must be crushed prior to installation. The cooling system sealing pellets can be added to the radiator or the pressurized coolant reservoir. Do not place the cooling system sealing pellets into a unpressurized coolant recovery reservoir. On these systems, the pellets must be added to the radiator. The sealant pellets may leave a film on the sides of the pressurized and unpressurized coolant recovery reservoirs. This film is normal.
- Fill the engine crankcase with 15W40 engine oil.
- Connect the battery cables to the battery terminals.
- Install a scan tool and check for DTCs on EFI models. Check and adjust the timing for the fuel injection pump mechanical fuel injection systems. (Refer to the Fuel Injection Pump Timing Adjustment step in chapter 2.)
- Perform the TDC offset timing procedure using a factory level scan tool on 6.5L EFI engines and the 6.5L upper engine cover.

44 Fill Coolant

Refill the cooling system using the vacuum suction method. Connect a vacuum suction device that uses air pressure to create a vacuum that will depressurize the engine cooling system. Connect an adapter to the radiator or expansion tank to pull a vacuum on the cooling system. Connect a clear plastic hose to a jug of 6.2 gallons of premixed Dex-Cool and water coolant to fill a dry system with the fill valve closed. Run the shop air with the top two valves open until the pressure gauge reads 20 to 25 inches of Mercury vacuum; then, push the pushbutton to off and close the valve going to the gauge. Then, open the fill valve from the coolant jug and let the coolant flow into the engine.

45 Install Hood

Install the hood on the vehicle using the marks made during engine removal.

Engine Setup and Testing

Once the engine is installed, follow these steps to set it up and test it. First, use a bar to turn the engine over several times, feeling for any evidence that any of the parts are binding. Start and idle the engine, listening for unusual noises. Once idling, operate the engine at about 1,000 rpm until the engine is at operating temperature. Listen for improperly adjusted valves, sticking valves, and other unusual noises. Finally, check for oil and coolant leaks while the engine is running.

DIAGNOSTICS AND MODIFICATIONS

The 1982–1991 6.2L diagnostic concerns dealt with both the engine mechanical problems and also the DB2 mechanical fuel injection system failures. This chapter contains a diagnostic guide at the beginning followed by a series of specific diagnostic concerns in no particular order. It covers all 6.2L engines and some of the mechanical-fuel-system 6.5L engines.

Mechanical System Diagnosis

These engines did not use factory-installed turbochargers, but many owners and rebuilders added either an aftermarket turbo or the later 6.5L turbo from a mechanical DB2 6.5L. This took place on both the civilian and military CUCV and HMMWV trucks. The 6.5L with the mechanical DB2 pump was used on civilian models from 1992 to 2001 with and without a turbocharger on both civilian and military HMMWV trucks. The HMMWV never used a turbocharger. The L49 had *F* as the eighth character of the VIN civilian engine that was not turbocharged.

More Than Normal Smoke After Startup (All 6.2L Engines)

Many engines were released with retarded timing and/or incorrect timing. The HPCA setup calibration was

Strategy-based diagnostics is a scientific and organized process of elimination. It directs you to look for the simplest causes to a problem first, before undertaking more difficult and time-consuming procedures.

The housing pressure cold advance (HPCA) system was designed to advance the injection timing 3 to 4 degrees before TDC when the engine is cold to reduce white smoke and improve starting.

set to reduce engine noise associated with cold advance. To fix this, replace the programmable read-only memory (PROM) on EFI engines and rotate the pump flange 1 mm clockwise toward the driver's side, which will provide 2 degrees advance.

Long Crank Time 1982–1991 (All 6.2L Engines)

Any fuel leak introduces air to the fuel system, even if liquid fuel is not found leaking. Check the throttle shaft seal, the pump servo seal, the line connections, the cracked leaking nozzles, and the filter drain seal. Replace the lift pump with the special check-valve mechanical pump (part number 25116503) or install an electric solenoid lift pump and replace the HPCA ball-check regulator valve (part number 10149645).

No Glow Plug Operation 1985–1991 (All 6.2L Engines)

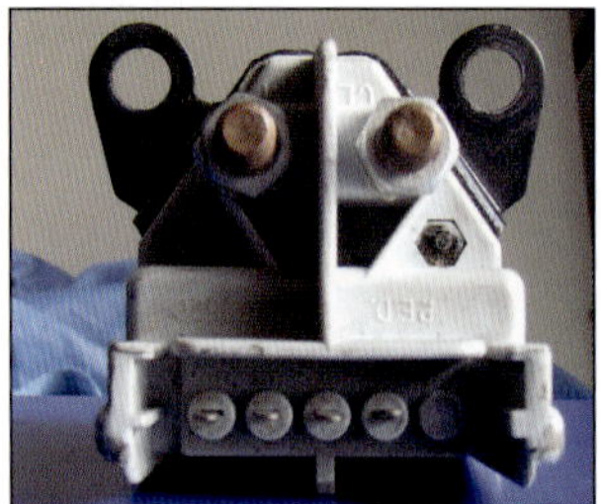

The black electronic glow plug controller needs to be replaced with the gray controller (part number 12088520) to fix glow plug operation on early 6.2L engines using the electronic glow plug controller.

White Smoke After Startup 1990–1991 (VIN C LH6 Light-Duty Engines)

In early 1990 production, some engines were released with retarded timing or incorrect timing marks and problems with the HPCA system. Changes were made in calibration to reduce noise when starting at the plant.

The front cover has a line scribed in it to represent the number-1 cylinder at TDC, and the injection pump has a similar mark on the housing flange also representing TDC for number-1. Initially, these two marks were lined up, but the engine plant began a program of microwaving fuel injection timing so these marks may not be lined up. One millimeter of movement equals a 2-degree change in injection timing. The best timing adjustment is to use luminosity or magnetic timing.

Replace the PROM and rotate the pump flange 1 mm clockwise toward the driver's side, which will provide 2 degrees advance to reduce white smoke at startup.

Loss of Power with White Smoke and Hard Starting (All 6.2L Engines)

Check the basics first, including the fuel filter, air and fuel injection pump climbing, and glow plug operations. If all of those are okay, check for a damaged cam or crank sprocket keyway, which cause incorrect cam and pump timing.

Engine Surge at 65 mph (RPO LL4 J 6.2L)

The number-1 cylinder was cutting out at between 3,100–3,400 rpm. The injection pump was sent to a pump shop to be tested and to be upgraded. Placing a luminosity probe in the cylinder showed the light of compression going out between 3,200 and 3,500 rpm. The injector lines, lifters, and prechamber missing and low compression, or a valve sticking were all possibilities for the misfire. Compression was tested on the number-1 cylinder and found to be below specifications. Upon disassembly, the cylinder was found to have to a 0.0025-inch taper from top to bottom. I replaced the engine with a short-block.

Engine Cranks Normally But Will Not Start

There are several reasons that an engine will crank normally but not start. They are:

1. Incorrect starting procedure: To fix, locate the proper procedure from the online service information.
2. Glow plug control system: Review the glow plug information found in chapter 2.
3. No fuel into cylinders: Remove one glow plug, press the throttle partway, and crank the engine for 5 seconds. If no fuel vapor comes out of the load flow hole, check for a plugged fuel system. If fuel vapors are noticed, remove the remainder of the glow plugs and see if fuel vapors are coming out of the glow plug holes when the engine is cranked. If fuel mist comes out of one glow plug only, clean and test the injector in that cylinder. If no fuel comes out of any of the glow plug holes, suspect a DB2 injection pump problem.
4. Plugged fuel filter: Check and replace the fuel filter.
5. No fuel to injection pump: Perform a fuel supply system check (chapter 2).
6. Restricted fuel filter: Replace the filter.

All 6.5L original engines were equipped with a cartridge-type fuel filter, which can become restricted and cause a no-start or low-power complaint. The fuel filter must be replaced at 30,000 miles.

7. Bad lift pump: Replace.
8. Clogged fuel tank stock: Clean or replace pump.
9. No voltage to the fuel injection pump ESO solenoid: Correct no voltage.
10. Incorrect or contaminated fuel: Change fuel.
11. Incorrect pump timing: Retime fuel.
12. Low compression: Locate cause.
13. Injection pump malfunction: Replace or rebuild.
14. Nozzle malfunction: Use the Glow Plug Resistance procedure or an infrared thermometer to locate the bad nozzle or nozzles. Remove the injection nozzle and pop test it for opening pressure.
15. Air in the fuel supply lines: Review the information in chapter 2 under Evaluation and Diagnosing the Fuel System.

Oil Leaks from High Crankcase Pressure

Check the crankcase for high pressure from a collapsed CDR hose or defective CDR. To do this, install a water manometer in the oil dipstick tube. At engine idle, it should read 1 inch of water; at full load or about 2,000 rpm, it should read 3 to 4 inches of water.

The CDR valve manages the engine crankcase pressure by depressurizing the crankcase, using this valve to regulate how much the intake sucks air out of the crankcase.

Stalling or Underrun

For stalling or underrun, check the following:
1. Check the injection pump metering valve for sticking and freedom of movement.

The injection pump metering valve is like a control spigot that regulates how much fuel is placed between the pumping plungers. When the governor guide stud is installed, it must be under the spring on top of the metering valve, and the valve must move freely in its bore.

2. Check for a twisted governor linkage spring.
3. Check for burrs on the metering valve arm in the area where the linkage rides.
4. Check for a failed flex ring by attempting to rotate the retainer at the governor weight cage. If it can be moved more than 1/16 inch, the governor weight retainer is bad and the pump will need to be overhauled.

Automatic Transmission TPS/VRV DB2 Systems

The 6.2L or 6.5L DB2 system uses either a throttle position switch/sensor (TPS) or a vacuum regulator valve (VRV) mounted on the passenger's side of the pump. The TPS is used when you have an electronic shift valve transmission, such as the 4L60E or 4L80E. It sends a throttle position signal to the transmission control module (TCM) for upshifts. It is an engine load indicator.

When the transmission is a Turbo-Hydramatic (THM400), a vacuum modulator is used as the engine load indicator. A diesel engine cannot retain vacuum (low pressure) in the intake manifold because it does not have a throttle valve, so there is no vacuum supply from the engine. SA mechanical vacuum pump is used to supply vacuum to the transmission vacuum modulator. The

The TPS is a variable resistor that varies the voltage as the throttle is opened and closed to the transmission control computer, telling it the throttle position.

VRV simulates gas engine vacuum by metering vacuum, such as a gas engine high and low, at wide-open throttle. The VRV and the TPS require an adjustment using special tools.

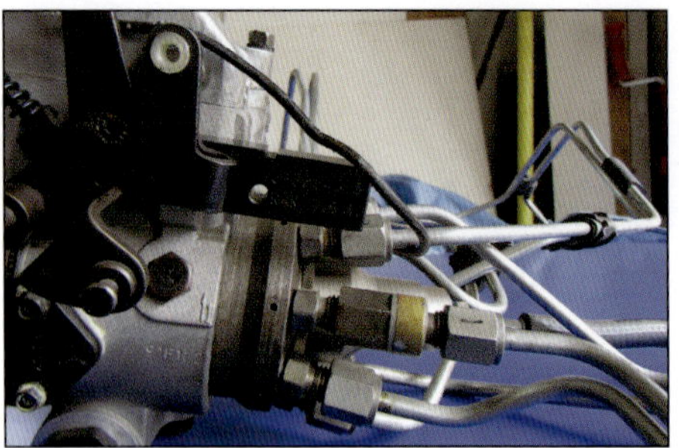

The TPS and VRV require a specific adjustment to provide the correct-position valves to either the TCM or the vacuum modulator. Two screws hold it to the injection pump, and it is slotted for adjustment.

TPS Adjustment

Use the following steps to adjust the TPS:

1. Disconnect the TPS connector and install jumpers between all three wires.
2. Turn the key on with the engine not running.
3. Install the TPS/VRV gauge block using the 0.646 size (GM Special Tool 33043-2 or make one).
4. Rotate the throttle and capture the gauge block between the WOT stop screw and the stop on the pump body.
5. Using a DMM, measure the voltage between TPS terminals A to C, which is the reference voltage (V-Ref). Next, measure the voltage between terminals B to C, which is the TPS voltage.
6. Compare the voltage reading to the chart

V-Ref	4.5	4.6	4.7	4.8	4.9	5.0	5.1	5.2	5.3	5.4	5.5
TPS Volts	2.84	2.9	2.96	3.02	3.09	3.15	3.21	3.28	3.34	3.4	3.47

7. The TPS voltage should be within plus or minus 0.03 of the voltage measured. For example, at a V-Ref of 4.6, the TPS voltage should be between 2.87 and 2.93 volts.
8. If not within range, loosen the TPS bolts and rotate the TPS until you get a good reading.
9. Tighten the screws to 53 in-lbs and reconnect the TPS connector.

VRV Adjustment

To adjust the VRV, perform the following steps:

1. Attach a Mityvac or any vacuum pump to the bottom nipple on the VRV.
2. Attach a vacuum gauge to the top nipple of the VRV.
3. Install the TPS/VRV gauge block using the 0.646 size (GM Special Tool 33043-2 or make one).
4. Rotate the throttle and capture the gauge block between the WOT stop screw and the stop on the pump body.
5. Pump up the vacuum to the bottom nipple to 20 inches of mercury (Hg).
6. Loosen the VRV bolts and slowly rotate the VRV body clockwise, facing the pump until the vacuum gauge reads 8 inches of Hg on 1982–1986 trucks and 11.5 inches on 1987–1991.
7. Tighten the VRV bolts to 4 to 5 ft-lbs.

6.5L DS4 EFI Diagnosis

The PCM calculates the start of injection and the duration of the injection period. The PCM controls the injection of the diesel fuel at the right moment and in

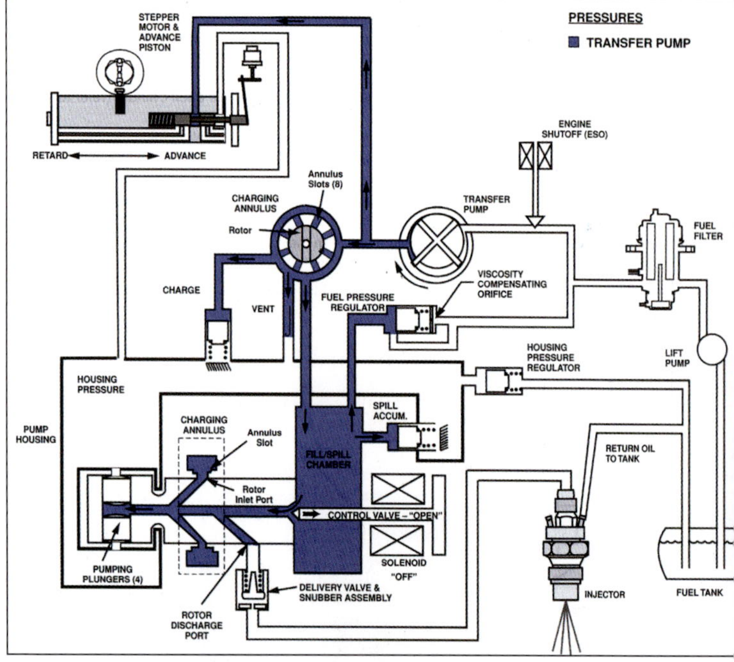

In 1994, the GM Powertrain Division released the 6.5L electronic fuel injection (EFI) version of this engine. This was a full-authority diesel fuel injection system using the Stanadyne DS4 rotary distributor-type electronically controlled pump to fuel the engine. The powertrain control module (PCM) manages fuel delivery and metering through a driver assembly mounted on the injection pump called a pump mounted driver (PMD). The PMD acts as a high-voltage switch to pulse on and off the pulse width modulated (PWM) fuel solenoid. (Photo Courtesy Stanadyne Diesel Systems)

the right quantities. The PCM uses a number of input sensors to manage the fueling. Some sensors include engine speed (optical), crankshaft position, fuel temperature, engine coolant temperature, manifold boost pressure, vehicle speed, mass airflow, intake air temperature, etc. The 1994 and 1996 versions used the onboard diagnostics (OBD) with the two-digit flash codes, and those from 1996 to 2000 used OBDII Class 2 serial bus system communication as a diagnosis interface. This permitted evaluation of the stored system data using the fifth-character diagnostic trouble codes (DTC) that can only be read using a scan tool.

DS4 Fuel Injection Pump

A single high-speed electronic spill-control solenoid controls fuel delivery through the PWM of a poppet control valve that spills off the fuel. Metering of the fuel using this poppet valve happens through a constant beginning of the radial plunger injection and a variable end of the injection (spill) as opposed to the previous mechanical DB2 pump's variable beginning and constant ending of fuel injection. Automatic timing advance occurs electronically through a hydro-mechanical piston moving the cam ring, which is controlled by a servo valve that is moved by a stepper motor.

Electric Shutoff Solenoid

The energized to run (ETR) electric shutoff solenoid (ESO) is located on the right side of the transfer pump and upstream of the transfer pump with the regulation downstream.

Fuel Control Solenoid

The fuel control solenoid is a high-current switching solenoid that receives injection commands from the PMD and sends a poppet (control) valve closure signal (injection pulse width) to the PCM. When a high-speed electromagnetic actuator is pulsed, it actuates a poppet (control) valve in the rotor to control fuel delivery at the rated speed of 3,400 rpm solenoid pulses 227 times per second.

Fuel Temperature Sensor

The fuel sensor is a thermistor that senses fuel temperature. Resistance is inversely proportional to temperature (as the temperature increases the resistance decreases). Low fuel temperature produces high resistance, and high fuel temperature produces low resistance. The PCM monitors the fuel temperature sensor circuits to detect faults. When the PCM detects a fault, it can take the following diagnostic actions:

- Stores DTC in memory (P0182 and P0183) or flash codes 42 and 43.
- Record data parameters related to the stored DTCs (Freeze Frame and Failure Record data).
- Turn on the malfunction indicator lamp (MIL) when the fault occurs under Type B DTC conditions.

Pump-Mounted Driver

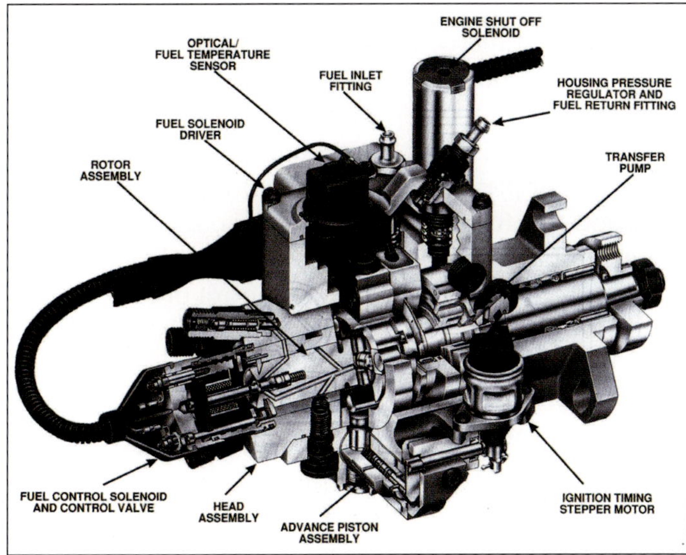

The DS distributor-type electronic solenoid injection pump is an eight-cylinder four-plunger radial pumping plunger rotary distributor pump. It uses a transfer pump just like the DB2, which provides regulated pressure for charging and advances operation, and the speed governor operates electronically not mechanically. (Photo Courtesy Stanadyne Diesel Systems)

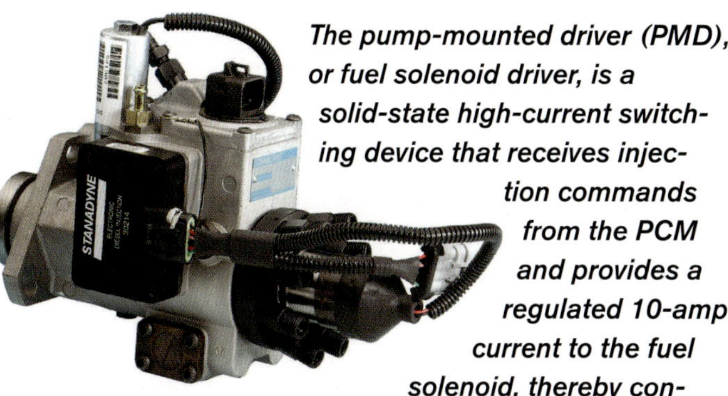

The pump-mounted driver (PMD), or fuel solenoid driver, is a solid-state high-current switching device that receives injection commands from the PCM and provides a regulated 10-amp current to the fuel solenoid, thereby controlling injection. It also sends a poppet valve closure signal (injection pulse width) to the PCM. (Photo Courtesy Stanadyne Diesel Systems)

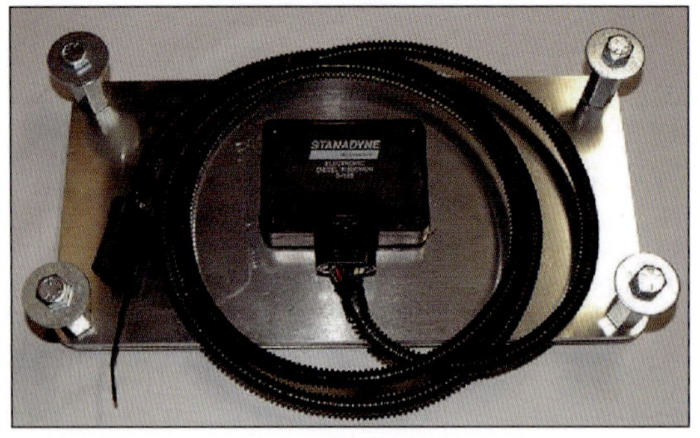

The PMD is one source of problems with the 6.5L EFI engine. It sits in the valley of the intake manifold, which is a very hot place. For this reason, the PMD will most likely fail. It is recommended that you purchase a remote location kit, remove the PMD from the pump, and mount it in a cooler place in the engine compartment. (Photo Courtesy Jim Halderman)

The DataTrack Disk contains two separate tracks that contain a series of notches or windows. The inner track or cam reference pulse has eight notches (windows), which provide individual cylinder references.

The PMD is a solid-state device that acts like an ignition coil or a step-up transformer to boost the voltage to the PWM control poppet valve solenoid, which controls the fuel injection.

Optical Sensor

The optical sensor provides RPM, cam and crankshaft position, and injection duration information to the powertrain control module (PCM). The optical sensor reads the high and low resolution tracks on the DataTrack Disk and sends signals to the PCM. The 1994 flash codes 17, 18, and 19 setting sensitivity was reduced with the January 17, 1994, PROM change. No problem in 1995. From 1996 to 2000, the OBDII DTCs were P0360 High-Resolution Reference error 512X signal (flash code 17), P0251 Cam Reference Pulse error 8X signal (flash code 18), and P0335 Crankshaft Position Sensor reference error missing a crank pulse (flash code 19).

The angular or optical speed timing encoder (ASTE/OSTE) is a two-channel optical sensor that is mounted on the pump cam ring that reads a two-track DataTrack Disk, which is mounted concentric to the pump driveshaft.

DataTrack Disk

The low-resolution track contains 8 windows that provide an angular relationship between TDC and the pump cam ring to synchronize the firing order for injection sequence and timing. A second (outer) track on the DataTrack Disk contains 512 notches, and their signals are sent to the PCM from the optical sensor. The PCM multiplies these signals 16 times through an angular clock mechanism to provide 0.044 degrees of angular resolution. This is called the high-resolution track.

The optical sensor has an angular resolution of 0.044 with 8,192 possible counts in a single revolution (e.g., 606 counts = 0.044 x 606 = 26.6 degrees) that can represent the off-delay (OFFDLYA) angle on the high-resolution track. The PCM uses this track information to map fuel delivery in an angular pie. This information provided enables the PCM and the fuel solenoid driver through the PMD to energize and de-energize the fuel control solenoid at precise intervals to achieve accurate control of fuel delivery at all throttle positions and vehicle speeds. (The 0.044 figure is derived as follows: 512 notches times x the 16x angular clock = 8192, and 360 degrees divided by 8192 = 0.044.) The optical sensor transmits these references to the PCM. When the PCM detects a fault, it can take the following diagnostic actions:

- Store Diagnostic Trouble Codes (DTCs) in memory: P0251 for camshaft position signal, which is an 8x signal; P0370 is the high-resolution signal, which is the 512X signal (flash codes 17 and 18 for 1994 and 1995 models); and P1635 or flash code 57 for the 5-volt reference circuit DTC and turns on the malfunction indicator lamp (MIL) or Service Engine Soon light when these faults occur.

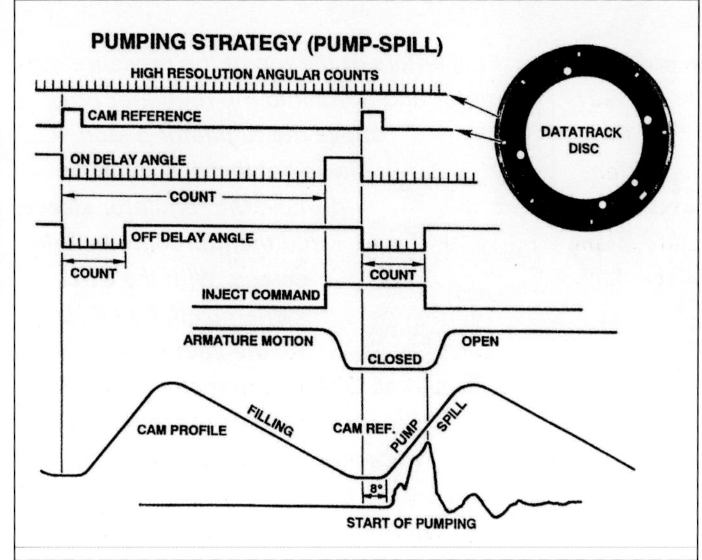

This track is also referred to as the low-resolution track and can provide an angular relationship between the crankshaft position (CKP) sensor and the pump cam ring for timing purposes. (Photo Courtesy Stanadyne Diesel Systems)

- On 1996 to 2000, OBDII models record data parameters related to the stored DTCs (Freeze Frame and Failure Record data).

Housing Pressure Regulator

This pressure regulator contains a positive sealing poppet valve–type regulator in the first stage and a spring-loaded glass ball-check regulator with a notched seat in the second stage. They are both rated at 5 psi. On engine shutdown, air could migrate through a porous return hose into the pump, generating air-in-fuel symptoms through the notched seat. The housing pressure regulator values are as follows:

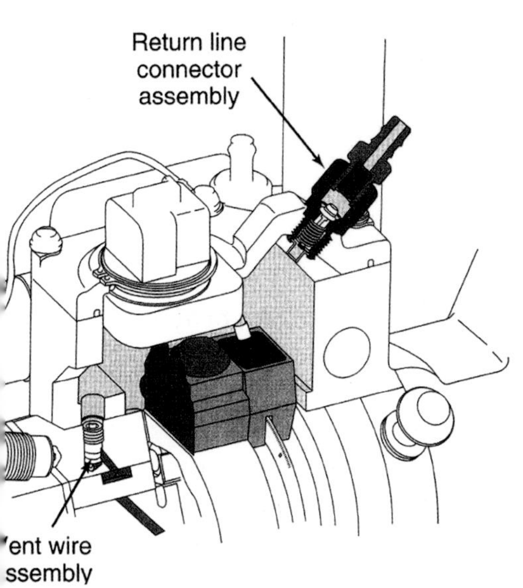

The housing pressure regulator or return line connector uses a two-stage positive seal regulator, which reduces drain back to the fuel tank. (Photo Courtesy Stanadyne Diesel Systems)

- Engine running 8 to 12 psi
- Test stand 6 to 14 psi
- Cranking 4 psi or lower
- Residual line pressure for both DS4 and DB2 is 600 to 800 psi

The housing pressure regulator (return line connector) uses a two-stage positive seal regulator. This reduces drain back to the fuel tank. This regulator contains the same positive sealing poppet valve type regulator used on the DB2 pump (6.2L/6.5L mechanical system) in the first stage and a spring-loaded glass ball-check regulator with a notched seat in the second stage. They are both rated at 5 psi.

On engine shutdown, air could migrate through a porous return hose into the pump, generating air-in-fuel symptoms through the notched seat. Note: The first design single-stage spring-loaded ball-check regulator with a notched seat was rated at 10 psi. The second design (GM service campaign) contains a positive sealing poppet valve–type regulator rated at 2 to 4 psi and a spring-loaded ball-check regulator with a notched seat rated at 6 psi.

The following are additional DS4 pump facts:

- DS4 transfer pump pressure range is 14 to 170 psi.
- Transfer pump pressure at idle (approximately 600 rpm) is in the 45- to 70-psi range. The value of 20 to 30 psi is for the mechanical DB2 pump.
- Peak injection pressure is 3,000 to 5,000 psi.
- The spill accumulator works like a shock absorber to absorb or snub possible high-pressure spikes.
- The charge accumulator is made to assist charging at high speeds to allow additional reserve fuel for high-rate periods, when time is a limiting factor. The original intent was anticipating a direct-injection application of the 6.5L, which was dropped.
- The electric shutoff (ESO) is located on the right side of the transfer pump. The ESO is upstream of the transfer pump, and the regulation is downstream.
- Similar nozzles used in the mechanical pump 6.2L/6.5L diesel engines are used in the EFI application. Yet, they contain a variable-rate spring to complement the EFI. There are two different nozzles, a purple band (opening pressure 1,500 psi) on the RPO engines L49 and L57 and the orange band (opening pressure 1,700 psi) on the turbocharged RPOs L65 and L56. The non-turbo RPO L57 now uses 1,500-psi nozzles to correct a hard-start condition.
- PROM enhancements include enhanced thin fuel tolerance (stalling and starting).

PCM Inputs/Outputs

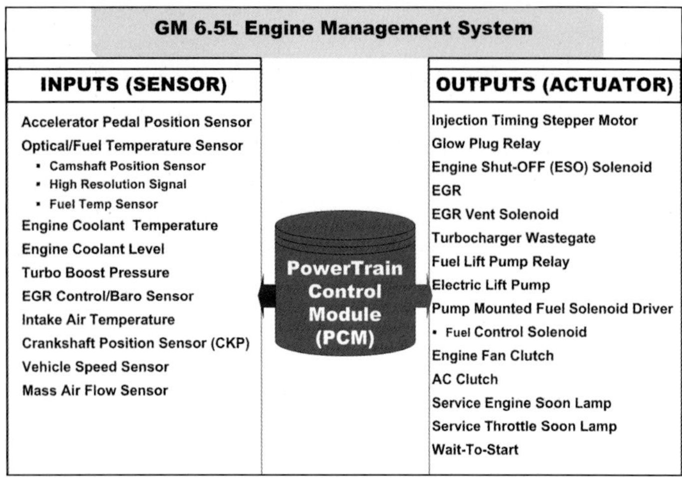

The PCM contains a fuel table for an engine over-temperature protection feature. When there is a loss of power when pulling loads, RPO engines L65/L56 after mid-December 1984 will subtract (up to 9 mm³) fuel as the temperature reaches 208°F. At 226°F, the maximum fueling of 9 mm³ is reached. When hard starting, a truck will have extended cranking time but does start hot. A 2- to 3-second hot restart time is normal. The reason is PCM wake-up time.

Fuel enters at the top of the pressure regulator and flows into the regulator bore above the regulator piston. It flows out through the four ports in the regulator sleeve, and then through the inlet screen. With the ESO energized, fuel flows to the inlet side of the transfer pump. Fuel is pressurized as the pump rotates. Pressurized fuel flows through the transfer pump porting screw and to a horizontal passage in the housing, to the head locking screw, and into the charge annulus in the hydraulic head. (Photo Courtesy Stanadyne Diesel Systems)

Fuel System Inputs/Outputs ECT Sensor

The ECT sensor is a thermistor where the resistance is inversely proportional to temperature. As the temperature increases, the resistance decreases. It changes its value based on temperature. Low coolant temperature produces high resistance; high coolant temperature produces low resistance. The ECT uses a voltage divider network.

Accelerator Pedal Position Module

The drive-by-wire potentiometer variable resistor controls fuel delivery that is requested by the driver through the accelerator pedal. Three sensors are used for redundancy to prevent breakdown.

DS4 Pump Fuel Flow

As the rotor turns, two (of eight) rectangular charging ports in the head bore align with two rotor charging ports. Pressurized fuel then flows into the central (angled) bore in the rotor and into the pumping chamber. Two charging ports are used in the rotor to ensure the maximum charge. The poppet valve is open (fuel solenoid de-energized) during the charging event, and pressurized fuel flows past the poppet valve to help assist in charging. The four rollers ride down the cam lobe to the base circle of the cam, permitting the four plungers to move to the maximum extended position (base circle of cam ring).

Crankshaft Position Sensor

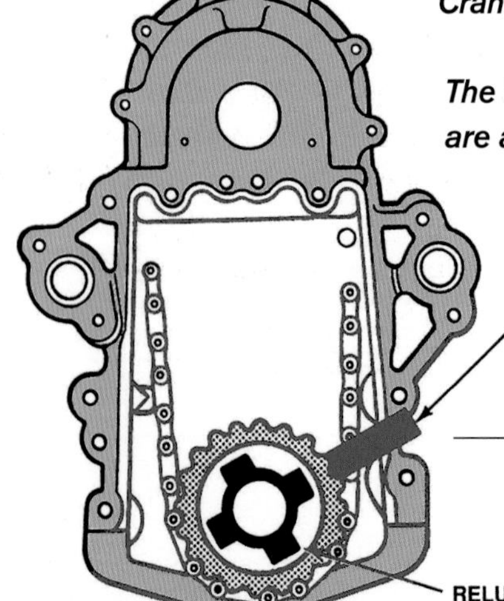

The CKP sensor is a Hall-effect sensor mounted on the front cover. When no teeth of the sprocket are aligned with the sensor, the sensor's magnetic field generates a voltage as it passes through the Hall-effect device, causing it to turn on with pulling the voltage high at 5 volts. When a tooth comes into alignment with the sensor, the magnetic field passes through the lower reluctance of the tooth instead of the Hall-effect device. This pulls sensor voltage to 0. This high–low variable provides crank positioning reference with the optical sensor DataTrack furnishing the number-1 signal.

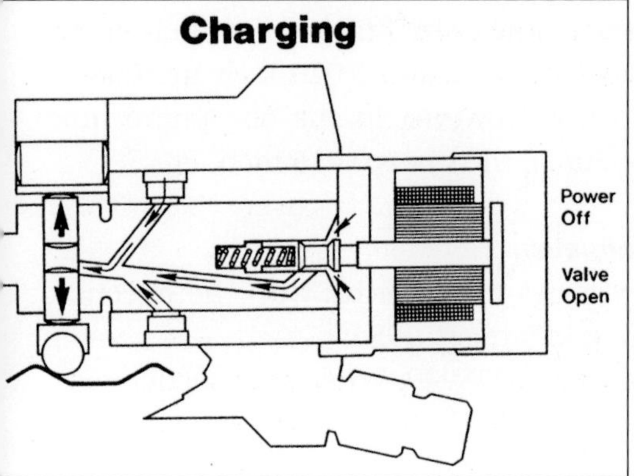

(Photo Courtesy Stanadyne Diesel Systems)

The pumping chamber is completely filled during each charging event. The rotor discharge passages are not in registry during the charging event.

Solenoid Energized/End of Fill

The on-delay (ONDLYA) clock determines when the fuel control solenoid will be turned on. The optical sensor also reads the high-resolution track, and when the prede-termined number of counts for the on-delay angle is measured, a command is sent to the PMD to turn on the fuel control solenoid.

The ONDLYA values are programmed to ensure that poppet valve closure occurs at the same point on the cam (approximately 8 degrees before the pumping ramp) throughout the speed range. As the speed increases, the ONDLYA value decreases (less time). This is done to always allow poppet valve closure to occur 8 degrees before the pumping ramp. The fuel solenoid is now on, the rotor continues rotation, and the charging (inlet) ports pass out of registry.

The rotor discharge port aligns with one of the eight high-pressure discharge outlets prior to roller contact with the cam lobe. The rollers contact the cam lobes and climb the cam ramp, forcing the plungers inward.

Pressurized fuel lifts the delivery valve and snubber plate that are located in the discharge fitting and flows out through the high-pressure line to the injector. High injection pressure lifts the needle valve in the injector and sprays atomized fuel into the

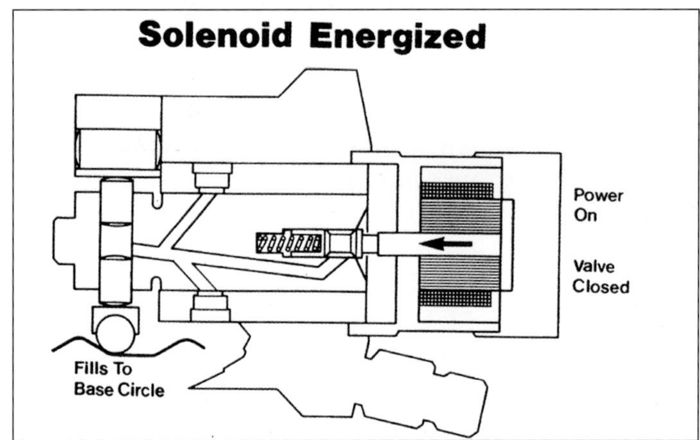

The command to energize the fuel control solenoid is generated as follows: The optical sensor reads the high- and low-resolution tracks on the DataTrack Disk and sends these signals to the PCM. The rising edge of the cam reference pulse (low-resolution track) sets several computer clocks in the PCM. (Photo Courtesy Stanadyne Diesel Systems)

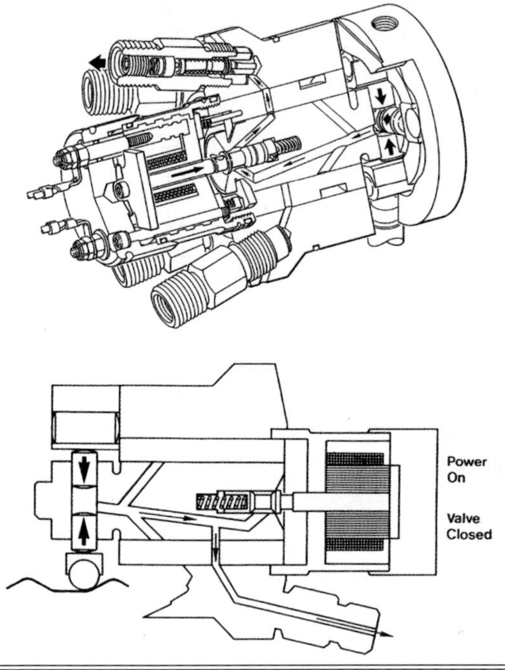

The fuel in the pumping chamber is pressurized and discharged through the central rotor passage and discharge port of the rotor, through a drilling in the hydraulic head, and out to the discharge fitting. (Photo Courtesy Stanadyne Diesel Systems)

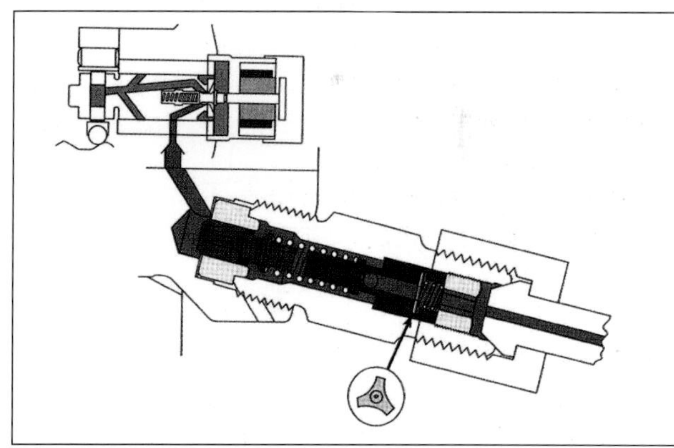

During the pumping event, the delivery valve and snubber plate rise off their seats. The retraction cuff of the delivery valve adds its volume to the spring chamber between the two valve seats. The triangular-shaped snubber plate permits fuel to flow around its edges. The fuel, while under injection pressure, is delivered to the high-pressure lines. (Photo Courtesy Stanadyne Diesel Systems)

---

engine's prechamber. During the pumping event, the delivery valve and snubber plate rise off their seats. The retraction cuff of the delivery valve adds its volume to the spring chamber between the two valve seats. The triangular-shaped snubber plate permits fuel flow around its edges; fuel, under injection pressure, is delivered to the high-pressure lines.

Spilling/End of Pumping, Solenoid De-Energized

When a predetermined number of counts for the OFF-DLYA is measured, a command to turn off the fuel solenoid is sent to the pump-mounted driver (PMD) by the PCM. The PMD de-energizes the fuel solenoid and the poppet valve opens. Cam rollers have not reached the end of the cam ramp. The discharge pressure spills into the cavity above the poppet valve seat. The pressure abruptly decays and pumping ends.

The delivery valve and the snubber plate move rapidly back to their seats. Volume displaced by the delivery valve during the pumping event is now removed from the high-pressure line. Pressure drops in the high-pressure line. The injector nozzle valve rapidly returns to its seat and fuel delivery ends. Reflected pressure waves generated in the high-pressure line are dampened (weakened) by the orifice in the snubber plate as the pressure equalizes above and below the snubber valve. Residual line pressure remains in the line at a value lower than injection opening pressure. It often varies from one application to another, but it is generally in the 600 to 800 psi range on both the DS and DB2 pumps.

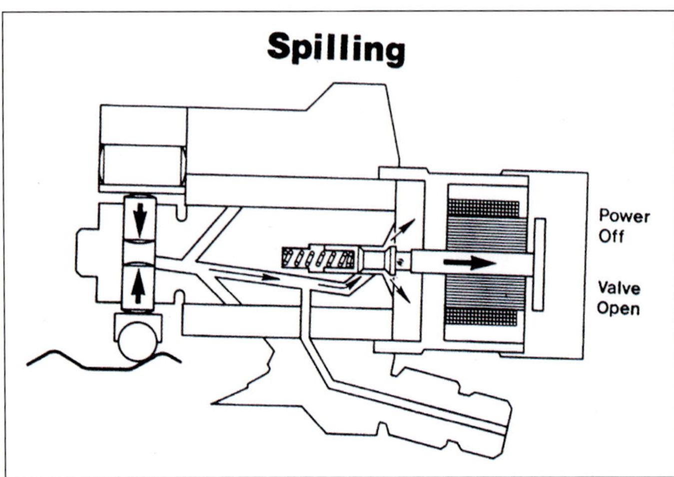

DS spilling takes place when the optical sensor counts the 512 notches with the angular resolution of 0.044 with 8,192 possible counts in a single revolution. This represents the off-delay (OFFDLYA) angle on the high-resolution track. (Photo Courtesy of Stanadyne Diesel Systems)

The snubber plate orifice size line is 0.016 inch in the 5067 or 10225930 Light Duty and 0.020 inch in 5068 or 10225929 Heavy Duty. However, in the one pump now used (10225930 or 5067), the size is 0.016 inch.

Injection Pump Information

Here are a few issues to watch for with the injection pumps built before mid-January 1984:

- Stanadyne #5068-HD-10225929: When incorrectly used on an RPO engine L49/L56, the engine will surge at idle and smoke excessively.
- Stanadyne #5067-LD-10225930: When incorrectly installed on an RPO engine L65, it will accelerate in park/neutral and be extremely sluggish. If the vehicle is put into gear, it will not move or will exhibit very poor launch.
- Mid-January: Fuel calibration will be adjusted with different PROMS (the latest PROMS were May 1994). Also in mid-January, injection pump part numbers were made common. All RPO 6.5L engines L49, L56, and L65 use part number 10225930 (Stanadyne #5067).
- Model DS4 pumps that were updated to include refinements for starting concerns are identified by a blue and silver ID label. Previous pumps had a black and silver label. GM TSB 4810299.

6.5L EFI Diagnostics

Scan tools can do the following:

- Conduct a selected test
- Retrieve or erase diagnostic data and DTCs
- Control a monitored function
- Reprogram the computer

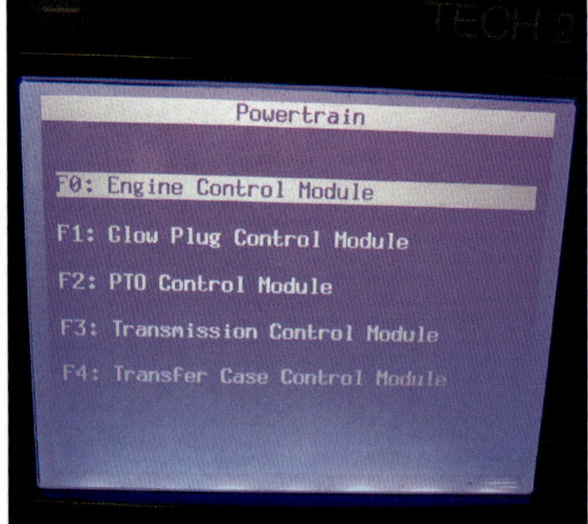

EFI diagnostics requires the use of a factory or aftermarket factory-level scan tool. This device is a handheld diagnostic computer that has both one-way and two-way communication with the PCM through a DLC (Data Link Connector) (Courtesy of Jim Halderman)

- View recorded data frames related to DTCs (Freeze Frame data and Failure Record data) on 1996–2000 trucks
- Conduct and review data snapshots recorded in multiple frames that are related to trigger conditions set by the technician on 1996—2000 trucks
- Perform special functions, such as output device commands

Scan tools talk with the PCM, reading DTCs and serial data. Serial data, or parameters, is a series of rapidly changing voltage signals pulsed from high voltage to low voltage. Serial data means that each word is read in order, one at a time, in a series. A typical serial data stream may have 20 words.

The PCM for a 1994–1995 engine used a removable PROM that stored software information, including calibrations to operate powertrain functions. During PCM replacement, a service technician is required to transfer the PROM to the replacement PCM. There were several TSBs in this book that listed replacement PROMS to fix 6.5L problems for 1994 and 1995 trucks.

You can also install aftermarket performance-based PROMS for better performance. The PCM for a 1996–2000 truck equipped with OBDII uses an electronically erasable programmable read-only memory (EEPROM). The EEPROM also stores software information that includes calibrations to operate powertrain functions. This EEPROM can be reprogrammed with fixes using a factory-level aftermarket scan tool for reprogramming.

6.5L Diagnostic Issues

This section will cover specific diagnostic issues concerning the 1994–2000 6.5L EFI engines, RPO numbers L56 and L65. The following diagnostic concerns will be addressed: starting concerns, DTC codes, stalling, missing/roughness, engine knock, fuel economy, smoke, and engine low power.

Starting Concerns

When starting, the PCM looks around, operates the glow plugs, and waits to see cranking RPM. When the PCM sees cranking RPM, it provides starting fuel and timing control. Foot pedal accelerator pedal position (APP) input has no effect during the start cycle. The PCM uses the optical sensor information to start unless it is in backup fuel mode. This involves setting flash code 17 (DTC P0370), which is the high-resolution reference pulse, or 512x signal, and flash code 18 (DTC P0251), which is the low-resolution reference pulse, or 8x cam pulse.

Situations Affecting Cold Starting Greater Than 4 Seconds

In the 1998–2000 6.5L EFI, the Passkey III anti-theft system uses a transponder inside the head of the ignition key. The exciter inside the ignition lock cylinder energizes this transponder when the ignition switch is turned on. The transponder transmits a unique signature to the theft deterrent control module. If the key signature transmitted is acceptable to the theft deterrent control module, the module will transmit a fuel-enable password to the PCM. If the fuel-enable password is correct, the PCM will start the vehicle. This can cause an "engine cranks but does not start" concern.

To fix the issue, do the Security System Relearn procedure, and the truck should start:

1. Insert a master key (black head) into the ignition switch and turn the key to the on position without starting the engine. The security light should turn on and stay on.
2. Wait for 10 minutes or until the security light turns off, and then turn the key to the off position for 5 seconds.
3. Turn the key to the on position without starting the engine. The security light should turn on and stay on.
4. Wait for 10 minutes or until the security light turns off, and then turn the key to the off position for 5 seconds.
5. Turn the key to the on position without starting the engine. The security light should turn on and stay on. Wait for 10 minutes or until the security light turns off.
6. Turn the key to the off position. The key transponder information will be learned on the next start cycle.
7. Start the vehicle. If the vehicle starts and runs normally, the relearn is complete.

Additional situations that affect cold starting include:
- Injection pump failure: Check online for this GM Campaign TSB
- Optical sensor (OSTE): GM Campaign TSB 41-65-33
- PMD failures: GM Campaign TSB 41-65-33
- Air leaks/fuel drain back at the housing pressure regulator: GM Campaign TSB 41-65-33
- Lack of fuel or air in the system: GM Campaign TSB 41-65-33
- Glow plug problem, wrong controller: GM Campaign TSB 41-65-33
- Optical sensor 5-volt reference noise: GM Campaign TSB 41-65-33
- Cranking speed—100 rpm minimum cold: GM Campaign TSB 41-65-33
- Pump timing/retarded timing: GM Campaign TSB 41-65-33
- Wiring connection issues

- Fuel quality/waxing issues
- Compression—380 psi minimum: Do a compression test. Engines were found to have excessive taper causing low compression.
- Block heater not plugged in

Situations Affecting Hot Starting Greater Than 4 Seconds

On DS4 pumps, hot starting is different in that up to a 4-second hot start is considered normal (this is measured with a scan tool snapshot). The GM campaign TSB stated to block off the air inlets and run to operating temperature. Restart while checking for a start time greater than 4 seconds. The following issues may cause poor hot starting:

- Internal injection pump leakage (black label pump): GM Campaign TSB 41-65-33
- Low cranking RPM (175–180 rpm minimum): GM Campaign TSB 41-65-33
- ESO pressure buildup (drain fuel filter): GM Campaign TSB 41-65-33
- Timing (if retarded): GM Campaign TSB 41-65-33
- Fuel quality (fuel rate at idle using scan tool, maximum amount is 13 mm^3 (manual transmission) and 15 mm^3 (automatic transmission): GM Campaign TSB 41-65-33
- Fuel availability (low-pressure system 3 psi at idle): GM Campaign TSB 41-65-33
- Compression, 380 psi minimum
- Wiring connections: (circuit 984 for voltage) Look for problems with the optical sensor, the CKP sensor, all grounds, and the PCM pinouts.

Diagnostic Trouble Codes Set

Here are some common DTCs:

- Flash code 18 (DTC P0251) and flash code 19 (P0335) may be caused by electrical disturbances on the 5-volt reference line to the pump. Install an electrical filter (part number 12553327) between the optical sensor and the engine harness to fix the issue.
- Flash code 35 (DTC P1216 solenoid response too short) and/or flash code 36 (DTC P1217 solenoid response too long) may set with flash code 18 (DTC P0251) and flash code 19 (P0335).
- 1994–1995 trucks: Flash code 34 (DTC stepper motor) may be caused by a sheared camshaft gear key (due to improper pump installation), allowing the timing to be incorrect.
- 1994–1995 trucks: Flash code 78 (wastegate) may be caused by the plastic vacuum lines being swapped in the rubber connector body at the solenoid.

Engine Stalling

A PROM change was available on 1994 and 1995 trucks and may still be available to fix manual-transmission vehicles that experience a de-clutch stall after a zero-throttle deceleration. Any diesel engine may stall if the lift pump pressure is incorrect. The causes for low pressure include:
- A plugged fuel filter
- An oil pressure switch problem: Test the fuel pressure at the fuel inlet; the pressure should come up quickly to at least 3 psi.
- An inoperative lift pump
- A plugged primary tank filter
- An open lift pump fuse
- A wiring or ground problem
- Contaminated or incorrect fuel

Engine Misfire or Roughness

You need to define when the engine misfires. Note that 1996–2000 EFI engines are OBDII and will set a misfire DTC at P0300, P0301, P0302, P0303, P0304, P0305, P0306, P0307, or P0308.

Misfire on cold startup may be caused by air in the fuel, poor fuel quality, glow plugs not working, or retarded timing.

Misfire while driving down the road can be caused by the PCM being in backup fuel mode, retarded timing, or an intermittent lift pump.

If misfiring all the time, check for fuel quality and crossed injection lines. For misfire at specific truck speeds, check the torque converter clutch.

For fishbite, which is a very random infrequent instantaneous miss, install an electrical filter (part number 12553327) between the optical sensor and the engine harness to fix. However, if it is a wiring problem (a bad connection or a short), you will have to trace and repair it.

Engine Knock

Right bank noise (tick) is characteristic of idle knock in the cab. Look for heater hose grounding. If it sounds like a rod knock, it is most likely an injection nozzle that is stuck open.

Smoke

Fuel burned without air is generally smoke. The tendency to produce black smoke is any variable that increases the amount of fuel injected or reduces the amount of air taken into the cylinder. These include any nozzle (injector) malfunctions, turbo failures, restricted airflow, etc.

White smoke is a mixture of water vapor and unburned or partially burned fuel. As a result of the lower temperature, the fuel ignites so late that combustion is incomplete at the time the exhaust valve opens and fuel is emitted in an unburned or partially burned condition.

Smoke also comes from improper fuel and air mixing, owing to the extremely short time available for mixing; as the air/fuel rate increases beyond a certain value, an appreciable fraction of the fuel fails to find the necessary oxygen for combustion and passes through the cylinder unburned or partially burned.

If an EGR system is causing smoke on PCM EFI engines, try the following:

- Remove the EGR system, but keep in mind that this would require modifications to the control system, requiring an aftermarket PROM to be installed.
- For RPO L56 VIN code S, check to see if the EGR tower gasket is missing: GM service bulletin 47-63-04.
- Check for the wrong PROM, such as a light-duty 5067 PROM operating in a heavy-duty 5068 pump.
- Look for advanced timing. This situation has high unburned hydrocarbons (HC) when the piston is down, so coming up on the compression stroke, the heat generated is low, which causes poor liquid fuel evaporation. Ignition delay (ID) is then increased, and fuel impinges on the cold wall surfaces and does not mix properly with the air.
- Determine if it is long ID or ignition lag, which puts more fuel than can mix with the air into the cylinder. During the period of controlled combustion, when the ID is longer than the injection time, the amount of fuel involved is affected only if it has not mixed with the necessary oxygen during the period of rapid combustion.

Low-Power Towing

The leading cause of low-power towing complaints are overloading. Keep the following towing capacities in mind:

- GCWR = 14,500 pounds for automatic, 4.10 axle; 12,000 pounds with a manual transmission
- Max fifth-wheel trailer weight = 9,000 pounds
- Max ball-hitch trailer weight = 9,000 2WD and 8,500 4WD
- Coolant temperature fuel pull-out changed

Use a chassis dyno to find maximum horsepower at the rear wheels. At WOT, it should be at least 140 hp. Check boost pressure using a scan tool. On a road test, go to WOT from a 35-mph roll and observe the max boost kPa recorded on the scan tool. (It should be around 159 kPa.) Subtract the barometric pressure value from the max boost value to obtain the boost developed. Convert this kPa amount to psi by multiplying the kPa value by 0.1450326 (e.g., 89 kPa x 0.1450326 = 12.907 psi).

Timing TDC Offset/TDC Learn

The injection timing stepper motor is located on the right side of the pump. The motor housing contains two coils that are controlled by voltage from the PCM through four circuits:

- CKT 564 for coil 1 low position
- CKT 565 for coil 1 high position
- CKT 566 for coil 2 low position
- CKT 567 for coil 2 high position

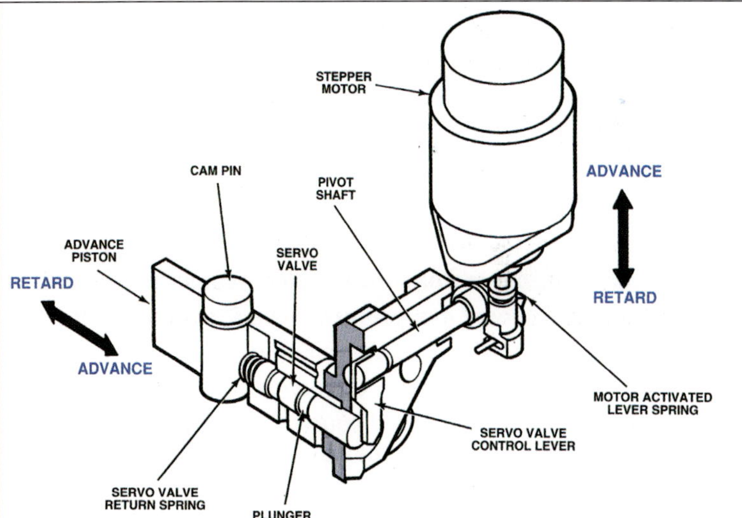

The stepper motor actuated dual-powered automatic advance allows the start of pumping to happen earlier to offset ID relative to piston TDC (speed advance) and delays of fuel injection (line lag). The best timing is where the minimum ID occurs, which is called minimum advance best timing (MBT). The system advances or retards the start of pumping in response to engine load changes. For example, light loads require reduced fuel quantities and produce lower cylinder temperatures. Lower cylinder temperatures at light engine loads require additional advance (irrespective of speed) to provide stable ignition and combustion (light load advance). (Photo Courtesy Stanadyne Diesel Systems)

1994–1995 6.5L EFI Diesel Backup Timing Procedure

Check the DS model pump timing procedure using TDC (offset) learn (backup timing procedure: TSB 476508 and 94C57A):

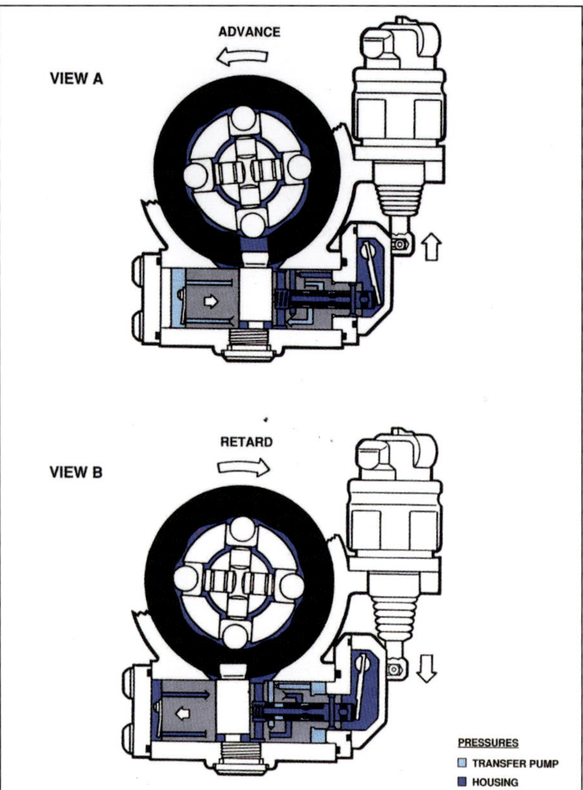

A DTC will set when RPM is steady and the PCM detects injection timing that is a five-step difference between desired injection and measured injection timing. This electric stepper motor converts electrical impulses into discrete rotational movements. It is a threaded shaft in a worm gear that moves up and down at 12 steps per revolution, where 1 step = 0.1 pump advance. For stepper motor response time, cold equals 50 steps per second (5 pump), and hot equals 120 steps per second (11 pump). This is due to the fact that increased torque is required to move the advance components during cold operation. As the step rate increases, the torque decreases. (Photo Courtesy Stanadyne Diesel Systems)

1. Idle engine until warm.
2. Install a factory-level aftermarket or "TECH 2" scan tool.
3. Activate "TDC offset learn" in the "output test/inj pump" section of the scan tool. If the engine stalls during the TDC learn activation, stop the engine, rotate the pump slightly toward the driver's side, tighten the

Offset Rotation

To achieve a negative number, rotate the pump toward the driver's side; for a positive number, rotate toward the passenger's side. A 1-mm (0.040-inch) pump movement equals approximately 2 degrees.

mounting nuts, and repeat this step.
4. If the learned TDC offset is between 0.25 and 0.75 degrees, the procedure is complete. If not, stop the engine, slightly rotate the pump, and retighten the mounting nuts. Repeat steps 3 and 4 until the TDC offset value is between 0.25 and 0.75 degrees.

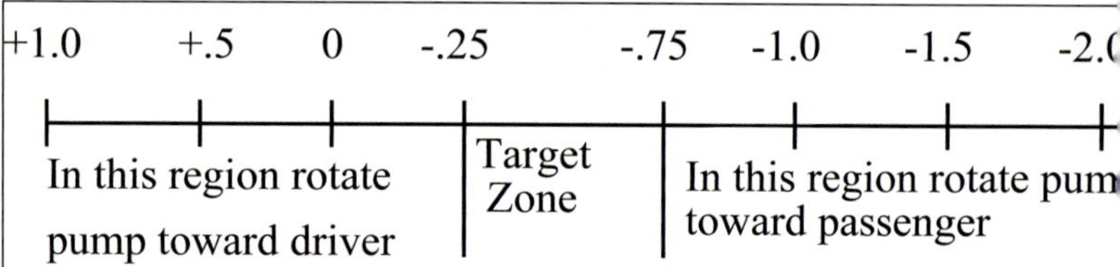

+1.0	+.5	0	-.25	-.75	-1.0	-1.5	-2.0
In this region rotate pump toward driver			Target Zone	In this region rotate pump toward passenger			

Notice: The manufacturing process for injection pump timing is different from the procedure available to the service field. Learned offsets between 0.75 and −1.75 on production-built engines are normal. Because a different technique is used for service injection pump timing, a different target zone is required, hence the value −0.25 to −0.75.

1996–2000 6.5L EFI TDC Offset Learn

The PCM in the 1996–2000 6.5L EFI engine learns the key TDC offset learn for injection timing and retains it in its memory. The procedure is listed here below:

1. Connect a factory-level aftermarket scan tool to the DLC and follow the scan tool directions to get to the engine main menu.
2. Select the data list from the main menu and look at the ECT data parameter.
3. Start the engine and run it until the temperature is greater than 170°F.
4. Clear all DTCS.
5. With the ignition switch and run engine off, push the accelerator pedal to WOT for at least 45 seconds to prepare the PCM for the learning process.
6. Turn the ignition switch to lock for 30 seconds, and then power down the PCM.
7. Check the data list, making sure that the PCM has cleared the TDC offset learn. If the value is zero, you can continue. If it's not, then repeat the previous steps.
8. Start the engine and run it until the engine temperature is greater than 170°F.
9. Allow the engine to run below 1,500 rpm so that the PCM will automatically learn the TDC offset.
10. Verify that the PCM has learned the TDC offset by selecting the data list and viewing the TDC offset data parameter. If the value is between −0.25 and −0.75, you are done. If the value is higher than this, stop the engine

and scribe reference marks on the front cover and the injection pump mounting flange. Loosen the injection pump mounting nuts and rotate the pump toward the driver's side by 1 mm, or 2 degrees. To retard, rotate toward the passenger's side 1 mm, or 2 degrees. Tighten the pump holds.

11. Redo the above procedure and check the TDC offset value to make sure it is between –0.25 and –0.75.

Air in the 6.2L/6.5L Engine Fuel System

Air in the fuel system causes rough idle, hard starting, and low performance. First, install a short, clear plastic hose in the return line at the top of the injection pump. Start the engine and see if air bubbles or film is in the line. When bubbles are present, proceed as follows:

1. Raise the vehicle and disconnect both fuel lines at the fuel tank.
2. Plug the smaller line, which is the return line.
3. Attach a low-pressure air pressure source, preferably a hand-operated pump, to the larger 3/8-inch fuel hose and apply 8 to 12 psi.
4. Observe the fuel pump reading of 8 to 10 psi. A decrease in pressure will indicate the presence of a suck leak that is most likely at the lift pump.
5. It's important that the proper-size clamps are used on all hoses. Also a burr on the edge of the pipe side of the line can create an air ingestion problem.
6. Fuel pressure is important. It is checked at the fuel pump outlet to the fuel injection pump and should be between 5.5 and 6.5 psi.
7. If you have one of the older, square-type fuel filters, replace it with a factory or aftermarket filter that has an air bleed and water drain.
8. After any filter change, it is absolutely necessary to purge the air from the system, otherwise you will have hard starting and rough idle. Follow whatever procedures are available for the type of filter your truck is using.
9. Remove the fuel filler cap and disconnect the fuel shutoff pink wire to the injection pump.
10. I recommend installing a solenoid electric lift pump. If you must use a mechanical pump, use the non-vented pump (AC Delco part number 4325 and GM part number 25116503).
11. On electric lift pump vehicles, open the air bleed, turn on the ignition, and let the pump run until clean fuel with no air comes out the vent.
12. On mechanical lift pumps, crank the engine for 10 to 15 seconds then wait 1 minute. Repeat until clear fuel with no air comes from the bleed valve.
13. If you are still getting air, the air leak must be found before proceeding.
14. Install the fuel filler cap and connect the fuel shutoff pink wire to the injection pump.
15. Try to start the engine. If it does not start, have someone crank it while you bleed the lines to the injection nozzles. If it starts and has a rough idle, bleed the lines.

Injection Nozzle Testing

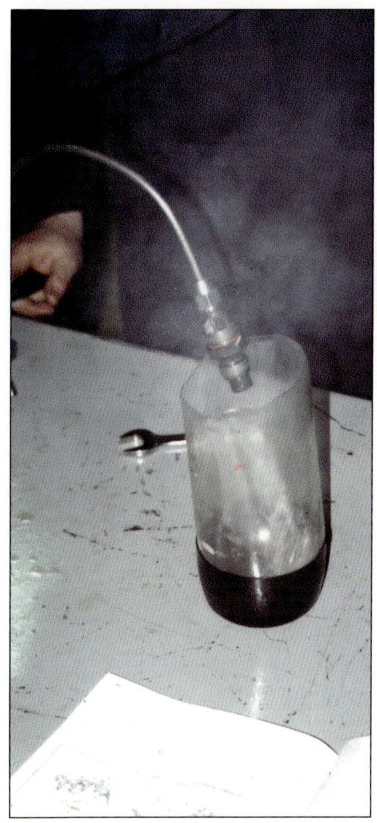

Bench test the injectors for three basic performance functions: pop-off pressure, spray pattern, and leakage. Does it meet specifications for pop-off pressure? General Motors 6.2L nozzles open at 1,810 to 1,960 psi; 6.5L nozzles open at 1,700 psi. The spray pattern must be uniform and atomized. For a 6.5L engine, there should be no leakage after 15 seconds at 1,360 psi (94 bar), and for a 6.2L engine, there should be no leakage after 15 seconds at 1,520 psi (105 bar). (Photo Courtesy Jim Halderman)

It is recommended to discard the older, square fuel filters and install a spin-on filter that contains a vent valve to bleed out the air along with a water drain valve to drain water.

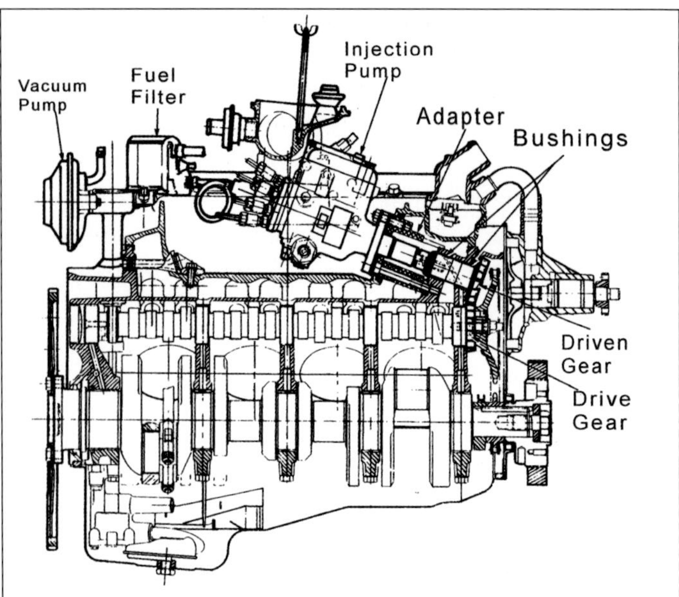

There was a 4.3L V-8 (260 ci) diesel that had a smaller bore and valves and was only offered in 1979 in the Oldsmobile Cutlass. In 1985, Olds offered a 4.3L V-6 version of this engine using a splayed crankshaft that contained all of the latest design features used on the 5.7L V-8.

Early 5.7L Olds Diesel Engines

The Olds 5.7L V-8 diesel engine is a four-stroke cycle, naturally aspirated configuration with overhead valves. Cylinder numbers 1, 3, 5, and 7 are on the left bank. Cylinder numbers 2, 4, 6, and 8 are on the right bank. The number-1 cylinder is at the water pump end. The firing order is 1-8-4-3-6-5-7-2.

The cylinder block, crankshaft, main bearings, rods, pistons, and pins are heavier duty because of the high compression ratio for spontaneous ignition. Diesel ignition occurs because of heat developed in the combustion chamber during compression. This eliminates the need for spark plugs and high-voltage ignition.

The intake and exhaust valves are of a special design and material for diesel operation. The stainless steel prechamber inserts in the cylinder head combustion chambers are serviced separately from the head. Glow plugs and injection nozzles are in the cylinder heads. The injection nozzles are calibrated to open at a specified PSI of fuel pressure.

The 4.3L and 5.7L V-8 diesels are both indirect injection engines. The fuel is injected indirectly into a precombustion chamber as opposed to being directly injected into the main combustion chamber.

In 1979, the 4.3L V-8 was also offered with a 5-speed manual transmission. The mechanical lift pump was crankshaft driven due to the injection pump drive system and later replaced with a solenoid electric lift pump. The fuel injection system on this engine used the Stanadyne DB2 injection pump and injection nozzles. Its operation is very similar to the 6.2L system.

The electrical system was modified significantly to provide the necessary starting power to control the glow plugs and to provide "driver aid" lights to assist the driver in starting the engine. They are located in the instrument panel.

Two batteries with copper cables are provided.

The recommended engine oil is 15W40 with the use of 10W30 for cold climates. Oil pressure at idle is 7 psi and 30 psi at 1,500 rpm.

Olds 5.7L Engine Block Identification

There is a method of positively identifying engine blocks (diesel or gas and size). Block identification is cast on one bank of the engine block. The sizes 260, 350, or 403 will appear on gasoline blocks. Diesel blocks are similar, with a *D* just below the size. The latest and most robust Olds diesel engine block is identified by 350 DX. The cylinder bore size code letter locations on the above engines are being changed in production as follows:

- For the 5.7L, the bore size code letters are stamped on the cylinder block pan rail surface only.
- Two letters are stamped on each corner of the block, representing the cylinder size for the two cylinders nearest that corner. There will be no stamp on the block cylinder head surface.

Overheat Olds V-6 or V-8 Diesel

If you have an overheating condition on a V-6 or V-8 diesel engine and no apparent cause can be determined, it may be due to an incorrect radiator fan that was installed. Due to the serpentine belt on the V-6 diesel engine, the fan blades on this engine rotate counterclockwise rather than clockwise, as on the V-8 diesel. Should these fan blades be installed on the wrong engine, it would cause reverse airflow and an overheat condition. Check the airflow in front of the radiator while the engine is running to determine if the direction of airflow is correct. Replace the fan blades with the correct part number to eliminate this condition.

Crankshaft Pulley Torque Compensator

A crankshaft pulley torque compensator, similar to that used on the V-6 diesel engine, is now being used in production on the 5.7L V-8 diesel engine. The torque compensator reduces the torque variations being transmitted to the drive belt and will increase drive belt life. The torque compensator is available for 1980–1983 5.7L V-8 diesel models with air-conditioning that use a two-groove crankshaft pulley. The torque compensator and four bolts required for installation are available through General Motors (part number 22521773).

Camshaft Thrust Button

Since the vacuum pump and the injection pump are both powered by the camshaft, it is possible that the power required for vacuum pump operation may coincide with injection pump pulses and set up a fore-and-aft action of the camshaft. This fore-and-aft camshaft movement can change the pump timing several degrees because the injection pump drive and camshaft gears mesh with a beveled cut and can cause a rough idle.

In a rough idle condition, disconnect the vacuum hose from the vacuum pump and observe the idle quality. If idle improves, reinstall the vacuum hose to the pump. Loosen the vacuum pump hold-down clamp. Rotate the pump in the engine. If idle improves, clamp the pump in that position. If idle does not improve, remove the vacuum pump and reinstall with the drive gear in a different relationship to the camshaft.

If idle still has not improved after reinstalling the vacuum pump, remove the engine front cover and the camshaft bolt. Install the revised bolt, camshaft button, and spring. This will minimize fore-and-aft camshaft movement and was used in 1978–1980 engines to correct a rough idle condition due to vacuum pump loading.

Broken Glow Plug Tip

A burned-out glow plug tip may bulge, break off, and drop into the prechamber when the glow plug is removed. When this takes place, the cylinder head and the prechamber must be removed from the head to remove the broken tip. Pencil nozzle heads can be blown out.

Surface Cracks in the Cylinder Head

Minor surface cracks in the valve port area of the cylinder head, especially between the intake and exhaust valve ports, are normal. These surface cracks do not affect the function of the cylinder heads, and they should not be replaced for this condition. The use of Magnaflux is not recommended, as cracks in the cylinder head that affect performance are readily visible to the naked eye. Therefore,

Magnafluxing is an unnecessary expense.

There is an indentation in the block and head surface where the sealing ring contacts both parts. While this appears to be deep, actual measurements have shown that the groove is only 0.001 or 0.002 inch deep and does not affect sealing. There are gaskets available that are used with 0.030-inch oversize pistons. These head gaskets will move the sealing bead outboard of the existing groove.

Head Gasket

Another condition is evident by looking at the gasket once it is located on the dowel pins on the block. The sealing bead is only slightly larger in diameter than the bore. The bead may extend into the chamfer at the top of the cylinder, which results in an uneven crush of the wire and, after a few miles, will result in a leak.

To check for this, lay the old gasket on the block. Look at each cylinder, the gasket should be concentric with the bore. It may help to pull the metal ring out of the gasket so the block is more readily visible. If the gasket is not concentric with the bore, look at the shield on the side next to the block. There will be a crease line in the shield. If the line shows up on the shield, you definitely have dowel pin shift. If you are unsure, play it safe anyway.

There are two options to correct this condition. The new gasket, which is used with 0.030 pistons, will result in the sealing ring moving outward 0.010 inch, which may be enough to correct the condition. Another method is to enlarge the dowel-pin holes in the head gasket until the gasket can be located with the ring concentric with the bores. However, the gasket will not stay in the correct position when the cylinder head is installed. To keep it in place, put a small daub of contact cement on each end of the gasket between the bolt holes. Place the gasket on the block, then remove it to allow the contact cement to become tacky. Then place the gasket in the proper location on the block. Care must still be exercised when installing the cylinder head.

Another condition that could exist is to try to put a cylinder head on the block without the aid of dowel pins. Service blocks do not contain dowel pins. The dowel pins are very difficult to remove. Service blocks should not be installed without dowel pins. It is essential that the dowel pins be transferred, for if they are not, the head gasket will leak. Should dowel pins be needed, they can be ordered using part number 585927.

Make sure that the bolt holes in the cylinder block are drilled and tapped deep enough. The head should be placed on the block without a head gasket. Then, run a 0.005 feeler

---

gauge around the edge of the head. There should be no clearance. This indicates that dowel pins are not holding the head off the block. Then, screw in each of the bolts by hand. The bolts should screw in far enough to contact the head. This will indicate that the holes are drilled deep enough.

The bolt threads should be cleaned with a wire brush and then oiled. Oil should be on the threads and under the heads of the bolts. Oil on the threads and under the head is critical so that the friction on the bolt is reduced during installation. Do not put the oil in the bolt hole, as an excessive amount of oil could cause a hydraulic lock and prevent the bolt from tightening. Do not paint the head gasket with a sealant. Sealants will sometimes attack the RTV sealer, which results in a leak.

1982–1984 Piston Differences

The 1982–1984 pistons have the following differences from the 1978–1981 pistons:
- Flame slot for better mixing of air/fuel and for reduction of particulate emissions.
- Same-size valve reliefs improve air/fuel mixing and eliminate the need of matching specific piston to cylinder.
- Chamfer at the bottom of the lower ring land is eliminated. This provides a sharper sealing edge against the cylinder wall and increases crankcase negative reducing pressure.
- Top land has a series of grooves used to break up carbon. This prevents ring scuff by picking up any stray pieces of carbon and trapping them in the grooves.
- Tighter skirt clearance of 0.0035 to 0.0045 inch.
- There is a 0.045-inch piston pin offset toward the major thrust area to reduce noise and piston slap.

Rapping or Knocking Noise: 1982–1984 Diesel Engines

The 1982–1984 V-6 and V-8 diesel engines have the piston pin moved 0.045 inch off-center of the piston. This change was made to reduce the noise level of the engine. If this offset is on the wrong side, a rapping or knocking noise will be heard and get worse as the engine warms up.

There are two ways that the piston offset could be on the wrong side:
- The piston could be installed backward.
- The piston could be mismachined.

The cast notch in the top of the piston should face toward the front of the engine. If the cast notch is properly located, then each piston should be removed from the engine and inspected. The direction of the piston pin offset should be the same for all pistons on each bank. If a piston is found with the offset on the opposite side from the other three on that bank, the piston should be replaced.

Calculating Diesel Cranking RPM

Cranking speed is extremely critical for a diesel to start, either hot or cold. Some tachometers may not be accurate at cranking speeds. A way to determine cranking speed and check tachometer accuracy is to perform the following procedures:
1. Install J-26999 compression gauge into any cylinder.
2. Disconnect the injection pump fuel shutoff solenoid lead at the injection pump or harness connector.
3. Install a tachometer.
4. Depress the pressure release valve on the compression gauge.
5. With the aid of an assistant, crank the engine for 2 or 3 seconds to get the starter up to speed. Then without stopping, count the number of "puffs" that take place at the compression gauge in the next 10 seconds. Multiply the number of puffs in the 10-second period by 12 and that will be the cranking RPM (speed).
   Example:
- 10 seconds = 1/6 of a minute
- 1 puff = 2 rpm
- RPM: # of puffs x 2 x 6 = cranking speed
- Or RPM: # of puffs x 12 = cranking speed
- Diesel engines start hot at around 200 rpm

Cleaning Procedure: Gasoline in the Fuel System

1. Drain the fuel tank and fill it with diesel fuel.
2. Remove the fuel line between the fuel filter and the injection pump.
3. Connect a short pipe and a hose to the fuel filter outlet and run it to a closed metal container.
4. Crank the engine to purge gasoline out of the fuel pump and fuel filter. Do not crank the engine for more than 30 seconds with 2 minutes between cranking intervals.
5. Remove the short pipe and hose and install fuel line between the fuel filter and the injection pump.
6. Attempt to start engine. If it does not start, purge the injection pump and lines by cranking the engine with the accelerator held to the floor. Crank until the gasoline is purged, and clear diesel fuel leaks out of the fittings. Tighten the fittings. Limit cranking to 30 seconds with 2 minutes between cranking intervals.
7. Start the engine and run it at idle for 15 minutes.
   If gasoline is inadvertently pumped into the tank, there will be no damage to the fuel system or the engine.

The engine will not run on gasoline. Gasoline has a feature called octane, which is defined as the ability of the fuel to resist ignition under high temperatures. Gasoline at any percentage will make the engine hard to start hot. In the summer, this could be a cause of a hot-start problem.

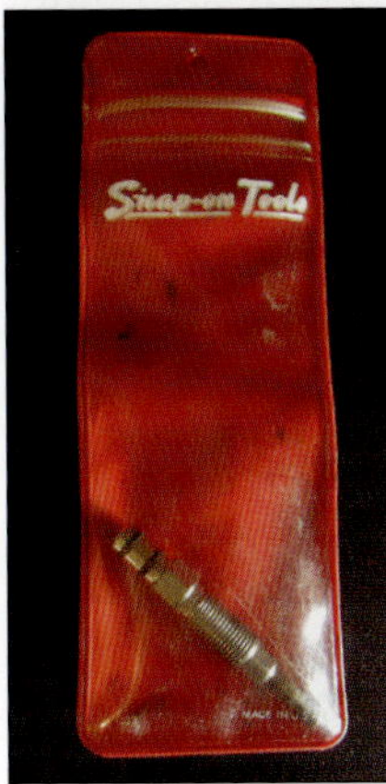

A Snap-on luminosity probe is used for the Olds 4.3L or 5.7L diesel engines. Remove the glow plug at the number-3 cylinder and install this probe. It is critical that the probe not be overtightened because if you do overtighten it, the quartz crystal will crack. This probe actually lets you see the light of combustion.

Dynamic Injection Pump Timing Using Luminosity

Certain engine malfunctions may cause incorrect timing readings. Engine malfunctions should be corrected before a timing adjustment is made. The marks on the pump and adapter flange will normally be aligned within 0.762 mm (0.030 inch) on a V-8 and 1.27 mm (0.050 inch) on a V-6.

1. Place the transmission selector lever in park, apply the parking brake, and block the drive wheels.
2. Start the engine and let it run at idle until fully warmed up. Then shut off the engine. Failure to have the engine fully warmed up will result in sooting of the probe, which will cause incorrect timing reading and adjustments.
3. Remove the air cleaner assembly and install cover J-26996-1. The EGR valve hose must be disconnected.
4. Clean any dirt from the engine probe holder (RPM counter) and crankshaft balancer rim.
5. Clean the lens on both ends of the glow plug timing probe and the lens in the photoelectric pickup. Use a dulled toothpick to scrape the carbon from the combustion chamber side of the glow plug probe. Look through the probe to make sure it's clean. Retarded readings will result if the probe is not clean.
6. Install the RPM probe into the crankshaft RPM counter (probe holder).
7. Remove the glow plug from the number-3 cylinder on a V-8 and number-1 on a V-6. Install the glow plug probe in the glow plug opening. Torque the probe to 11 Nm (8 ft-lbs).

8. On the V-8, set the timing meter offset selector to B (99.5). On the V-6, set the selector to A (20).
9. Connect the battery leads: red to positive, black to negative.
10. Disconnect the generator two-lead connector.
11. Start the engine and adjust the RPM to the speed specified on the "Vehicle Emission Control Information Label."
12. Observe the timing reading. At 2-minute intervals, again observe the reading. When the readings stabilize over the 2-minute interval readings, compare that reading to one specified on the vehicle emission control information label. The timing on the base 5.7L is –5 degrees ATDC at 1,250 rpm.
13. The timing reading, when set to specification, will be negative (after top dead center).
14. Disconnect the timing meter and install the removed glow plug. Torque the glow plug to 16 Nm (12 ft-lbs) on the V-8 and 21 Nm (15 ft-lbs) on the V-6.
15. Connect the generator two-lead connector.
16. Install the air cleaner, being certain to reconnect the EGR valve hose.

Poppet Nozzles (Microinjector)

The poppet nozzle is a miniaturized form of a fuel injector that is designed for use in high-speed, indirect injection diesel engines. Screwing directly into the engine cylinder head, the poppet nozzle is equipped with a nozzle having an outward-opening, spring-loaded poppet valve in contrast with the inward opening valve of a pencil diesel fuel injection nozzle.

Since engine compression and combustion pressure forces on an outward-opening valve are added to that exerted by the nozzle spring, opening pressure settings of the poppet nozzle are correspondingly lower than those of the pencil nozzles. This nozzle is not required to seal against injection pressure; the poppet nozzle does not require a return line.

Testing Glow Plugs

Checking continuity of a glow plug with a test light or an ohm meter may not detect a marginal glow plug. Measure the current draw or the resistance to be sure. Values should be approximately as shown:
- Slow glow system current: 7.5 amperes, Resistance 1.8 ohms
- Fast glow system current: 15 amps, Resistance 0.8 ohms

An induction-type ammeter is used for dynamically checking the operation of the glow plug system. You can go from plug to plug and measure 15 amps or connect the induction clamp around the glow plug harness and measure 120 amps. If you only read 115 amps, you have one bad glow plug. Then, go from plug to plug to find it.

Glow Plug Resistance Test for Power Balance
(Also can be used on 6.2L)

1. Use a quality digital multimeter (DMM).
2. Select scales to "OHMS" on the 200-ohm scale.
3. Start the engine, turn on the heater, and allow the engine to warm up. Remove all the feed wires from the glow plugs.
4. Disconnect the generator two-lead connector.
5. Using Mag-Tach J-26925, adjust the engine speed by turning the idle-speed screw on the side of the injection pump to the worst engine idle roughness, but do not exceed 900 rpm.
6. Allow the engine to run at the worst idle speed for at least 1 minute. The thermostat must be open and the upper radiator hose hot.
7. Attach an alligator clip to the black test lead of the multimeter.

Important!

This clip must be grounded to the fast-idle solenoid. It must remain grounded to this point until all tests are completed.

8. On a separate sheet of plain writing paper, write down the engine firing order.
9. With the engine still idling, probe each glow plug terminal and record the resistance values on each cylinder in firing sequence. Most readings will be between 1.8 and 3.4 ohms. If these readings are not obtained, turn the engine off for several minutes and recheck the glow plugs. The resistance should be 0.7 or 0.8 ohms.
10. If this reading is not obtained, check the meter for the correct settings, check for low or incorrect battery in meter, and check the meter ground wire to the engine. The resistance values are dependent on the temperature in each cylinder, and therefore indicate the output of each cylinder.
11. If the reading on any cylinder is about 1.2 or 1.3 ohms, check to see if there is an engine mechanical problem. Make a compression check of the low-reading cylinder and the cylinders that fire before and after the low cylinder reading.
12. Correct the cause of the low compression before proceeding to the fuel system.
13. Examine the results of all cylinder glow plug resistance readings, looking for differences between cylinders. Normally, rough engines will have a difference of 0.3 ohms or more between cylinders in firing order. It will be necessary to raise or lower the reading on one or more of these cylinders by selection of nozzles.
14. Remove the nozzles from the cylinders in which you wish to raise or lower the ohm reading. Determine the pop-off pressure of the nozzles as well as checking the nozzle for leakage and spray pattern.
15. Install nozzles with a high pop-off pressure to lower the ohm reading, and nozzles with lower pop-off pressure to raise an ohm reading. Normally, a change of about 30 psi in pressure will change the reading by 0.1 ohm. Nozzles normally will drop off in pop-off pressure with miles. Use nozzles from parts stock or a new car. Use broken-in nozzles on a car with 1,500 or more miles, if possible.
16. Whenever a nozzle is cleaned or replaced, before installing the injection pipe, crank the engine and watch for air bubbles at the nozzle inlet. If bubbles are present, clean or replace the nozzle.
17. Install the injection pipe, restart the engine, and check the idle quality. If idle is still not acceptable, recheck the glow plug resistance of each cylinder in firing order sequence. Record the readings.

Performance Upgrades

In the source guide, you will find a number of aftermarket sources for engine replacement parts as well as performance upgrades. For example, you can buy studs for your motor from Automotive Racing Products (ARP) or Summit Racing Products. You can consult with BorgWarner Turbo Systems to find the best turbo for your engine build, or you can contact Banks to find the best turbocharger for your project vehicle.

Turbocharger Works

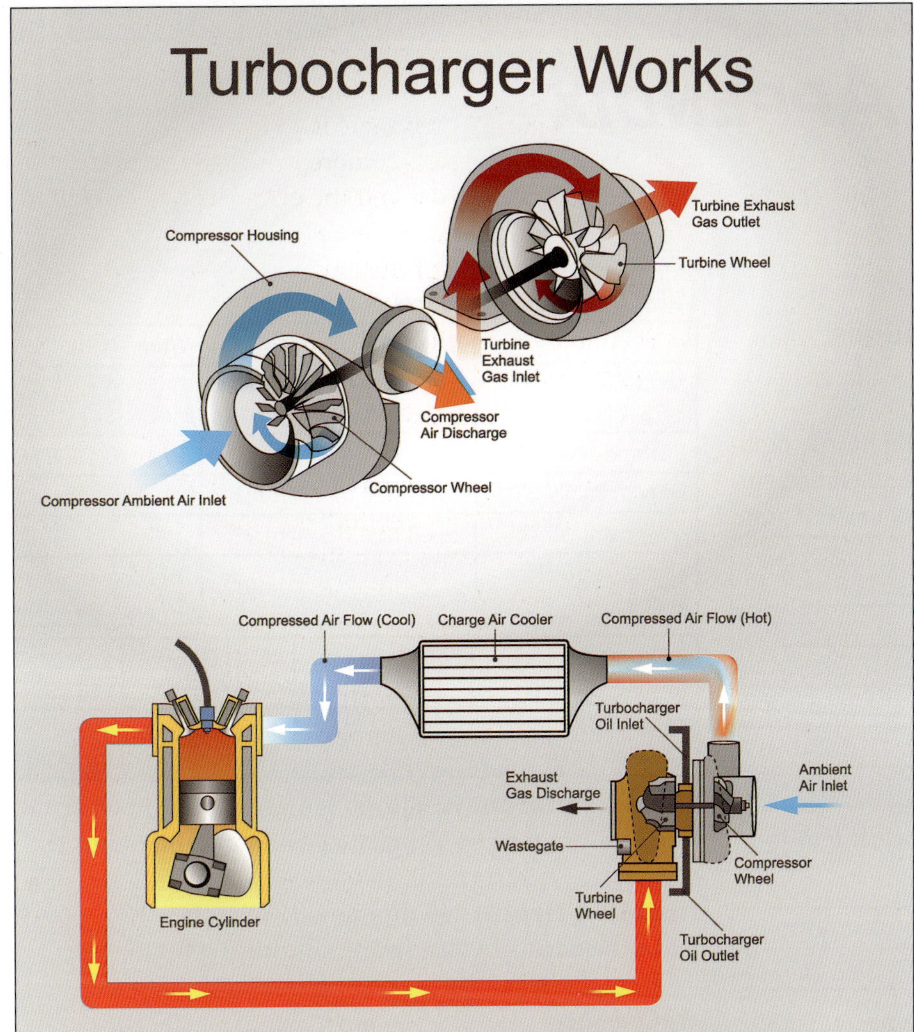

Turbocharging is used to produce higher power output, lower emissions levels, and improved efficiency from a diesel- or gasoline-fueled engine. The turbocharger charges the intake manifold at pressures above atmospheric to make the charge denser, thereby packing more molecules in the air/fuel charge and creating greater combustion pressure when the mixture explodes and pushes the piston. This higher pressure is called boost. A turbine wheel is driven by the exhaust, which in turns drives a compressor turbine wheel that compresses the intake air above 14.7 psi. A wastegate device, such as an open door in the exhaust stream, is used to control the boost pressure. You can also use a charge air cooler to lower the air temperature to make it cooler and therefore more dense for more power. You either cool the air before it enters the turbo or after.

Warner Ishi also makes a series of turbochargers for the 6.2L or 6.5L, such as the RHB6 that has a built-in wastegate and six different area-to-radius (A/R) ratios. My recommendation is to use one from a production 6.5L engine, a Banks kit, or the Holset HX35.

In 1992, when General Motors introduced the 6.5L turbocharged engine with a mechanical DB2 pump, it used the GM4 turbocharger. Later, it was upgraded to a GM8, or you can use the Holset HX35.

APPENDIX

Most Current Engine Specifications

Camshaft

The Moraine 6.2L engine plant experienced chronic problems with holding bored-in-place cam bearing tolerance currently at 0.025 mm. They increased this tolerance to 0.038 mm.

Finished cam bearing ID #1–#4	55.051–55.088 mm (2.1673–2.1688 inches)
Finished cam bearing ID #5	51.039–51.076 mm (2.0094–2.0109 inches)
Diameter tolerance	0.055 mm (0.0022 inch)
Cam journal diameter #1–#4	54.970–55.025 mm (2.1642–2.1663 inches)
Cam journal diameter #5	50.970–51.025 mm (2.0067–2.0089 inches)
Diameter tolerance	0.055 mm (0.0022 inch)

Note: These specifications will maintain the bearing to journal clearance as listed:

#1 to #4	0.026–0.118 mm (0.0010–0.0046 inch)
#5	0.014–0.106 mm (0.0006–0.0042 inch)

Intake and Exhaust Valves

	New	Worn
Face angle/both	45 degrees	
Intake thickness	1.94 mm (0.0764 inch)	0.8 mm (0.0315 inch)
Exhaust thickness	2.04 mm (0.0803 inch)	0.8 mm (0.0315 inch)
Intake stem diameter	8.661 mm (0.3410 inch)	
Exhaust stem diameter	9.436 mm (0.3715 inch)	
Stem to guide clear	0.026 mm (0.0010 inch)	0.130 mm max (0.0051 inch)
Intake protrusion	1.143 mm max (0.045 inch)	Same
Exhaust protrusion	0.889 mm max (0.035 inch)	Same

Valve Operating Mechanism

	New	Worn
Shaft diameter	24.15 mm (0.9508 inch)	24.12 mm (0.9496 inch)
Pushrod bend	5 mm (0.1968 inch)	5 mm (0.1968 inch)
Lifter diameter STD	23.41 mm (0.9217 inch)	
Lifter diameter O/S	23.66 (0.9315 inch)	
Lifter-to-bore clearance	0.04–0.08 mm (0.0015–0.0031 inch)	0.11 mm max (0.0043 inch)

Valve spring compression closed	356 Newtons	46 mm	80 pounds	1.811 inches
Valve spring compression open	1025 Newtons	35.3 mm	230 pounds	1.390 inches

Spring squareness: Spring length should not vary more than 1.59 mm (0.0626 inch) when being rotated in the free state.

Installed Height: 46 mm or 1.8110 inches

Note: Replace all valve springs during a rebuild.

PreChamber

Diameter in the Head STD: 39.650–39.675 mm (1.5619–1.5620 inch) O/S 39.676–39.701 mm (1.5720–1.5730 inch), Flange STD Diameter 39.676–39.701 mm (1.5620–1.5630 inch), O/S Flange Diameter 39.930–39.955 mm (1.5720–1.5730 inches)

Year	Dots	Class	Protrusion	
1982	1 or 3	M, N, P	0.050 mm (0.002 inch)	Press Fit
1983	1 or 3	M, N, P	0.050 mm (0.002 inch)	Press Fit
1984	1 or 3	M, N, P	0.050 mm (0.002 inch)	Press Fit
1985	1, 2, or 3	M, N, P	0.050 mm (0.002 inch)	Press Fit
1986	2 or 3	N, P	0.050 mm (0.002 inch)	Press Fit
1987	1, 2, or 3	M, N, P	0.050 mm (0.002 inch)	Press Fit
1988	1, 2, or 3	M, N, P	0.050 mm (0.002 inch)	Press Fit
1989	1, 2, or 3	M, N, P	0.050 mm (0.002 inch)	Press Fit
1990	1 or 3	M, P	0.050 mm (0.002 inch)	Press Fit
1991	1 or 3	M, P	0.050 mm (0.002 inch)	Press Fit
1992 6.5L Turbo	2 DOTS, Word Turbo	L, M	0.050 mm (0.002 inch)	Press Fit

6.2L Pistons

	Grade	Millimeters	Inches
Piston skirt diameter standard grade	C	100.911–100.924	3.9729–3.9734
	D	100.924–100.937	3.9734–3.9739
	E	100.937–100.950	3.9739–3.9744
	H	100.963–100.976	3.9749–3.9754
	O/S GRADE 2	101.687–101.700	4.0034–4.0039
	O/S GRADE 3	101.700–101.713	4.0039–4.0044
Piston-to-bore clearance		0.89–0.115	0.0035–0.0045

Cylinder Block

	Millimeters	Inches
Maximum out-of-round	0.020	0.0008
Maximum taper	0.020	0.0008
Crosshatch angle	45 to 46 degrees	

6.2L Piston Pin Bore ID

PIN Code	Millimeters	Inches
Green	31.0088–31.0114	1.2208–1.2209
Orange	31.0114–31.0140	1.2209–1.2210
Blue	31.0140–31.2210	1.2210–1.2211
Piston-to-pin clearance	0.0101–0.015	0.0004–0.0006
Protrusion	0.99–1.50	0.0390–0.0590

6.2L Piston Rings

	Millimeters	Inches
Side clearance (top ring)	0.076–0.178	0.0030–0.0070
Side clearance (second ring)	0.039–0.080	0.0015–0.0031
Oil control	0.040–0.096	0.0016–0.0038
Ring gap	0.300–0.550	0.118–0.0216
Ring gap (second ring)	0.750–1	0.0295–0.0394
Ring gap (oil control ring)	0.250–0.510	0.0098–0.0201

Connecting Rod and Piston Pin

	Millimeters	Inches
Rod pin bore ID	33.10–33.14	1.3031–1.3047
Pin bushing ID	31.012–31.027	1.2209–1.2215
Pin to bushing clearance	0.0081–0.0309	0.0003–0.0012
Crankpin bore ID	64.124–64.150	2.5246–2.5256
Bend	0.25 max measured at 76.2 mm (3 inches) from rod center line	0.0098 max
Twist	0.38 max measured at 76.2 mm (3 inches) from rod center line	0.0150 max
Side clearance	0.17–0.63	0.0067–0.0248
Green	30.9961–30.9987	1.2203–1.2204
Orange	30.9987–31.0013	1.2204–1.2205
Red	31.0013–31.0039	1.2205–1.2206

Cylinder Head

	Millimeters	Inches
Firedeck flatness longitudinal	0.152	0.006
Firedeck flatness traverse	0.076	0.003
Surface finish	1.6–2.8	63–112 microinches
Head thickness	97.87–98.13	3.8530–3.8630
Valve guide ID intake	8.705–8.730	0.3427–0.3437
Valve guide ID exhaust	9.480–9.505	0.3732–0.3742
Valve to guide clearance	0.026–0.069	0.0010–0.0027
Valve seat angle	46 degrees	
Seat runout	0.05 max	0.002 max
Seat width	0.89–1.53	0.0350–0.0600

Crankshaft

	Millimeters	Inches
Main journals #1–4 diameter	74.917–74.941	2.9495–2.9505
Main journal #5 diameter	74.912–74.936	2.9493–2.9502
Taper	0.005 max	0.0002 max
Out of round	0.005 max	0.0002 max
Journal to rod clearance	0.045–0.100	0.0018–0.0039
Crankshaft end play	0.010–0.250	0.0039–0.0098

SOURCE GUIDE

Accurate Diesel Automotive Parts Store
1512 S. Division Ave.
Orlando, FL 32805
407-843-7045

ARP Automotive Racing Products
1863 Eastman Ave.
Ventura, CA 93003
805-339-2200
arp-bolts.com

Banks Power
546 S. Duggan Ave.
Azusa, CA 91702
800-601-8072
bankspower.com

BorgWarner Turbo Systems
3800 Automation Ave.
Auburn Hills, MI 48326
828-684-4000
turbo.borgwarner.com

Diesel Power Products
5204 E. Broadway Ave.
Spokane Valley, WA 99212
888-993-4373
dieselpowerproducts.com

GM Genuine Factory Parts
gmpartscenter.net

JEGS Performance
101 Jegs Blvd.
Delaware, OH 43015
1-800-345-4545
jegs.com

Pure Diesel Power
2600 S. Galvin Ave.
Marshfield, WI 54449
715-254-1833
PureDieselPower.com

Quadstar Tuning LLC
quadstartuning.com

RockAuto
rockauto.com

Summit Racing Equipment
1200 Southeast Ave.
Tallmadge, OH 44278
800-230-3030
summitracing.com

US Diesel Parts
2400 Palmer St.
Missoula, MT 59808
800-823-4444
Email: clint@usdieselparts.com
usdieselparts.com